Branding Brazil

Branding Brazil

· ·

Transforming Citizenship on Screen

LESLIE L. MARSH

Rutgers University Press

New Brunswick, Camden, and Newark, New Jersey, and London

Library of Congress Cataloging-in-Publication Data
Names: Marsh, Leslie L., author.
Title: Branding Brazil: transforming citizenship on screen / Leslie L. Marsh.
Description: New Brunswick: Rutgers University Press, 2021. | Includes bibliographical
    references and index.
Identifiers: LCCN 2020031069 | ISBN 9781978819290 (paperback) |
    ISBN 9781978819306 (cloth) | ISBN 9781978819313 (epub) |
    ISBN 9781978819320 (mobi) | ISBN 9781978819337 (pdf)
Subjects: LCSH: Brazil—Cultural policy—History—21st century. | Branding (Marketing)—
    Brazil. | Arts and society—Brazil—History—21st century. | Brazil—In motion pictures. |
    Brazil—In mass media. | Brazil—History—2003-
Classification: LCC F2538.3 .M362 2021 | DDC 981.06/7—dc23
LC record available at https://lccn.loc.gov/2020031069

A British Cataloging-in-Publication record for this book is available from the British Library.

www.rutgersuniversitypress.org

Manufactured in the United States of America

For my parents, for their love and support at the start
For my husband, David, for his love and support to the finish

Contents

Branding Brazil

Introduction

∎∎∎∎∎∎∎∎∎∎∎∎∎∎∎∎∎∎∎∎∎∎∎

Welcome to the "New Brazil"

The images presented here operate as visual bookends to an intense period in Brazil's recent history from approximately 2003 to 2014. They reference critical moments, marking the opening and closing performances in a complicated narrative that unfolded during those years.

In the first (figure I.1), we see the presidential inauguration of Luiz Inácio Lula da Silva (or Lula) in January 2003. Lula's inauguration represents the first democratic transfer of presidential power in Brazil's history from one democratically elected president (Fernando Henrique Cardoso, 1995–2002) to another (Lula) who served a full term in office. In the second (figure I.2), we see a mural painted on a wall before the 2014 World Cup matches held in Brazil. The painting foregrounds the sad face of a young fan of the Brazilian national team who apparently cries because his dreams of another World Cup championship have ended.[1] The painted words lament that his community will be destroyed because of the World Cup and refer to the displacements caused by urban development projects on the heels of international mega-events. The image of the soccer ball overlaid by a skull further suggests misery and destruction. A boy wearing a backpack and presumably walking to or from school passes before the mural, suggesting there are important social needs (such as education, housing, and health care) that must be addressed. Juxtaposed, the two images capture the contradictions of the period, including the utopic and dystopic moments, the highs and lows, the hopes and dreams alongside the traumatic markings left on surfaces and people.

1

FIG. I.1 Democratic handover. (Sérgio Lima/Folhapress.)

FIG. I.2 Fraught dreams. (Movimento de Decoração Anti-Copa (Anti-Cup Decoration Movement), Rio de Janeiro, Homenagem à favela Metrô-Mangueira.)

By many accounts, Brazil was becoming a different nation in 2003. Cardoso had come to power when effective social and economic reform seemed implausible. As finance minister, he introduced the Real Plan, which aimed to curb inflation and bring financial stability to the country (de Oliveira and Nakatani 2000; Fonseca 1998). As president, Cardoso led a neoliberal agenda of market reforms. Generally, neoliberalism is characterized by policies of economic liberalization that include privatization, deregulation, and free trade, to name a few measures (Wilson 2018). In Latin America, neoliberalism is frequently associated with austerity measures and reductions in government spending (Kingstone 2018). Under Cardoso, Brazil privatized state-owned companies (like mining) and introduced free trade with Mercosul,[2] a customs union including Brazil and other South American countries. Despite some successes in market reforms and social initiatives, the Cardoso administration was unpopular before the 2002 elections, as the government was deemed ineffective in overcoming economic stagnation and social divisions (Saad-Filho 2003).

Lula largely adhered to neoliberal policies implemented under Cardoso, but his administration inaugurated a "neodevelopmentalist" model that favored growth through commodity exports. Armando Boito Jr. describes this approach as the developmentalism of the era of neoliberal capital that was made possible in part because neoliberalism achieved "a significant ideological impact on various segments of the working classes" (Boito 2007, 122).[3] What, however, is the broader ideological impact of this development model on cultural identity? And what new ways of being and participating in the social, economic, and political life of the nation were promoted at this time? As governments shrink themselves by instituting austerity plans, privatizing, and outsourcing oversight of welfare programs to private groups and nongovernmental organizations, to what do citizens pledge allegiance? Neoliberalist thought conceives of society in terms of markets and not civil spheres. It would seem that as authority is ceded to the market, citizenship then follows. The market defines values and provides liberty, and people become competitive participants in cost-benefit calculations.

By the time Lula took office in January 2003, Brazilians (and citizens elsewhere) were prepared to believe in a time of (and the need for) significant change. Global events certainly helped motivate this process. Just over two months after the September 11, 2001, terrorist attacks on the World Trade Center in New York City, Jim O'Neill, as director of the global economics research division for the investment firm Goldman Sachs, published the now-famous report *Building Better Global Economic BRICs*, in which Brazil was signaled as one of the most important economies of the future. In this influential position paper, O'Neill not only called for global economic organizations to include new members (Brazil, Russia, India, and China) but also used the term "building," which suggested the possibility of renewal and reconstruction. Established North-South geopolitical relations seemed disrupted, and there were new opportunities for emerging nations to assert themselves, especially after the global financial crisis of 2007–2008.

Indeed, a new Brazil was under construction. Notably, culture would be utilized to construct a new nation and cultural identity would become a commodity for development. Fueled by global economic shifts, Brazil appeared to have a new story to tell. In his inauguration speech as the newly appointed minister of culture, Gilberto Gil offered a broader definition of culture that crossed class lines (i.e., rejected divisions between "high" and "low" culture). He vowed that cultural policy would be part of a general project of "constructing a new hegemony in our country" or, in more tepid language, the project to establish a truly democratic, plural, and tolerant Brazil (Gil 2003). This more integrative view that defined culture as a space to realize citizenship set in motion a new regime of visibility whereby formerly marginalized groups and manifestations of culture gained attention. This view of culture was met by significant socioeconomic change. During the first decade of the twenty-first century, millions officially entered the middle class, identified as composing over half the nation's population (Neri 2011, 25–29). This demographic shift can be attributed in part to social programs (like Fome Zero and Bolsa Família) but is largely credited to a booming economy of commodities exports to China. As China's economy and demand for Brazilian exports began to slow in 2011, the popular classes began to slowly lose illusions of progress and political alliances began to unravel. Yet more than a democratic platform, cultural production became a strategic mechanism of economic development and sovereign affirmation of Brazil's role in the world.[4] The country was embarking on an intense period of nation branding in which notions of a new, improved Brazil were cultivated and debated in cultural policies and productions.

This book explores the branding of Brazil to reveal how market principles influenced the status and practices of citizenship during this unique, historic period. Given the reliance on the visual image as a support to a brand, I explore how narratives of a "new Brazil" were cultivated (and contradicted) in selected works of film, media, and television. Brazilian cultural identity was being produced anew for local and global consumption, and cultural production was conceived of as a way to achieve social and economic profits, especially greater inclusion of previously marginalized people and places at home and greater inclusion of the nation as a whole in the global landscape. What is more, a utopian impulse drove nation-branding practices that are readily apparent in international mega-events like the World Cup (2014) and the Olympic Games (2016). Yet nation-branding practices are also internally directed and involve the cultivation of affinities and values, such as with the mobilization of consumer desires and beliefs in social mobility. The state certainly played a role in promoting new ideas about Brazil. Yet I aim to complicate how we understand this process by evaluating how ideas about a new Brazil (concerning race, gender, sexuality, urban spaces, and class) were engaged with in different forms of media (film, television, and photography) by major production companies, nongovernmental organizations, and individuals. These different modes of media were arenas for developing ideas about a new Brazil at this time.

Branding has often been studied in terms of specific campaigns surrounding a product or service. In chapter 1, I address strategic efforts by state and nonstate actors, outlining cultural policies, agencies, and initiatives. However, scholars of branding located primarily in media studies have argued that the discursive practices of branding have moved beyond corporate-style strategy and entered multiple arenas of contemporary life, including religious groups, movements for social justice, political parties, educational institutions, geographical spaces, and so forth. The increasing marketization and commodification of everyday life means that portrayals with a profit motive are on the rise. Thus, the critical challenge is to broaden the approach to analyze branding and its discursive practices.

Andrew Wernick has argued that promotional discourse has become the dominant symbolic language in contemporary capitalism, and geographic spaces—including nations and cities—are increasingly framed by promotionalism (1991, 188). If this is true, then how might scholars approach the task of analyzing the promotional discourses surrounding an emerging nation like Brazil? What is more, how might scholars approach an analysis of nation branding but with an expanded view that looks beyond specific campaigns? Theoretical discussions of branding contribute to an understanding of the contemporary intersection of art, politics, and commerce. Thus, this book proposes a framework that draws on theoretical discussions of branding to analyze the portrayals of Brazil as an emerging nation. Rather than examining specific campaigns, I offer a model that considers three key discursive practices: promising progress, cultivating buy-in, and resolving contradictions regarding the development of new social and spatial relations. These are the most salient and recurrent practices of nation branding that link back to fundamental utopic beliefs about Brazil and its potential during the period from 2003 to 2014. Although focused on Brazil, this study contributes to an analysis of other emerging nations whose cultural policies and practices have also cultivated financialized fictions to change perceptions of their citizens and countries. What is more, Brazil serves as a limit case to analyze shifting power relations between the state, the market, and citizens.

This expanded understanding of branding coheres with the current phase of capitalism, whereby intangible economic and political value is increasingly linked to perceptions. While some nation-branding campaigns are more overt, not all nation-branding practices are clearly organized, centralized, or conspicuous.[5] Indeed, this book examines the less obvious side of the dialogue taking place visually in various modes of audiovisual production that not only offer the more compelling stories of this period but also reveal the deeper local and international tensions involved in seeking greater sociopolitical and economic inclusion. That is, one of the key issues at stake in a discussion of nation branding as manifested in contemporary audiovisual works from this period is the nature of local and global citizenship.

To characterize the period further, it is one framed by ambivalence. It is a period that can be described as one of creative destruction or of destructive re-creation, depending on the perspective. It is a period of celebrating what was great and new and leaving scars on surfaces and subjectivities. Between moments of victory and defeat, the period in question was primed for a new presentation of the nation and cultural identity. During this period, intense symbolic disputes took place over the meaning of Brazilian cultural identity and belonging. What is at stake is an exploration of the tensions involved in developing a new narrative of the nation, as well as the challenges to the status and practices of citizenship that did not result in a successful reorientation of society but eventually gave way to increased social division and political backlash, which became evident in the impeachment of Dilma Rousseff in 2016 and election of right-wing presidential candidate Jair Bolsonaro in 2018.

The period from 2003 to 2014 was also fueled by a utopian impulse, with all the successes and shortcomings that utopian impulses bring to bear. Utopian aspirations have underscored the history of Latin America generally. According to Kim Beauchesne and Alessandra Santos, utopian thought and its dystopic consequences are a persistent, intermittent theme in Latin America (2011, 2–10). They encourage other scholars to analyze these recurrent moments, and argue that in times of crisis, "the *practice* of utopia becomes particularly pertinent, even in the age of globalization" (7). Indeed, the practices of utopia are perhaps more significant in the midst of economic globalization. Brazil as a country and Brazilian cultural identity were embraced and celebrated during recent global economic and political crises that emerged parallel to marked shifts in politics and economics at home. In other words, Brazil's contemporary utopian impulse was shaped by apparent openings in global politics and economics, by a newly empowered middle class, and by (ostensibly) new political, democratic practices. A utopian impulse in Brazil from approximately 2003 to 2014 drove desires to conceptualize a more ideal nation (consonant with long-held beliefs of the country's unfulfilled potential), to reform local civic and international relationships, and to believe in the possibility of systematic transformation.

Taking a cue from Beauchesne and Santos, I address the practices of utopia and its contemporary aesthetic strategies. The practices of utopia in this period are best understood as nation-branding practices. For a newly identified emerging nation, this is particularly the case. Shedding their past labels as "Third World" and "underdeveloped," these nations are like actors who are eager to step out from behind a curtain to play new dramatic roles on stage. Lacking military might or industrial independence or being held in suspicion by more advanced industrialized nations for either, so-called emerging nations have turned to culture as their soft-power strategy to reshape opinions at home and abroad. As discussed further in this chapter and throughout this book, nation branding fundamentally involves cultivating messages that offer profitable readings. It is a utopian impulse that drove the soft-power strategy to make culture the central tool and venue to redefine Brazilian identity (or "build a better Brazil," as cultural policy documents frequently suggested) at home and to place Brazil as a nation on the global landscape. Consequently, a very particular era of spectacle emerged in Brazil that was linked to seeking economic, political, and social gains. Theoretical discussions of branding allow us to see how spectacle operated and the profits that were sought during this period.

Perspectives on Branding

Branding draws out new questions regarding the intersection of art, politics, and society, but an expanded understanding of branding necessitates clarification of terms, especially with regard to apparent overlaps with marketing, propaganda, and stereotyping. As concepts and practices, each of these involves spreading ideas, but they differ in subtle and important ways. Marketing aims to increase profits from sales of an object and involves a strategic approach that employs a number of techniques, including research, advertising campaigns, and the development of logos. Marketing primarily seeks tangible, measurable rewards. Marketing may contribute to the brand, but the brand precedes and supersedes marketing efforts. Conversely, branding is a communicative practice that involves the cultivation of perceptions, values, and identities. Branding involves the development of profitable—in the multiple senses of that word—narratives and is linked to lived experiences, affective relations, hopes, promises, and histories.

Branding may be seen as related to propaganda but differs in intent. Simply stated, propaganda is a persuasive mode of communication that not only promotes but also demands a certain way of thinking primarily for the benefit of an individual or group in a position of authority. That is, propaganda aims for control and sustaining ideological hegemony. By contrast, branding is the cultivation of associations and perceptions and ideally results in a broad range of profits (social, cultural, political, and economic) for multiple participants. Where propaganda seeks to constrain human liberties and aims to manufacture consent, branding strives to capitalize on human liberties and aims to stimulate desire and participation. In terms of its economic dimensions, a brand is an identity with an exchange value.

Branding differs from stereotyping in that branding is far more dynamic. Stereotypical portrayals are static (by definition) and repeat established ideas about a place or people with an intent to control or oppress. Branding promises renewal, cultivates buy-in, and aims to sustain affective associations with tangible objects and the immaterial world. Lastly, a brand (as noun) is a discursive object representing a constellation of ideas, myths, and values linked to social, political, and economic concerns. Meanwhile, branding (as process) concerns the mobilization, engagement, and assembly of ideas, myths, and values.

Owing in part to its multifaceted, multidirectional communicative potential, scholars have developed new approaches to theorizing branding that highlight expansive, participatory, and transformational aspects. The publication of Naomi Klein's *No Logo* in 2000 is frequently cited as a turning point in recent discussion of brands and branding. Klein defined the moment of the new millennium as a new, globally linked, "branded world" in which one lived entangled in a "web of brands" where advertising, corporate sponsorship, and market-oriented intellectual activity increasingly encroached on everyday life and civic institutions (2010, xxxiii–xxxli). Klein was addressing a debate that Arjun Appadurai had developed nearly a decade earlier concerning the social and cultural aspects of the economy. Defining the economy as a social form that consists of the *exchange* of values, Appadurai deemphasizes the form of what is exchanged in the economy and moves away from a limited definition of commodities as merely products and production. By contrast, Appadurai broadens the definition of a "commodity" and theorizes that what is immaterial can also be exchanged (1986, 3–16).

This discussion of an economy of ideas has contributed greatly to discussions of branding. Brands and branding have become understood not as a static mark or labeling on a surface (of an animal or inanimate object) but as part of dynamic exchanges. Indeed, brands became seen as gaining a tangible existence through social relations and interactions with the information they convey (C. Lury 2004, 1–16). Unlike propaganda, brands are "owned" by multiple stakeholders and, subsequently, hold the potential for being more participatory in their construction (Ind 2001, 2003; C. Lury 2004; Arvidsson 2006; Moor 2007). Partly due to this relational aspect, brands have been theorized as holding the potential for reasserting the identities of previously marginalized groups (Chin 2001). At stake, then, is not only the development of a new Brazil but also how people participated in developing the idea of a new Brazil.

Yet this participatory aspect is not neutral or necessarily liberating. As an increasingly common practice to manage people, branding seeks to induce individuals to "buy in" to participate in and belong to a larger organization or effort (Ind 2001; Ind, Fuller, and Trevail 2012; Ind and Iglesias 2016; Brannan, Parsons, and Priola 2011), but this process may in fact seduce individuals to be disloyal to their authentic selves (Banet-Weiser 2012, 1–14, 58–89). (This tension is considered in chapters 3 and 4 of this book.) Subsequently, scholars have examined how people interact with brands as ideas and values associated with places and objects and, in a late capitalist period, how branding has become part of daily experiences and identities. What is more, these scholars see brands to represent an ordering logic (or logos) of contemporary politics and economics (C. Lury 2004, 10; Arvidsson 2006, 124–137; Moor 2007, 15–38). While Celia

Lury (2004, 10) sees brands as both cultural forms and modalities of economic power, given the retreat of the state in economic functions, Adam Arvidsson (2006, 125) asserts that brands are forms of informational capital that operate like institutions that manage and organize people. In this regard, Liz Moor (2007, 19–38) cites a long history of branding and makes a link between brands and national or imperial projects, which leads her to assert that branding has transformed into a mode of governance. (This idea is explored especially in chapters 5 and 6.)

These scholars have pushed for new approaches and the placement of new arenas of experience in the analysis of branding. Indeed, more recently, scholars have urged us to consider the impact of branding beyond the business world, examining how branding has evolved from a corporate plan into a strategy for international diplomacy and public policy (Aronczyk and Powers 2010, 2–3). Observing that national cultures and territories have been increasingly seen as resources of economic value and part of a soft-power paradigm, Melissa Aronczyk has called for thinking about how the nation has been conceived of as a brand and how the nation has been "reorganized" by understandings of neoliberalism and globalization. For Aronczyk, the nation is like a brand in that it is a category of discourses and practices that can be mobilized for various ends (2013, 3, 10–14, 30). For example, chapter 1 in this book explores contemporary cultural policy and efforts to make Rio de Janeiro an attractive site for international film production to bolster the creative economy. Meanwhile, chapter 6 considers contemporary Hollywood films that set their narratives in Brazil to capture new middle-class audiences and global interest in Brazil.

In terms of tangible outcomes, nation branding deals in perceptions of attractiveness (as a dimension of global competitiveness) for foreign direct investment to sustain or strengthen economic development. Logistically, nation branding also aims to establish a voice—presumably greater, more respected, and influential—in international affairs and decision-making bodies. That is, nation branding seeks to help nations matter in the global world. Geographer and anthropologist David Harvey has written extensively on the link between the accumulation of capital and geographic locations.[6] Nation branding involves communicative practices that seek the accumulation of real and symbolic capital for specific locations by way of various cultural forms. For instance, a number of nations in transition from formerly communist bloc and emerging nations have directly and indirectly engaged in nation-branding practices to establish a new role in global economics and politics (Kaneva 2012; Surowiec 2017; Prieto Larraín 2011; Yang 2016; Fung 2016). Cities, regions, and smaller geographic locations (such as the shantytowns of Colombia and the *favelas*[7] of Brazil) have also taken to branding as a way to reorganize, remap, and jumpstart development programs (Greenberg 2008; Kalandides and Hernandez-Garcia 2013; Torres 2012).

It is a programmatic, if-then approach toward nation branding by purported experts and consultants that merits (at times negative) critique. Moor calls for considering less the "effectiveness" of particular campaigns and thinking more about "the impact of branding on a wider environment" (Moor 2007, 64). Indeed, nation branding demands consideration of its intangible consequences, as it raises a series of philosophical questions. For instance, as certain values are adopted and cultivated for nationalist or unifying goals, how does this affect a sense of belonging and loyalty to a geopolitical unit? That is, what are the consequences for citizenship? With state agencies frequently involved in branding discourses, what becomes of their political legitimacy and democratic practices? And as ideas regarding the nation are restructured and reveal the imprint of neoliberalism and globalization, how do these transformations and reorientations play out in self-understanding in a contemporary context? In this way, nation branding should be seen in terms of its external and internal flows and exchanges as a way to evaluate how the discursive practices of branding reconfigure social and political identities and redefine geographic imaginaries with a profit motive.

Broadly speaking, Brazilian cultural identity has been shaped by previous periods of branding and propaganda as manifested in internal and external communicative practices. Starting with the nation's "discovery" by Portuguese sailors in 1500, the inhabitants of Brazil were depicted as barbarous cannibals, but the region was also portrayed as an Edenic paradise and home to valuable commodities. In fact, the name Brazil refers to the dyewood, also known as brazilwood, that was the first commodity exported by the Portuguese.[8] Flash forward five hundred years and the Goldman Sachs report declaring Brazil a BRIC nation resembles a modern-day version of Pêro Vaz de Caminha's letter to the Portuguese Crown extolling the virtues and potential of a newly (re)discovered land.[9] These portraits of Brazil frame a history of the country's being the target of external cultural productions both as a (not always so sophisticated) way to curry favor with the local population and as a way to assert and sustain geopolitical hierarchies. That is, external actors located primarily in the global North have historically portrayed Brazil in ways that favor them (i.e., sustained a sense of economic, political, and cultural superiority while looking for new prospects for capitalist exploitation). This is apparent in the hundreds of Hollywood and European films where Brazil has been portrayed as a land of opportunity marked by lawlessness and lust.[10]

The twentieth century in Brazil is particularly notable for the proliferation of publicity campaigns seeking to sustain and legitimize political and ideological hegemonies at home and in partial synchronicity with the global North. Daryle Williams examines how populist dictator Getúlio Vargas (1930–1945) created several cultural institutions and agencies that operated to gain control of *brasilidade* (Brazilianness) as a way to govern. Cultural management of the

Vargas era sought to minimize diversity and conflict in a context of frequent rebellions (D. Williams 2001, 1–25). Notable among the agencies established under Vargas are the Departamento Nacional de Propaganda and the Departamento de Imprensa e Propaganda (DIP), the latter of which never hid its propagandistic intentions but established itself at the center of Brazil's culture through a blend of repression and collaboration with (or co-opting of) artists and artistic agencies. For example, the Cine Jornal Brasileiro newsreels created by the DIP were obligatory at screenings in Brazilian cinemas and promoted optimistic visions of Brazil and its modernizing progress under Vargas (D. Williams 2001, 84–85; Shaw 2006; D. Rêgo 2007). Indeed, both film and radio were key vehicles for the dictatorship's messages that Brazil was a modern and progressive nation (M. Bastos 2001, 15–17).

Notwithstanding internal contradictions over the meaning of Brazilianness, Williams observes that the Vargas regime sought to increase foreign attraction to Brazilian culture. In other words, cultural relations during Vargas "joined commercial propaganda as a vehicle for improving Brazil's stature in the international community" (2001, 199). Brazil's state-sponsored cultural renewal was met with U.S. foreign cultural policy of the Good Neighbor era (1933–1945), which sought to develop diplomatic relations with Brazil, a strategically important nation during World War II. These soft-power strategies on the parts of both nations may have ended with World War II, but the publicity campaigns and the propaganda machines put into place under Vargas have continued to influence the national and international imaginaries of Brazil (D. Williams 2001, xvii). We do not see the replay of Vargas-era and Good Neighbor–era cultural renewal but rather the legacy of it in recent productions from Hollywood and France about Brazil. Chapter 6 in this book reflects on this tension between celebrating and welcoming Brazil as part of the global community and the developed North's desire to reassert its authority in contemporary action and animated films.

The generals who ruled Brazil in a civil-military dictatorship from 1964 to 1985 did not want a centralized agency like the Vargas-era DIP because they did not wish to appear to be a dictatorship. This was particularly important since the military had justified its role in assuming power to restore democracy, economic progress, and stability (Schneider 2014, 9, 14). Instead, the regime established the relatively small organization the Assessoria Especial de Relações Públicas (1968–1974), which was replaced by the Assessoria de Relações Públicas (1976–1978), largely to outsource the production of materials— primarily short films screened in cinemas and on television—to the private sector (Schneider 2014, 16–17; Fico 1997, 18). Unlike the DIP and the precoup propaganda organizations Instituto de Pesquisas e Estudos Sociais and Instituto Brasileiro de Ação Democrática, the Assessoria Especial de Relações Públicas and Assessoria de Relações Públicas orchestrated a subtle approach, and the films' optimistic messages, emphasis on the concept of "Great Brazil" (Brasil Grande), celebratory ideas regarding the nation's natural resources, and treatment of everyday themes (like public safety, the importance of a good work ethic, and personal cleanliness) made them seem relatively apolitical. However, as propaganda, the films channeled the virtues that the regime wanted people to embody (Schneider 2014, 8, 15–16, 24–64). The tactics of encouraging people to embody the ideals of a new Brazil and celebrating of the nation's resources are taken up especially in chapter 3, where I discuss programs by the Globo Network that focus on women and their social roles as a way to think through changing cross-class relations and an increasingly market-oriented citizenship.

The military dictatorship strategically and subtly deployed propaganda to give new meanings to Brazilianness. According to historian Carlos Fico, the regime's project for the nation was driven by recurrent ways of thinking about Brazil: the idea that some "course corrections" were necessary to put the nation on the right track, the idea of a "moral crisis" in which the nation's problems could be attributed to the personality flaws of individuals, and a long-standing preoccupation with the image of Brazil held by foreigners (Fico 1997, 38–50). Civilian actors eventually reclaimed symbols of the nation and gave them new legitimacy and authority toward the end of the regime (58–61). In Fico's assessment, a new historical moment was inaugurated in Brazil at the end of the dictatorship that is best characterized as one of a spectacular politics in which citizens fervently and publicly reclaimed the symbols of the nation (such as the flag and national hymn), in contrast to a solemn and repressive symbolic agenda established by the military (58–67). Clearly, the military regime engaged in a spectacular politics, but what is particularly interesting is the way in which civilian actors engaged with spectacle to seek change. This book builds on this period, which is in fact a precursor to the nation-branding period found during the Lula and Rousseff administrations, in which we can further trace the trajectory of spectacle in cultural and political life in Brazil.

Practices of Utopia, Strategies of Branding

While it may be possible to identify branding practices at different moments in time, the nature of those practices and the ideas that drive them differ. The period addressed in this book certainly resembles but does not precisely replicate the practices of the past. What are the unique drivers *now* for branding Brazil during the period in question? To broaden our analytical view to assess the wider impact of promotional discourses, I offer a three-part approach to the branding of Brazil in different modes of media during this period. As noted earlier, these practices include promising progress, cultivating buy-in, and resolving contradictions. In the text that follows, I provide a brief sketch of these three key discursive practices in relation to Brazil and found in selected works of film, television, alternative media, and photography. I then refer to case studies expanded on in the chapters. While each chapter highlights one of the three strategies, these practices generally overlap. Ideally, the framework I propose will expand a discussion of nation branding beyond a focus on specific programs or campaigns while also offering an interpretation of aesthetic practices that reveals how neoliberal capitalism influenced the social imaginary at this time.

Promising Progress (or, The Future Is Now)

If nations have foundational myths, one recurrent myth for Brazil is its status as a country of the future that is full of potential and on the verge of greatness. Among various historical points of departure, the most salient of the twentieth century is the 1941 text by Stefan Zweig, *Brazil, Land of the Future* (*Brasilien: Ein Land der Zukunft*), published concurrently in Portuguese as *Brasil, o país do futuro*. In his travelogue, Zweig extols the beauty of the nation, its unexplored landscapes, and he points to Brazil as a nation to emulate for its peaceful way of being and lack of racial animus (7–12). At a time of crisis in Europe, Zweig describes Brazil as a haven for humanity. However, the sense of optimistic potential has since been accompanied by sarcastic remarks that Brazil is the country of the future and always will be, suggesting its perennial inability to fulfill its destiny and achieve greatness. The idea of Brazil as a country of the future is not just optimistic; it is highly utopic and linked with notions of becoming modern. At the start of the Lula administration and into the first Rousseff administration—and notwithstanding the *mensalão* (literally, "big monthly payment" or a vote-buying scheme) scandal (2005–2006) during the first Lula administration—it seemed as if Brazil was embarking on a new political path and was finally going to achieve its forecast potential.[11] Past failures would be set aside and the nation would embrace the present as a politically stable, democratic nation that was en route to overcoming its violent, authoritarian past and marked inequality. The nation's newfound political stability and economic potential would attract flows of foreign direct investment.

Branding puts the utopic into practice, and one of its discursive strategies is promising progress. Ruth Levitas, in *The Concept of Utopia* (1990, 8, 86), asserts that utopias offer "dreams of a better life" and mobilize desires for "a better way of being and living." Meanwhile, brands and branding also point toward the future. Aronczyk and Powers (2010, 11) assert that a brand is predicated on the future and the promise of a positive future experience. Aronczyk (2013, 1–14, 34–61) further argues that to be competitive in the global marketplace, national cultures and territories become potential resources of economic value and nations are induced to become "new and improved."

Chapter 1 ("Branding Brazil through Cultural Policy") serves as a departure point for discussing the idea of promising progress and considers how government policies sought to reshape Brazilian cultural identity and present a new Brazil on the verge of achieving its long-idealized potential. If branding is a discursive process that uses certain strategies to communicate ideas, then cultural policies in Brazil served as one of these communicative tools. The fundamental purpose of cultural and public policies is to organize and develop (or give shape to) social life in geopolitical units (such as towns, cities, and nations). Cultural policies can offer practical as well as discursive interventions, meaning they set the tone for cultural production as much as provide structures on which creative efforts can be built.

Thus, I argue in chapter 1 that cultural policies functioned as a way to brand Brazil for domestic and international audiences. I offer a critical interpretation of cultural policy during the Lula and Rousseff administrations as engaging in a complex process of nation branding. I briefly map the key tendencies of contemporary cultural policy and their relationship to the audiovisual sector, focusing on the film industry. Film in Brazil is a particularly important creative industry to examine, as the film sector had reemerged in the 1990s after the dismantling of state support to the industry. Cultural policies specific to the audiovisual sector sought to make Rio de Janeiro, which frequently serves as metonym for all of Brazil, a key site for the new creative economy. My analysis of cultural policies also reveals efforts to make Rio a film capital of Latin America and a site for global consumption. While the key ideas concerning the emphasis on the creative economy presented in chapter 1 gain resonance in chapters 3 and 4, the discussion of place-branding efforts examined in chapter 1 are complemented by discussions of filmic representations of Rio de Janeiro in chapters 5 and 6 that further contributed to the development of a city brand for Rio and a broader nation brand image..

In contrast to the discussion of cultural policies in chapter 1, chapter 2 ("Negotiating the Past in the Dictatorship Film Cycle") continues the discussion of how a new nation was being conceptualized in a more diffuse way. Indeed, part of "promising progress" was asserting that the nation had entered a new political era. In chapter 2, I examine a cycle of films that focus on the military dictatorship (1964–1985). Beauchesne and Santos observe that utopian thinking in Latin America has frequently involved symbolically neutralizing past horrors (8). As noted earlier, a new nation brand demands a "new and improved" version that emphasizes progress and future potential. After a long redemocratization process and delayed reconciliation for violence that took place during the dictatorship in Brazil, starting in the late 1990s, a cycle of films appeared in Brazil that focus on the military dictatorship. The majority of these films appeared around the time of the fortieth anniversary of the military dictatorship in 2004, meaning that most were produced and released in a very particular context in which looking toward the future held great sway. The cycle closed around 2012 on the eve of the official installation of the Truth

Commission, and a new cinema of intimacy regarding the past emerged. Many of these films certainly aim for reconciliation, but they are also engaged in developing a new mediated nationhood.

The discussion of these films focuses on the particular investment in the past found in selected feature-length fiction films, which have preceded, in some instances, state and nonstate initiatives and demands for an accounting of the dictatorship. The dictatorship film cycle includes three phases. In addition to mapping key tendencies of the first two phases, I offer close readings of *Zuzu Angel* (2006), *O ano em que meus pais saíram de férias* (*The Year My Parents Went on Vacation*, 2006), *Quase dois irmãos* (*Almost Brothers*, 2004), and *Os Desafinados* (*Out of Tune*, 2008). I argue that we find in these films a politics of the present that either contains or reinterprets the past in ways that recalibrate the imaginary of Brazil as a stable, democratic nation. Works in the third phase like *Hoje* (*Today*, 2011) and *A memória que me contam* (*Memories They Told Me*, 2012) offer reflective, intimate considerations of the past. While these films can be seen as residing at the intersection of mediated nationhood, sociopolitical reconciliation, and the memory market, they are also engaged in a broader process of constructing a new nation brand of Brazil. In terms of the transformation of citizenship, the films discussed here portray the process of democratization in a triumphant but incomplete way. The portrayal of the dictatorial past in these films has taken on particular relevance in recent years, characterized by calls (by some) for a return to military rule, increased authoritarianism under Bolsonaro, and militarized control of urban spaces.

Cultivating Buy-In

As part of the promotion of a new Brazil, citizens were called on to participate in the improved nation and seek utopian dreams of a better life, which seemed entirely plausible during this historical period. Places and people were drawn into the construction of a more democratic, plural, and tolerant country. Government policies and external demand for commodities improved the overall gross domestic product and helped millions of Brazilians move into the middle class (*classe C*). Greater political stability and a booming economy brought new conditions for citizenship and new lifestyle practices. Indeed, many scholars have theorized the link between citizenship and consumerism or social class in Latin America.[12] Individuals who had been economically marginalized possessed greater disposable income and gained unprecedented access to consumer credit. With an improvement to their socioeconomic standing, people of the lower-middle and middle classes began entering new spaces (like malls and airports) and engaging in new leisure activities (like going on cruises, frequenting the cinema, etc.) (Rocha and Rocha 2016). That is, with their newfound disposable income, the new middle class was called on to embody new sociopolitical subjectivities of the emergent citizen in an emerging nation (Marsh and Li 2016).

In terms of branding practices, we find audiovisual works and initiatives that cultivate or even solicit buy-in to the ideals of a new and improved nation promoted in part through the cultural policies discussed in chapter 1. Cultivating buy-in is a central goal of branding, and encouraging citizens to "live the brand" is key to nation branding (Aronczyk 2013, 77–79). For Slavoj Zizek, appeals to participate in these new financialized fictions constitute a capitalist utopia. For him, there are two types of utopia, one that is idealized and will never come into being and the other, a capitalist utopia "in the sense of the new perverse desires that you are not only allowed but even solicited to realize" (*Zizek!*, Astra Taylor, 2005). Branding operates as the engine that mobilizes and solicits desires to participate in a capitalist utopia.

Cultivating buy-in also characterizes the political moment inaugurated by Lula. Lula's election as president of Brazil coincided with the rise of other populist, left-leaning leaders in Latin America that has become known as a "pink tide" (Lievesley and Ludlam 2009). Lula, who had run for presidential office previously in 1988 and was a founding member of the leftist Partido dos Trabalhadores (Workers' Party), was not elected in 2002 by a wave of populist support. Rather, his bid for the presidency was supported by an "alliance of losers," or a coalition of groups that had experienced some sort of loss under Cardoso's neoliberal reforms (Saad-Filho 2007).[13] Consequently, Lula's administration can be characterized as a regime because of its "blend of socio-economic alliances, political-economic institutions, and its public policy profile" (Wylde 2012, 177). Lula sustained support by "recruiting and seducing" markets and individuals to his national development policies (Burges 2009, 196). Thus, stimulating desire to participate in the idea of a new Brazil can be seen as an extension of politics at this time.

Chapters 3 and 4 address the practice of cultivating buy-in. Chapter 3 ("Courting the New Middle Class on Primetime TV") considers programs from TV Globo that address the new middle class and encourage them to embody the ideals of a new Brazil. TV Globo mapped its programming onto the techno-cultural zeitgeist to appeal to the new middle class and address challenges to its audience market share. This chapter explores how selected television programs attracted (or courted) viewers to new ideas about belonging, especially as consumers and laborers. I focus on selected episodes from the miniseries *As cariocas* (2010) and its sequel, *As brasileiras* (2012), as well as the groundbreaking show *Cheias de charme* (2012).

More specifically, chapter 3 examines the contemporary cultural economy of stardom in Brazil, aiming to understand portrayals of the new middle class in television at this time and their relation to broader economic and political outcomes. In the case of *As cariocas* and *As brasileiras*, the Globo Network drew on its pantheon of famous actresses whose existing star status provided a matrix on which ideas about contemporary society were promoted. Globo's female stars embodied particular *femotypes*—geopolitically and socioeconomically favorable portraits of women that uphold the notion of a reinvented nation with global aspirations. In the case of *Cheias de charme*, we find an unprecedented effort to build an intermedial, digital experience around a TV Globo show, which included a contest for viewers to select the most charming maid from hundreds of video submissions by maids across Brazil. I explore the underlying class tensions and broader significance of these efforts at cross-media, engagement marketing, which took place amid a "maid crisis" widely reported in the press and at a time when legislators debated new labor laws to protect domestic workers. These television programs raise questions about how ideals of selfhood (along lines of race, gender, and cross-class relationships) are supported and how women are called on to perform new ideals of citizenship.

Chapter 4 ("Selling Citizenship in Alternative Media") further explores the practice of cultivating buy-in to realize the ideals of a new Brazil. Here I consider two alternative popular media projects sponsored by the Observatório de Favelas (Slum Observatory), a nonprofit organization located in the North Zone of Rio de Janeiro: a photography project called Imagens do Povo (Images of the People), and the Juventude Marcada Pra Viver (Youth Marked to Live), an affirmative publicity campaign developed by the Escola Popular de Comunicação Crítica (Popular School of Critical Communication). Both projects promote a new regime of visibility and a new urban sociability.

Both also reflect on citizenship in terms of race and place. Consistent with the goals of the creative economy, the Imagens do Povo program trained photographers to enter the for-profit marketplace, and it maintained an archive for commercial and nonprofit use. My discussion of selected photographs considers how an aesthetics of the everyday is mobilized as a way to include favelas and their residents in the new Brazil. The Juventude Marcada Pra Viver affirmative publicity campaign, which includes several photos from the Imagens do Povo project, draws attention to the rights of young, Black men and the horrific levels of violence committed against them. The concept of affirmative publicity draws from the idea of affirmative action developed in the United States (and intensely debated in Brazil) and the language of advertising. My discussion of this affirmative publicity campaign explores the significance of using the practices and language of branding as tools for social advocacy and considers how these practices counter the social invisibility wrought by neoliberal policies and chronic urban violence.

Resolving Contradictions: New Spaces, New Relations

Brazil is known for its marked income inequality, which is correlated with spatial, ethnic, and racial segregation. During the 1970s, economists coined the term "Bel-India" as a way to describe how regions and sectors of Brazil were developed and on par with advanced nations like Belgium while others were underdeveloped and registered levels of destitute poverty comparable to levels found in India (Bacha 1973; Bacha and Taylor 1976). In the new Brazil, this division was one to overcome. Utopian thinking in Latin America frequently conceives of spaces as arenas of resolution where opposites and fundamental contradictions are neutralized (Beauchesne and Santos 2011, 33–37). For scholars of nation branding, the success of a nation brand depends largely on its ability to overcome tensions, especially internal divisions, to gain a competitive advantage through perceptions (Aronczyk 2013, 37). A third discursive strategy I examine is how audiovisual works from this period address tensions and contradictions regarding the cultivation of new understandings of spaces and new social relations.

The favelas of Rio de Janeiro have been a nodal point for thinking about Brazil both internally and externally. In the works examined in chapters 5 and 6, the favela becomes a space of contradictions and tensions that must be overcome in order for Brazil to become a new and improved nation. The favelas of Brazil are born from historic inequality. In Rio de Janeiro, agglomerations of humble brick homes cling to hillsides. They also exist alongside wealthier neighborhoods or are isolated from urban centers. This division between prosperity and poverty, between tropical luxury and urban fear, between asphalt avenues and dirt ditches, has become an integral part of the associations with Rio de Janeiro and Brazil more broadly. To quote anthropologist Erika Robb Larkins, Rio de Janeiro has become a place where "the allure of tropical Brazil merges with Rio's illicit narco-glamour" (2015, 81). Indeed, the favela has become a highly spectacularized site and a significant component of the nation's identity in recent cultural productions that range from media and video games to fashion and tourism.

Chapter 5 ("Favela, Film, Franchise") takes these tendencies as a point of reference but examines more closely the contradictions apparent in recent films that portray favelas as political and economic emerging spaces. What is the cultural logic underlying the repeated portrayals of these urban spaces? This chapter takes the favela as a branded place in contemporary media and considers how it as brand operates in a larger socioeconomic exchange. I depart from the idea of the "divided city" introduced by journalist Zuenir Ventura in the mid-1990s and draw on the concept of the franchise to reflect on the action-crime thriller *Tropa de elite* (*Elite Squad*, 2007), its sequel and record-setting box office hit *Tropa de elite 2—O inimigo agora é outro* (*Elite Squad 2: The Enemy Within*, 2010), and the documentary *5x pacificação* (*5x Pacification*, 2012). Considering Moor's point referenced earlier concerning how branding becomes a form of governance, the idea of a franchise allows for thinking about political and economic incorporation into a larger organization as well as the rights of membership in a larger entity. In turn, my discussion of these films considers how these works not only enter into a market of hate but also map political discontent before the election of Bolsonaro in 2018.

My discussion of these three films addresses the territorial, commercial, and political inclusion of the favela in the idea of a new Brazil. Both *Tropa de elite* films directed by José Padilha are notable for their violent, spectacular treatment of efforts to "pacify" the favelas. Meanwhile, the documentary *5x pacificação*, which is a production directed by several residents of Rio de Janeiro's favelas, stands in critical dialogue with the *Tropa* films regarding inequality and urban violence. Structured as a conversation with multiple stakeholders involved in the pacification process, the documentary focuses on the economic insertion of the favelas into the city, its impact on residents, and the development of new relationships between police and favela residents. Indeed, all three films reflect on the entrance of official urban security forces (or, since 2008, the establishment of Unidades de Polícia Pacificadora [Police Pacification Units]) and how their implementation has affected cultural life and the economy of Rio de Janeiro's favelas. Thus, in chapter 5, I offer a critical reading of these films at the intersection of recent cultural and urban policy and I examine how they have engaged in efforts to rebrand Rio's favelas by redefining these urban spaces as sites for economic and cultural exchange.

Chapter 6 ("Another Good Neighbor? U.S.-Brazil Relations Revisited On-Screen") continues the discussion of the new nation brand of Brazil and reflects on issues of global citizenship. National identities do not exist in isolation. Brazilian national identity has been influenced by the cultures and the politics of other nations, especially France and the United States (Sadlier 2008, 4). For instance, during the years of the Good Neighbor Policy (1933–1945), many Hollywood films incorporated Latin American characters or were set in Latin American locations, such as *Flying Down to Rio* (1933) and musicals like *The Gang's All Here* (1943). What is more, animated films such as Disney's *Saludos Amigos* (1942) and *The Three Caballeros* (1944) played a vital role in supporting Good Neighbor era policies. While animated features presented Latin America as a friendly and inviting place to North American visitors, live-action films frequently portrayed Latin America as an erotic playground for thrilling adventures or a refuge for outlaws. More recent Hollywood action thrillers and animated features offer portrayals of Brazil similar to those found in the Good Neighbor era.

Just as Hollywood has been at the heart of creating "Brand America," international cinema has been actively engaged in creating "Brand Brazil" for decades. Hundreds of films from numerous countries across the globe have made Brazil a central character (Amancio 2000). Promotion of Rio de Janeiro as an international site of film production was a goal of cultural policies (discussed in chapter 1). Hollywood heeded the call. Thus, chapter 6 complements the discussion of place-branding efforts addressed in chapter 1 by specifically considering the renewed international gaze on Brazil during a time when it appeared that the nation was a significant new global player. I focus on four contemporary Hollywood action-adventure films set in Rio de Janeiro, including *Fast Five* (Justin Lin, 2011), *The Incredible Hulk* (Louis Leterrier, 2008), and the animated features *Rio* (2011) and *Rio 2* (2014) by director Carlos Saldanha. Each of these films was a box office success in Brazil and internationally. What is more, *Rio 2* was strategically released before the start of the World Cup matches in 2014 and participated in the lead-up to promote Rio de Janeiro as a global city.

Despite their formal differences, these works reference new geopolitical relations (North-South, South-South) and trends in transnational cinemas such as portraying poverty and efforts to capitalize on new audiences who embrace moviegoing as a middle-class lifestyle practice. Continuing the discussion from chapter 5, I investigate how each film imagines the global through the local and takes up the favela as a site for interpreting international identities. However, these films also reveal tensions surrounding a shift in established North-South relationships. White, Anglo-American women still find freedom and romance below the equator while men with U.S. military-style force impose their own versions of justice and order over a presumably lawless, corrupt land. Thus, my discussion of global citizenship in chapter 6 reveals conflicts between "Brand America" and "Brand Brazil" and the contradiction that the established global order is not willing to accept a new and improved Brazil.

The concluding chapter ("States of Upheaval: The Marks That Linger") offers a reflection on events since 2014. The branding period came to a gradual and then abrupt closure. First, citizens took to the streets to manifest discontent in June 2013. Initially, the Movimento Passe Livre (Free Pass Movement) organized protests against an increase in bus fare in São Paulo, but the demonstrations also developed in other major Brazilian cities, reflecting an array of complaints and including a range of people of different backgrounds. If there were unifying factors, they were disgust with corruption and a crisis of political leadership (Lattman-Weltman 2015, 44). As many nations have discovered in recent years, infrastructure investment in the World Cup and Olympic Games left a financial hangover. Indeed, the branding period whereby a new Brazil was being symbolically constructed has revealed marked class tensions and triggered a cultural and political backlash. The shortcomings of a neodevelopmentalist model became apparent when economic growth slowed in 2011 and 2012, prompting a loss of illusions for the popular classes and inciting an orthodox neoliberal camp to initiate a "restorative agenda" that resulted in the impeachment of Rousseff in August 2016 (Boito 2018, 13, 282–285). In March 2014, a massive corruption scandal in the state-led petroleum company Petrobras was discovered, prompting ongoing investigations into inflated construction contracts and bribes. Whereas the period from 2003 to 2014 can be characterized by the creation of cultural policies that have supported the democratic expansion and diversification of cultural production, funding for the arts, education, and social programs has been markedly reduced and social progress has been slowed. Since taking office in early January 2019, Bolsonaro has instituted a series of perplexing, if not authoritarian, actions that have made the arts a national enemy and seem to indicate a determination to undo the democratic advances made over the past decades since the end of the military dictatorship.[14]

Recent increases in urban violence, an ongoing economic downturn, and divisive political rhetoric from the Bolsonaro administration seem to contradict the words years ago of Gilberto Gil, who advocated for a more tolerant, democratic, and plural Brazil. Yet the promises of progress and social mobility presented during the branding period have not been forgotten. Between victory and defeat, the significant transformations that took place during the branding period have left an indelible mark on Brazilian society. As noted in the conclusion to this book, branding involves discursive practices informed by capitalism and, as such, may fall short of achieving socioeconomic equality. What is key is to consider the impact of cultivating utopic ideas of a new Brazil in the wider audiovisual environment and how these works challenged and negotiated the boundaries of local and global belonging.

1

Branding Brazil through Cultural Policy

■ ■

The day after Luiz Inácio Lula da Silva was sworn in as president in January 2003, Gilberto Gil became the head of the Ministry of Culture. In his acceptance speech, the acclaimed and politically committed singer and songwriter from humble northeastern origins (similar to Lula) asserted that the nation had expressed popular support at the polls for an essential and strategic change. The new minister outlined several notable themes and promoted lines of action. While celebrating foundational ideas about Brazil as a nation (its racial, ethnic, and geographic diversity; its syncretism; the people's inherently peaceful nature and creativity), Gil first called for a cultural opening. This would be achieved by the Ministry of Culture's fostering of a broader definition of culture that crossed class lines (i.e., breaking down divisions between "high" and "low" cultural manifestations) and stimulation of access to cultural production as a matter of citizenship rights.

More than likely aware of the history of cultural management as a tool for social control and renewal of power, Gil rejected multiple times the notion that the state was invested in making culture. It was, nonetheless, deeply committed to cultural production as a vehicle for national construction and integration. The state would act not through culture per se but through cultural policy and cultural institutions. Indeed, cultural policy would be the pivot point for redefining culture and the role of culture in Brazilian society. As a pivot point, one finds policies that rotated between neoliberalism and neopopulism while aiming for a break from the past and a deeper development of cultural and political democracy. Gil clearly announced that cultural policy would be seen as part of a general project of constructing a new hegemony in Brazil ("a construção de uma nova hegemonia em nosso País") or, in more tepid language, the project to establish a truly democratic, plural, and tolerant Brazil ("uma nação realmente democrática, plural e tolerante") (2003). This new comprehension of culture and cultural policy would join a new configuration of actions working in tandem with other ministries (of tourism, education, environment, work, sports, and national integration) with the larger purpose of not only meeting domestic needs but, notably, seeking a new insertion of Brazil in the world. However, a judicious balance between social and economic development is not easily achieved. Tereza Ventura (2014) describes Brazilian cultural policy starting in 2003 as walking a fine line between a neoliberal economic logic that seeks social integration by way of the market and a neosocialist logic of distribution and expansion.

The fundamental purpose of cultural and public policies is to organize and develop (or give shape to) social life in geopolitical units (such as towns, cities, nations). Cultural policies can offer practical as well as discursive interventions, meaning that they set the tone for cultural production as much as they provide structures on which creative efforts can be built. Branding is also a discursive process that involves fictionalization, mythmaking, and creating profitable affective associations with a product, place, or people. As noted in the introduction, the concept of branding has evolved beyond the corporate world and its meaning as an image or reputation to include other aspects of the marketization and commodification of everyday life, as a strategy for international diplomacy, and as a form of sociopolitical expression and organization (Aronczyk and Powers 2010; Aronczyk 2013; Arvidsson 2006; C. Lury 2004).

Nation branding involves the mediation of a geopolitical space and can best be defined as a contingent, relational phenomenon that communicates new notions of national and cultural identity in the current context of economic globalization. Notably, place branding involves the development of new geographical imaginaries (Pike 2011), and it has become particularly important as a driver of economic and political development for countries in transition (Anholt 2006, 2007; Szondi 2007). A nation's brand is an amalgam of perceptions of and associations with a given country that affects socioeconomic investment—from direct economic flows to having a voice in international forums. A central claim of place and nation branding is that if perceptions about a place can change, then a given location can change its role in a broader economy. Fundamentally, branding involves communicative strategies that are promotional (i.e., wanting to "sell" something) and that intervene in value systems. These discursive strategies seek a socioeconomic profit or advantage.

Cultural policies have sought to intervene in symbolic and economic processes by motivating new values (linked to Brazil as a place and its people) and stimulating participation in the cultivation of new markets. Like the narratives they motivate, cultural policies are open to ideological critique. Whereas other chapters in this book consider how the idea of a "new Brazil" was manifested in different modes of media (film, photography, and television), this chapter takes cultural policy in Brazil as a strategic, communicative tool to foster new ideas about citizenship and cultural identity. I offer a critical interpretation of contemporary cultural policy as engaging in a complex process of nation branding. I first map key tendencies of contemporary cultural policy in Brazil from 2003 to 2014, focusing on efforts to affirm cultural diversity and expand cultural production. I also outline how cultural policies adopted principles of the creative economy. I then focus on significant trends in the film industry that aimed to expand production and distribution, as well as place-branding efforts to make Rio de Janeiro a key site for a new creative economy and film capital of Latin America.

A New Regime of Visibility

The Lula administration's approach to culture heralded a new era for Brazil in which cultural policies would be retooled to intervene in the shape of national and cultural identity as well as develop a new model of development. That is, cultural policy would be a strategic tool to seek multiple profits: social, economic, and political. Cultural production was central to creating a cultural democracy, overcoming social exclusion, and it was defined as a way to generate employment and attract investment in the country. Programs sought to affirm diversity, expand access and production, and change the regimes of visibility in the country. The Lula administration saw culture "in all its dimensions, from the symbolic to the economic," and government began a period of culture-led regeneration (Brazil, Ministério da Cultura 2006, 5). The Ministry of Culture launched a series of initiatives to diversity cultural expression, expand access to culture, and stimulate internal consumption of culture, including the programs Cultura Viva (2004), Mais Cultura (2007), and Vale Cultura (2012).[1] Whereas the Cultura Viva program emphasized diversity and inclusion, the Mais Cultura program reflected increased attention to culture as a mode of socioeconomic development.

Cultura Viva

The Cultura Viva program was created in 2004 to stimulate cultural production and administration, with the Pontos de Cultura (Culture Points) serving as the base of a nation-wide network. In other words, the Cultura Viva program acted through proposed cultural projects designated as Pontos de Cultura. All projects were linked back to the Pontos de Cultura network through a system of agreements (*convênios*) between municipal or state and federal governments. Funds for projects were initially awarded through a system of public grant competitions (*editais*) that projects would apply for. The network of Pontos de Cultura projects was conceived of as a way to create dialogue between citizens and the government and was also motivated by the goal to support cultural manifestations and practices outside areas with an existing concentration of cultural offerings and production.

The network of cultural projects was dedicated to creating a new political culture whereby sociopolitical exclusion would be confronted and broad cultural citizenship would be confirmed. According to Célio Turino (2010, 14–16, 52), who, as secretary of cultural citizenship, formulated the Cultura Viva program, culture was defined less as a product and more as a process, flux, and pulsation, with flows between and among urban territories being key. As the periphery and the favelas were the clear focus of action for the Cultura Viva program, there were some concerns that initiatives may simply create new isolated nuclei. However, critics have asserted that the program has been highly successful in stimulating an unprecedented level of sociocultural interrelations in that it has motivated participatory dialogue between artists, social movements, and official institutions (Lopes et al. 2014; Paschoalick and Rodrigues 2014).

Nearly ten years after its implementation, the Cultura Viva program gained a presence throughout the nation, supporting Pontos de Cultura led by institutions and independent groups. The program introduced the idea of urban networks and demonstrated that cross-cultural exchange is vital. What is more, it revitalized urban social movements and increased dialogue between and among urban areas. In this way, the Cultura Viva program contributed to creating a new political and urban culture, as well as changing the relationship between cultural consumers and producers. At the end of 2014, there were over three thousand Pontos de Cultura in the national network and nearly five thousand initiatives had been awarded funds.[2] When the Cultura Viva program began, it was seen as an innovative and powerful democratizing agent. It grew to become one of the largest cultural programs in Brazil in terms of its reach and the number of people involved. It not only allowed broad access to cultural goods but also sought to provide the knowledge and access to resources that would allow target populations to produce cultural goods of their own. In this, the program was not only concerned with the democratization of culture (or granting access to cultural productions) but also engaged in forming a cultural democracy (or stimulating cultural production across all sectors of society). Thus, the Pontos de Cultura network was linked to a broader, more inclusive belief that culture could help change Brazil by restructuring society. Again, the program's founder, Turino, asserts that the Pontos de Cultura would potentiate a process of change—political and cultural (2010, 16). Indeed, one finds two key political and cultural changes: the strengthening of cultural production as democratic practice and the dislocation and diversification of cultural expression.

The Cultura Viva program, executed through the Pontos de Cultura network, set the agenda to dislocate culture and diversify expression. As noted earlier, the effort to democratize culture was about not only granting access to existing cultural production and venues concentrated in wealthier or developed urban areas but also permitting the production of cultural goods outside these territories. The program has aimed to reduce cultural asymmetries in cultural production in terms of financing and representation, and a method for diversifying cultural expression was to make the target population for this program those living in the urban periphery. Indeed, Turino stated that one of the goals was to "desesconder o Brasil" (un-hide Brazil) (2010, 14). In the case of a city like Rio de Janeiro, this translates into recognizing and supporting cultural manifestations and practices in underserved areas, especially the North Zone, the West Zone, and the favelas spread throughout the metropolitan area. As critics have observed, state-sponsored Pontos de Cultura projects recognize the general stereotypical representation of the culture of the periphery and acknowledge that the favelas are a source from which culture has been extracted. However, by granting access to production know-how to members of these communities to construct their own images, the regimes of visibility are redistributed (Lopes et al. 2014). Notably, audiovisual production represents a significant percentage of activities in the Pontos de Cultura (W. Santos 2014).[3] Indeed, this book explores the tensions and exchanges surrounding this new regime of visibility developed in and through creative, audiovisual practices. This subject is taken up further in chapters 4 and 5.

Mais Cultura: Toward the Creative Economy

A second phase began around 2006 and was characterized by an economic turn to cultural policies that continued to the end of the first Rousseff administration (2011–2014). Brazilian scholars characterize the shift in cultural policy during the first Lula administration as a watershed, democratic moment (Calabre 2013; Rubim 2010) but critique the more recent embrace of economic-driven policies as a "backward march" (Silveira, Machado, and Savazoni 2013). Whereas the first Lula administration prioritized a diversity agenda, the second administration took steps toward further positioning cultural production as part of a creative economy.

The Ministry of Culture published the *Programa cultural para o desenvolvimento do Brasil* (Cultural plan for the development of Brazil) in 2006, which states that cultural and economic development are interrelated and that public policies should simultaneously aim for the general cultural development of Brazilian society, contribute to social inclusion, generate income and employment, and affirm Brazil's unique position in the world (Brazil,

Ministério da Cultura 2006, 13). That is, cultural production was invested with a strategic social, political, and economic role to construct a more just society and affirm Brazil's sovereign place in the world. Thus, cultural production became a space for realizing four aspects of citizenship—cultural, political, class (or economic), and global.

Following the publication of the cultural plan in 2006, the Ministry of Culture launched the Mais Cultura program in October 2007. The program more fervently defended and elevated culture as a basic human right and necessity alongside food, shelter, health care, education, and the right to vote. It consists of partnerships between the federal government and various government ministries, publicly traded banks, international organizations, and civil society organizations and institutions that collaborate on projects that articulate the three dimensions of the Mais Cultura program: culture and citizenship, culture and cities, and culture and economy. Although the program sustains the idea that culture would be a way to affirm citizenship, the influence of the 2006 text is evident. It clearly emphasizes culture as a strategic tool for sustainable economic development. Whereas the Cultura Viva program emphasized access and inclusion through the creation of Pontos de Cultura, the Mais Cultura program highlighted cultural projects as an important vector of economic development for the country. In this, the Mais Cultura program reflects the beginnings of the turn toward principles of the creative economy.

The Lula administration's adoption of these principles can be understood within an international framework. First, a number of scholars debated the idea of the creative economy, creative industries, and the creative class, defining them as integral to the current global economy (Florida 2002; Howkins 2001). Several developed nations also adopted the premises of a creative economy to jump-start their postindustrial economies (e.g., the United Kingdom and Australia). International, creative cities have been cited as the nodal points of global flows of a creative economy (Flew 2012), and their creative industries are central to urban development (Flew 2013). Adding to these international examples, the United Nations Conference on Trade and Development (UNCTAD) promoted the notion of the creative economy among emerging nations. In 2000, the audiovisual sector and related culture industries were identified as prime areas for developing countries to improve their trade in services (UNCTAD 2000, 43). In 2002, the agency further encouraged improving the participation of developing countries in audiovisual services, framing audiovisual production as a "nation building instrument" and "a pillar of the new economy" (UNCTAD 2002, 2). In 2004, at a meeting held in São Paulo, UNCTAD asserted that creative industries can "open up new opportunities for developing countries to increase their shares of world trade and to 'leap-frog' into new areas of wealth creation" (2004, 3). Lastly, the international zeitgeist also helps explain the adoption of creative economy principles. Around 2004, predictions seemed to be coming true that Brazil was a significant emerging (or BRIC) nation. It is at this time that the growth rate of Brazil's gross domestic product began to surpass the United States' and slightly outpace global averages. A need for greater socioeconomic integration at home was met with increasing international interest, which took on desperate tones during the economic crisis of 2007/2008.

The creative economy was embraced as one way to restructure society at home and reposition Brazil on the global stage. Principles of the creative economy were integrated into the 2010 Plano Nacional de Cultura (National Culture Plan). In 2011, the Ministry of Culture published the *Plano da Secretaria da Economia Criativa: Políticas, diretrizes e ações, 2011–2014*. Ana de Hollanda, as minister of culture (2011–2012), called for a secretariat of the creative economy to develop a national plan called Brasil Criativo (Creative Brazil) that would capitalize on Brazil's international reputation as a creative nation and simultaneously craft a new mode of development (Brazil, Ministério da Cultura 2011). In 2012, the federal Secretariat of the Creative Economy was officially established and charged with developing policies to realize the strategic potential of the creative sector. Regarding the turn to the creative economy in Brazil, Ana Carla Fonseca Reis offers two explanations. First, the creative economy was to have a role in promoting the image of Brazil (2008, 17). Second, the failures of the traditional economic system, which had not promoted development and inclusion, prompted the search for a new economic model to enable new social and economic relations (2008, 130).

Thus, culture-led regeneration in Brazil involved three interconnected processes on two stages—local and global. First, cultural policies were formulated to make cultural production part of the creative economy. Second, a creative economy lent support to a neoliberal economy of branding. Third, cultural policies became strategic interventions to achieve broader sociopolitical integration and communicate as well as celebrate new notions of cultural identity. This would make cultural policies seem simply a tool for contemporary nation building. Yet from the perspective of nation branding, cultural policies in Brazil at this time sought this goal en route to broader profitable symbolic reformulations of the nation, cultural production, and cultural identity. Brazil and Brazilianness (*brasilidade*) became flexible commodities for local and global consumption during a fervent period of redefining Brazil as an emerging nation.

New Paradigms for the Audiovisual Sector

The 2006 cultural plan defined the audiovisual sector as a strategic area for cultural policy and as a broad field that included filmmaking, television, and new digital technologies. Furthermore, audiovisual production was defined as a vehicle to enact change domestically and it was cast as having the external reach to reposition Brazil internationally. Policies and programs were implemented that sought to diversify and expand production as well as expand the exhibition sector to support the growth of the film industry.

Following the general trajectory of cultural policy at this time, support for audiovisual production emphasized diversity and inclusion and then became more integral to government development plans. As head of the Secretariat of Audiovisual (SAv) sector, Ana Paula Dorado Santana called for an expansion of audiovisual activities in 2012 and declared that one of the goals of the SAv is to transform the audiovisual sector into "a major factor contributing to the fulfillment of the main goals of the Federal Government" (2012, 66). She further affirmed that policies concerning the audiovisual sector must be aligned with government's programs Brasil Sem Miséria (Brazil without Poverty) and Brasil Maior (Bigger Brazil) in order to effectively "include production, income generation and the due recognition of audiovisual concerns as part of strategic state policy for economic, social and cultural development within these goals" (66).

Funding mechanisms allowed for some diversification of expression, but they focused increasingly on creating commercially viable products. Broadly speaking, a modest fiscal incentive period was followed by consistent steps to provide economic support to make filmmaking part of a creative economy. During this transition, one finds a focus on producing commercially successful films and capturing a greater share of the internal market. The Agência Nacional do Cinema (Brazilian Film Agency, ANCINE) reported a "constant and significant" increase from 2002 to 2006 in funding for audiovisual production (2006, 70). However, the more significant trend is the emphasis on the production of more economically successful works. For instance, the Banco Nacional de Desenvolvimento Econômico e Social (Brazilian Development Bank) conducted an analysis of the audiovisual sector in 2005 and subsequently changed the selection criteria for those projects in which it invested. Projects had to show commercial potential and the production company had to provide a clear business plan and a consistent business strategy (Gorulho 2012).

Diversifying Expression

A central premise of the creative economy is that creative industries generate employment and wealth. For the Brazilian government, broad participation in cultural production celebrates the nation's diversity and aims to realize greater socioeconomic inclusion. Both São Paulo and Rio de Janeiro have been centers of audiovisual production for decades, but there have been efforts to expand production outside both cities. A push to geographically diversify audiovisual production received federal support. In 2004, the SAv initiated the program Revelando os Brasis (Revealing Brazils), which provides audiovisual training workshops to members of small and medium-size communities with the intention of mobilizing communities around the production of videos and incorporating new points of view on Brazil's cultural diversity.

During the years when notions of the creative economy were developing and taking root in cultural policy, there were some early attempts to broaden access to audiovisual production. The program Brasil Som e Imagem (Brazil Sound and Image) was proposed early in the configuration of ANCINE and was assigned the objective of developing Brazilian cinematographic and audiovisual activities as an instrument for social inclusion, citizenship, and the generation of employment and income (ANCINE 2006, 68). In practice it was more dedicated to meeting goals related to managing incentive programs and financing audiovisual and cinematographic activities as opposed to fostering broader participation in the field. Under the direction of the SAv, a number of programs were subsequently developed that contributed to the diversification of audiovisual productions in underserved areas. The SAv developed the Política Nacional de Conteúdos Digitais (National Policy on Digital Content), which aims to strengthen the productive networks of different audiovisual sectors (i.e., cinema, television, animation, music, and electronic games). Among its five lines of action, one is specifically dedicated to regional development and another is dedicated to education and training.

Two notable initiatives managed by the SAv include the programs Olhar Brasil (Brazil Gaze) and Nós na Tela (Us on Screen). Both programs are initiatives to make Brazil a producer of content and reverse the nation's cultural history whereby it had been a traditional consumer of imported content (Brazil, Ministério da Cultura 2006, 21–22). Previous efforts by the SAv to support young participants in audiovisual training programs became formalized as the Nós na Tela program in 2008. Participants or graduates of programs run by popular social movements dedicated to producing audiovisual works are the intended audience for the Nós na Tela program. Since its consolidation under the SAv, the program has successfully helped develop projects in all regions of Brazil, ensured the distribution of these works through community channels, held competitive festivals, and assisted in securing internships for outstanding participants (SAv 2010, 24).

The Olhar Brasil program spearheads the regionalization of audiovisual production and supports independent production, which it primarily achieves through the creation of Núcleos de Produção Digital (Digital Production Nuclei). Since 2006, the program has developed agreements with institutions in eleven states. Among its notable successes is the collaboration with the Centro Audiovisual Norte-Nordeste (North and Northeast Audiovisual Center) that has provided cinematographic equipment to filmmakers in the region and offered various audiovisual training programs. The collaboration further contributes to changing the regimes of visibility in Brazil. The northern and northeastern regions, which are home to significant Afro-Brazilian and indigenous populations, have historically been more the subject of cinematic representation by predominantly White directors and producers located in the South and Southeast (Rio de Janeiro and São Paulo). Providing the tools and skills for production in this region significantly increases the possibility of future productions by regional producers about their own cultures.

What is more, these efforts would potentially open audiovisual production to Brazilians of African and indigenous descent, whose experiences and voices have been notably limited in the Brazilian audiovisual landscape. For instance, recent surveys indicate that 54 percent of the Brazilian population identifies as "black" (*preto*) or "brown" (*pardo*) (Instituto Brasileiro de Geografia e Estatística 2016, 39–40). Yet a study conducted by ANCINE of feature-length films released in 2016 reveal an egregious absence of Black and Brown people on screens and on production teams (as writers, directors, cinematographers, producers, and so forth) (ANCINE 2018). In sum, these efforts to expand access to training and regionalization of audiovisual production have begun the process of expanding the sector beyond the traditional centers (São Paulo and Rio de Janeiro) and have been particularly effective thus far in stimulating audiovisual cultural production in historically underserved areas.

Notably, these federally supported programs to diversify film and media production follow on the heels of several preexisting efforts that had developed in Rio de Janeiro. The 2002 film *Cidade de Deus* (*City of God*) is a watershed work not only in the sense that it closes the *retomada*[4] period in Brazilian film history but also because it functions as a departure point for thinking about the diversification of access to cinematic production and efforts to use audiovisual production as a path to greater social and cultural inclusion. Directors Fernando Meirelles and Kátia Lund collaborated with the urban cultural organization Nós do Morro (Us from the Hillside), a community-based theater company and school founded in 1986 and located in the Vidigal favela of Rio de Janeiro. Numerous actors from the organization took on roles in *Cidade de Deus*. Youths from Vidigal who had participated in the workshops offered by the directors in 2000 as part of the casting process wanted to continue their work in audiovisual production.

Subsequently, the group Nós do Cinema (Us of Cinema) was established in 2002 and the Popular Cinema School focused its efforts on youths with the objectives of producing films that treat topics with aesthetics familiar to lower-income groups and inserting youths into the film labor market. In 2006, the organization changed its name to Cinema Nosso (Our Cinema), relocated to the center of Rio, and gained support from the federal government. Cinema Nosso has become one of the largest popular film schools in Latin America, and films produced by its students have participated in hundreds of national and international festivals. Cinema Nosso is joined by many similar efforts to democratize audiovisual production with a focus on youths and young adults from low-income backgrounds.[5] These programs allow a diverse population to gain skills in audiovisual production, enter the creative economy, and contribute to the symbolic and economic reformulation of suburban locations. Such is the case with *5x favela—agora por nós mesmos* (*5x Favela, Now by Ourselves*, 2010) and *5x pacificação* (5x pacification, 2012)—discussed in chapter 5. Both are multidirector works by filmmakers from the favelas of the North Zone of Rio that critique narratives of favelas as violent zones and affirm them as complex, creative urban spaces.

Expanding Exhibition

As it renewed its dialogue with the film industry in Brazil, ANCINE declared that distribution and exhibition were vital to the expansion and sustainability of the Brazilian audiovisual sector. The federal agencies ANCINE and the SAv have worked in tandem to support film as an important sector in the creative economy by increasing access and supporting the expansion of the market base (i.e., assisting in the construction of hundreds of new cinemas throughout Brazil). A series of programs—Cine Mais Cultura (More Culture Cinema), Cinema Perto de Você (Cinema Close to You), and Cinema da Cidade (City Cinema)—sought to change the geography of cinema and democratize access to Brazilian productions. Two notable initiatives are the Programadora Brasil (Brazil Programmer), which distributes Brazilian works to alternative venues throughout the nation, and the Cine Mais Cultura program, which provides projection equipment, Brazilian content, and training to cine clubs to screen Brazilian films throughout the nation. What results is a vast network of alternative exhibition spaces especially in the periphery of urban centers, as well as in the rural interior of the country. These venues provide low-cost or free admission to view Brazilian works. The program is an example of the democratization of access to culture, and according to the SAv, the Cine Mais Cultura network is poised to be the world's largest noncommercial exhibition circuit (SAv 2010, 27–28). Yet expansion of the exhibition sector responded to the growth in the new middle class during this time period. Indeed, the program Cinema Perto de Você focused on inviting the legion of new members of the middle class into theaters, as it was seen as the social group with the greatest potential for consumption. If the program concerned democratizing access to culture, it was also invested in strengthening the internal market for national productions. It also concerned shifting lifestyle experiences in cities located especially in the interior, where there were markedly fewer cinemas than in the more urbanized regions of the South and Southeast.

An example of the alternative exhibition venues just described is the Cine-Carioca initiative sponsored by RioFilme. The program focuses on building low-cost cinemas in suburban areas of Rio de Janeiro. To date there are two theaters in the network, with plans to develop an additional ten. In 2010, Rio-Filme inaugurated the first 3-D theater located in a favela, the CineCarioca Nova Brasília in the middle of the Complexo do Alemão favela, a former bastion for Rio's drug traffickers. In 2012, the CineCarioca Méier was opened in a poor area of the city at the site of the former Cine Imperator, a movie theater from the 1950s that used to screen *chanchadas*[6] by the company Atlântida Cinematográfica. With 2,400 seats, the Cine Imperator had been the largest cinema in all of Latin America, but it closed in 1986 because of falling ticket sales. The investment in these cinemas is consonant with broader national policies to democratize access to cultural production and, it is believed, overcome ingrained inequalities. Theaters show primarily blockbuster Brazilian and foreign films and ticket prices are held low (at approximately two dollars) to ensure affordability and access. The CineCarioca venues certainly democratize access to culture and stimulate new urban experiences, but they also promote an aspirational middle-class lifestyle and cultivate an interest in going to the cinema.

In addition to stimulating the habit of going to the movies, these neighborhood cinemas play a role in restructuring urban spaces, making them more just and dynamic locations. If cinema was born in the streets of urban metropoles, then its resurrection in suburban locations can potentially rejuvenate them. Indeed, there are a number of historical precedents in Brazil for using cinema exhibition as a vehicle for modernization in the early decades of the twentieth century (Conde 2012; Navitski 2017). In the past, the renovation and construction of new exhibition venues led to material urban transformations both in terms of new buildings and public plazas and in terms of social and economic development. Just as people's occupation of public spaces stimulates greater social interaction, businesses near cinemas benefit from increased customer traffic. The CineCarioca theaters have certainly had an impact on the local urban environment, and they join a broader effort to develop the creative economy in Rio's favelas. Next to the Nova Brasília cinema, the Praça do Conhecimento (Knowledge Park) was built, providing local residents with training in audio, visual, and digital skills.

Brasil Todas as Telas

In 2014, the federal government announced the ambitious program Brasil Todas as Telas (Brazil All Screens). The program was an unprecedented, multifaceted government project to transform the country into a major center of audiovisual production. It was defined by four lines of action to expand the exhibition sector, further training and education programs, and stimulate the development and distribution of Brazilian audiovisual content. The program specifically targets cinema and television production with the goal of developing regional production centers throughout the nation. It furthered initiatives that had begun nearly ten years earlier. And like those efforts, the program sought to capitalize on the remarkable growth in the middle class, which represented a significant audience for Brazilian productions.

Yet the external market was also of great importance at this time of heightened attention on Brazil. Several programs were created to support the exportation of Brazilian audiovisual productions abroad, including Cinema do Brasil, which worked in collaboration with the state-run Agência de Promoção de Exportações e Investimentos (Agency to Promote Exports and Investments, APEX). Created in 2006 by the Sindicato da Indústria Audiovisual do Estado de São Paulo (São Paulo Audiovisual Industry Union), Cinema do Brasil is a private-sector association of Brazilian producers that aims to internationalize Brazilian cinema by assisting coproductions, assisting films selected for international festivals, and assisting distribution of Brazilian films abroad. Although Cinema do Brasil has played an important role in helping develop international coproductions and advanced Brazilian cinema at key international film festivals like Cannes, APEX threatened to withdraw financial support in March 2019, but the government claimed it would renew APEX funding a month later (Hopewell 2019). The threat to defund APEX and Cinema do Brasil reflects the chaos in cultural policy inaugurated by the Jair Bolsonaro administration and is reflected on further later.

Rio de Janeiro as a Creative, Audiovisual City

Scholars of the creative economy and creative industries note overlaps with place and nation branding. Justin O'Connor and Xin Gu (2013, 43) see creative industries as parts of the knowledge economy that are also geographically rooted and exemplify local histories and cultures. These authors argue that creative industry policy should be seen as a sort of urban policy. They emphasize how creative industries contribute to developing new symbolic values tied to places and participate in the generation of new narratives about urban spaces. What is more, they contend that creative industries benefit from and contribute to the image of a city (52).

As part of a culture-led development model, creative cities and creative territories become the locus of new cultural productions, with urban spaces themselves becoming enmeshed in the process of transforming into new cultural constructions. Rio de Janeiro has long been a center of audiovisual production and, more generally, a cultural center for Brazil given the historical concentration of government agencies and financial investment in cultural activities in the city and state. Despite Brazil's being a nation of continental proportions, Rio de Janeiro often serves as metonym for all of the country. Yet Rio de Janeiro has been at the center of efforts to develop a creative economy in Brazil in which the audiovisual sector was defined as a key creative industry. Drawing on the case of Rio de Janeiro and efforts to make it a creative, audiovisual city allows for exploring salient themes in cultural policy: the diversification of expression, stimulation of the internal market through exhibition and production, and efforts to seek external projection. Notably, the audiovisual sector has joined other initiatives of urban redevelopment.

The federal government as well as local and international institutions and agencies have collaborated to define Rio de Janeiro as a creative city and international cultural hub. They also help define the city as spectacle. In 2012, UNESCO declared the entire city of Rio de Janeiro a World Heritage site, a decision that made the city one of the first in the world to be honored in this way. A series of mega-events (e.g., the United Nations Rio+20 of 2012, World Catholic Youth Day of 2013, the FIFA World Cup of 2014, and the Olympic Games of 2016) originally orchestrated during the Lula administrations have stimulated significant (and controversial) urban development projects but have also cultivated Rio de Janeiro as a focal point for international attention.

Rio de Janeiro began efforts to define itself as a creative city in 2000 with the inauguration of the Superintendency of the Cultural Economy. More recently, support of Rio as a creative city has also come from two key regional institutions. The first is Rio Criativo (Creative Rio), an incubator for the creative economy in the state of Rio de Janeiro that was established by the State Secretariat of Culture with support from the Pontifícia Universidade Católica do Rio de Janeiro (Pontifical Catholic University of Rio de Janeiro). Not only is Rio Criativo the first incubator of the creative economies in Brazil, but UNCTAD has cited it as one of the most relevant examples in the world of fostering the creative economies. The success of Rio Criativo has served as an example for the development of a national network of creative economy incubators as part of the Brasil Criativo program. Another institution is the regional economic entity the Federação das Indústrias do Estado do Rio de Janeiro (Federation of Industries of the State of Rio de Janeiro). According to a study conducted by the federation in 2008—the first of its kind in the nation to map out the creative sector—the creative industries represent approximately 18 percent of all economic activity in Rio de Janeiro and audiovisual is a top sector (4, 15).

RioFilme

Defining Rio de Janeiro as a creative city in terms of audiovisual production and making the city more consumable in audiovisual works have been the goals of two key agencies, RioFilme and FilmeRio–Rio Film Commission. In short, the audiovisual industry in Rio de Janeiro has on its agenda the rebranding of Rio de Janeiro as a creative city and appealing regional and global audiovisual hub. This effort to redefine cities as creative audiovisual centers is also seen in the cities of other emerging nations, such as Shanghai and Beijing in China.

Over the course of its existence, RioFilme has transitioned from being a more limited, regional distributor to becoming a key player in the nation's audiovisual sector. In 1992, the city of Rio de Janeiro founded RioFilme, which operated at the time as a regional distributor of films during the *retomada* in the 1990s. During the cultural transition period inaugurated by the Lula administration, RioFilme developed a number of programs that were consistent with federal cultural policies informed by ideas of the creative economy and that were intended to create a stronger cultural democracy and democratize access to culture.

In 2009, efforts significantly increased to sell and shape the audiovisual and urban landscape in Rio de Janeiro. In broader context, 2009 also marks the culmination of an extended bidding process to secure Rio as the site for the 2016 Olympics and a moment when emerging nations took center stage as profitable territories after the global economic crisis of 2007/2008. At this time, RioFilme was reorganized and developed a proactive role in the funding of cinema and television production, as well as collaborating with other local agencies to promote and market Rio-based audiovisual productions. If RioFilme had been a minor agency, it was becoming a key investor in cinema, television, and new media. RioFilme's former commercial director, Adrién Muselet (personal communication, May 15, 2014), confirms that in 2014 the agency signed an unprecedented contract with YouTube to develop digital media content; at least 30 percent of the YouTube-RioFilme projects will come from audiovisual initiatives developed in Pontos de Cultura. In this way, RioFilme sought to open new venues for Brazilian content and develop future audiovisual practices. To gain this foothold in supporting audiovisual production, RioFilme has created two lines of funding for cinema and television. One line supported commercial productions, while the other provided funds for projects of great artistic value but with less probability of significant box office success. Muselet also reports that RioFilme's budget jumped from R$1.1 million in 2008 to R$50 million in 2012; as a result, the agency invested in 22 projects in 2008 and 124 in 2013. Subsequently, RioFilme became the second-largest investor in filmmaking in the nation (behind federal funding lines) and helped fund some of the highest-grossing Brazilian productions.

In essence, RioFilme invested in blockbusters as a way to generate steady income to invest in future blockbusters and, in theory, support its "nonrefundable" line of investment in less commercial works. Film and media studies scholar Courtney Brannon Donoghue (2014, 537) notes that local blockbusters have become a trend not just in Brazil but also among emerging media industries outside the Anglophone market. However, she underscores that Brazilian filmmakers do not simply replicate Hollywood but adapt strategic elements "to reimagine the scale and commercial nature of a national cinema within global terms" (538). For instance, RioFilme has invested in a good number of culturally specific comedies, which have been some of the highest-grossing films in recent years. In 2013, RioFilme invested in nineteen films, of which eight (42 percent) were comedies (RioFilme 2014).

According to agency documents, having reestablished itself in the local and national arenas, RioFilme aims to make Rio de Janeiro a Latin American center for cinema, television, and new media production (RioFilme 2014). Indeed, film trailers advertise RioFilme's role in making the city a site for local and global film production. RioFilme promotional flyers further promote Rio as a filmmaking mecca. One in particular includes white letters of Rio de Janeiro at the foot of the green mountain (Corcovado) on which the famous Christ the Redeemer statue stands. The white lettering for Rio de Janeiro in the promotional flyer clearly resembles the Hollywood sign clinging to the hills outside Los Angeles and announces Rio as a powerful international center of production that aims to capture more share of a market that has previously been dominated by foreign productions. Whether or not Brazilian production reiterates Hollywood blockbuster models, there remains a complicated relationship with Hollywood as an influence chronically looming over the audiovisual space and serving as a cultural point of reference. RioFilme's recent slogans demonstrate the intent to take a more self-defining role and insert Rio into the local and global audiovisual markets.

FilmeRio–Rio Film Commission

The year 2009 also marks when the agency FilmeRio–Rio Film Commission was established. As an official unit of the city government, the Rio Film Commission is charged primarily with drawing foreign productions to Rio de Janeiro and assisting production crews when on location in the state or city of Rio de Janeiro. Representatives of the Rio Film Commission attend film festivals and international content markets such as Cannes and Berlin. Steve Solot, former president of the Rio Film Commission and former vice president of the Latin American operations of the Motion Picture Association, has outlined in various essays the prime opportunities that the audiovisual sector in Rio de Janeiro can take advantage of given the increased attention and interest in the region that has resulted from the series of international mega-events. That is, unique opportunities exist to develop the creative economy to promote the image of Rio and Brazil more generally.

Unlike other film commissions in Brazil that have formed recently, the Rio Film Commission offers some modest production subsidies to foreign film productions. For instance, in 2012 it offered nearly $1 million to productions based on their marketability and their promotion of Rio de Janeiro. Despite the clear uptick in interest on the part of foreign production crews and producers, film commissions in Brazil need greater structure and organization to meet external demands. Solot advocated for ensuring that trained professionals be employed at Brazil's film commissions and called repeatedly for creating financial incentives to attract productions, which generate significant revenue for local businesses. Solot (2012) notes an overall strengthening of film commissions in other regions of Latin America (e.g., Mexico, the Dominican Republic, Colombia, and Chile) in terms of their organization and development of financial incentives to attract foreign production companies, but this has not occurred at the same pace in Brazil. In 2015, the organization joined forces with the Rede Brasileira de Film Commissions (the Brazilian Film Commission Network) to attract international productions to Brazil. More recently, the Rio Film Commission furthered its efforts to internationalize Brazilian audiovisual production at the 2019 BRICS Film Forum, an event joining film industry representatives from Russia, India, China, and South Africa. And the organization has represented Rio de Janeiro at Rio2C, the Rio Creative Conference, the largest event dedicated to innovation and creative work in Latin America.

Besides reshaping the audiovisual industry of Rio de Janeiro, in recent years the work of RioFilme and the Rio Film Commission has engaged in two significant trends by contributing to an upswing in the international promotion of Rio de Janeiro and its audiovisual sector and taking on a role in local urban development. Both trends are clearly engaged in further branding Rio de Janeiro as a creative city. In 2013, RioFilme joined the Films from Rio initiative, which is a consortium of Rio's top film and television institutions that serves as an international promotional agency for the region's film and television industries (Hopewell 2013b). The work of Films from Rio parallels that of the promotional agency Cinema do Brasil, which is based in São Paulo but promotes films from all over Brazil. In addition to promoting Rio-based productions, Films from Rio coincides with the Rio Film Commission in its goal to promote Rio de Janeiro as a prime location for international shooting and coproductions. Despite these efforts to promote the audiovisual sector in Rio de Janeiro, Muselet (personal communication, May 15, 2014) feels that there has not yet been an effective place-branding strategy and that the city needs to do a better job of this to more proactively compete in the global audiovisual market.

Creative Industries and Urban Development

The activities of both agencies have directly and indirectly intervened in developing the urban landscapes of Rio de Janeiro. The CineCarioca program is only a modest indication of the plans that RioFilme has for converting culture-led regeneration into urban renewal. While mega-events have been at the forefront of stimulating urban development projects and stimulating local and national economies, the audiovisual sector in Rio has been defined as a key area of economic activity and one that would take the lead in development post-2016—after the Olympics. In order to do so, the audiovisual sector must improve its infrastructure. In 2013, RioFilme announced plans at the Cannes Film Festival to develop an Audiovisual City in a derelict area of the city known as São Cristóvão. This is a clear merging of cultural policy and urban development and shows an evolution in the activities of RioFilme. Indeed, the then president of RioFilme, Sérgio Sá Leitão, states that RioFilme has evolved from financing production to financing distribution and, more recently, television series production. Now it is moving into infrastructure development and training (Hopewell 2013a). RioFilme signed a thirty-five-year rental agreement in September 2013 to occupy an abandoned police headquarters, and the Audiovisual City is to be located in an abandoned postindustrial area near Rio's port, adjacent to the Porto Maravilha (Marvelous Port) development area and close to where Trump towers were planned to be erected. This project joins the previously announced plans to expand and develop the Rio Film and Video Pole in the area of Barra da Tijuca to the south of Rio's center (Mango 2013). The Pole, which was initially developed in the early 1990s to become a cinema city akin to a Brazilian Hollywood, had remained an unfinished project.

Since 2013, little has been reported on these projects, likely owing to recent economic and political crises. Whether or not the Audiovisual City eventually becomes a reality, other institutions (of other sectors of the creative industries) have taken root in Rio's central urban districts as part of the Porto Maravilha redevelopment project, which merges cultural and urban development to modernize Rio's central urban landscape. The project is presented within a creative economy framework in that it reinforces the preservation of cultural heritage and the fostering of socioeconomic inclusion. Considered one of Latin America's largest urban redevelopment projects to date, the Porto Maravilha project aims to redevelop Rio's postindustrial waterfront area, much like projects that have been completed in European cities like Barcelona and Rotterdam. Like many redevelopment initiatives, the Porto Maravilha project aims for "urban upgrading," or adding value to urban districts, which it will achieve in part through the development of cultural institutions (Prefeitura do Rio n.d.). For instance, the project included the construction of the Rio Museum of Art, which opened in 2013, and the Museum of Tomorrow (Museo do Amanhã), dedicated to science and technology and opened in 2015.[7] In what is a clear strategy of place branding, the project aims to develop cultural venues in an effort to make the district a more attractive destination for tourists as well as local residents while also increasing real estate values.

While more modest, the Rio Film Commission has also taken on a role to intervene in urban development through its connections with local tourism boards. In the course of encouraging and assisting productions to come to Rio de Janeiro, it has developed partnerships with TurisRio, a public company linked to the Secretariat of Tourism, Sports and Leisure; RIOTUR, the municipal tourism agency of the city of Rio de Janeiro and part of the Special

Tourist Secretariat of Rio de Janeiro; and the Rio Convention and Visitors Bureau. On its website it promotes various prime shooting locations (e.g., beaches, cathedrals, and colonial plantations). Solot (2015) has promoted "cinematographic tourism" in Brazil in order to take advantage of increased on-location shooting in Brazilian municipalities. In short, cinematographic tourism consists of receiving visitors to a location used in an audiovisual production and seeks additional economic benefits. It is a form of urban development that evolves out of the audiovisual branding of a place and the economic benefits brought by curious fan-tourists.

There is a history of promoting and developing cinema tourism. While fans of the Kevin Costner film *Field of Dreams* (1989) flocked to rural Iowa in the United States, hundreds of tourists have made Highclere Castle, which was made famous in the British series *Downton Abbey*, a travel destination. If cinematographic tourism develops in Rio de Janeiro, it can take advantage of the documents prepared by RioFilme that identify significant sites in the city that are part of Brazilian cinema history. The promotion of former location shooting sites as tourist destinations clearly engages in place-branding activity and furthers the idea of Rio de Janeiro as a creative city. Taking a cue from the efforts of RioFilme and the Rio Film Commission, the Ministry of Tourism created a task force in 2018 to promote cinematographic tourism, hoping to merge efforts to attract foreign film productions and visitors to Brazilian settings. These efforts to make Rio de Janeiro a creative city through audiovisual production align the city and region with the demands and opportunities of the global marketplace. However, the Bolsonaro administration took these efforts a perplexing step further in late 2019 and reorganized the film industry under the Ministry of Tourism.

Not all have been pleased with the efforts and programs developed by Rio-Filme and the Rio Film Commission. In a statement posted online in 2014 and publicized during the Rio Film Festival of that year, the movement calling itself Rio: Mais Cinema, Menos Cenário (Rio: More Cinema, Less Setting, RMCMC), formed by approximately two hundred professionals from the audiovisual sector—including Júlia Murat, Maria Augusta Ramos, Daniel Caetano, and Anna Azevedo—called on local and regional officials to develop more democratic, transparent policies that were attentive to the city's cultural diversity.

The RMCMC reiterated the tone and objectives set forth in 2003 by Gilberto Gil as minister of culture, described earlier. Noting that current policies prioritize and concentrate funds in a few already well-established production companies, the open letter called for increased funding overall for the audiovisual sector in Rio de Janeiro and, perhaps more importantly, demanded the deconcentration of resources to allow for more diverse audiovisual production (RMCMC 2014). The group notes that since 2008, RioFilme has directed a third of its funds to only 10 production companies; the remaining two-thirds of funds have been piecemealed out to 147 companies (2014). To further illustrate the imbalances, the group cites RioFilme's 2014 budget of R$42 million, of which R$18 million (43 percent) was invested "automatically" in projects that were selected exclusively based on economic criteria with little or no regard for artistic or social merit; meanwhile, only R$6 million (14 percent) of the budget went to projects that underwent a selective process (RMCMC 2014). Notably, these figures contradict the claim of a more equitable distribution made by the then director of RioFilme, Sergio Sá Leitão.

RMCMC has rejected the notion that it pits market-oriented cinema against independent or "art" films. Rather, it has called for a more balanced approach to government policies and has critiqued the current model that focuses on supporting a competitive audiovisual industry, which promotes Brazilian films that may bring box office success but follow pre-established genres and formats. In essence, RMCMC rejects recent strategies to promote a particular type of Brazilian cinema that not only conforms to a supply-and-demand logic of the local and global marketplace but also homogenizes and simplifies the cultural diversity of the city.

Cultural policies during the Lula and Rousseff administrations sought a strategic rearticulation of Brazil and Brazilianness. They also sought to strengthen the relationship between state and civil society, overcome social and cultural divides, and redefine the role and nature of cultural production in the economy of Brazil. Yet this fervent period of transformation slowly came to a close before the door seemed to shut soundly. Whereas the June Days of 2013 manifested a variety of complaints about the nation's political and economic development, it was in 2014 that culture-led regeneration began to unravel. In March of that year, the Petrobras corruption scandal of bribes and inflated construction contracts broke. Historically, the state oil company had been a significant supporter of Brazilian culture, cosponsoring both major international film festivals (held in Brasília, Rio de Janeiro, and São Paulo) and local community organizations. Petrobras's funding of the arts decreased in 2014 as criminal investigations commenced, but its role in the arts has been significantly cut under orders from President Jair Bolsonaro (2019–present).

If the Petrobras scandal and the victory of Germany over Brazil in the final of the World Cup did not tarnish the idea of a new Brazil, it has been dismantled by the Bolsonaro administration. Under Bolsonaro, culture and the arts have become an enemy. Although Michel Temer had tried to close the Ministry of Culture in 2016 and failed, Bolsonaro succeeded in eliminating the government agency on January 2, 2019, and relocated its activities to the Ministry of Citizenship. In late 2019, several government entities dedicated to the cultural sector were also transferred to the Ministry of Tourism.[8] Additionally, Bolsonaro modified the Lei Rouanet, a 1991 fiscal incentive law that has allowed companies to offset their tax liability by contributing to the arts. Notably, the Lei Rouanet had been an important source of financing and rebirth for the audiovisual sector during the redemocratization period. Bolsonaro's perplexing actions have not gone without a response from artists, politicians, academics, and members of the public. In July 2019, nine former government ministers (including five former ministers of culture) since the end of the military dictatorship in 1985 united in opposition to Bolsonaro's attack on the arts. They expressed concern that the current president's approach to culture was reversing democratic advances made over the past thirty years. They reiterated that culture is a fundamental right and expression of citizenship in Brazil.

2

Negotiating the Past
in the Dictatorship
Film Cycle

■■■■■■■■■■■■■■■■■■■■■■

On May 16, 2012, Dilma Rousseff installed Brazil's Comissão da Verdade (Truth Commission) with the stated goal of accounting for human rights violations that took place between 1946 and 1988. This period includes the end of the Estado Novo (1937–1945) under populist dictator Getúlio Vargas, the military dictatorship (1964–1985), and the period of redemocratization (1985–1988). In her remarks, Rousseff noted that the initiative was not intended as an act of revenge but was an effort to reveal the recent history of the country. She further asserted that the word "truth" is the contrary of forgetting and that truth does not harbor ill will, hatred, or forgiveness (A. Souza, Alencastro, and Damé 2012).

The Truth Commission, which was inaugurated the same day that an information access law (Lei de acesso à informação) took effect, was framed as the fruit of nearly thirty years of constructing and consolidating democracy in Brazil. These official measures appeared after what some have defined as a delayed consideration of the dictatorship or unfinished democratic transition. This is owing to factors such as a "depoliticized ethos" (Oricchio 2003, 119–120), the penetration of the authoritarian regime into the new democracy (Zaverucha 2010), and the fact that the naturalization of violence brought about the lack of transitional justice, transparency, and reconciliation (Teles and Safatle 2010, 9–12; Kehl 2010, 124). Both initiatives are important steps in the reinvention of political institutions that come on the heels of significant changes in civil society's attitudes regarding the very concept of citizenship.[1]

Installation of Brazil's Truth Commission is also remarkable given that Rousseff made the announcement. Not only had Rousseff participated in a Marxist guerrilla resistance movement (Movimento Revolucionário 8 de Outubro [Revolutionary Movement, 8th of October, MR-8]), but she also had been detained and tortured by the military regime. The Truth Commission is part of an effort to seek justice and political transparency, acknowledge human rights and violations thereof, and further strengthen civil society. But it is notable that Rousseff spoke against a backdrop that day in which the word *futuro* (future) took a prominent place alongside larger concepts such as *país* (country), *cidadania* (citizenship), *democracia* (democracy), and *direitos humanos* (human rights). This official effort to look at the past is framed as a solidification of rights. It is also an effort to make a break from the past. Addressing the recent history of the nation is also about promising progress, rethinking Brazilian cultural identity, and developing a "new Brazil."

Shortly after its inauguration, family members of victims celebrated but military groups harshly critiqued the commission as an act of revenge that failed to uphold the 1979 Amnesty Law. They proceeded to establish a parallel truth commission and promised (or threatened?) to monitor the activities of the state-sponsored Truth Commission. Responding to complaints from the military, a group of over one hundred filmmakers signed a declaration in defense of the proposed objectives of the Truth Commission (Barbar 2012).

The vocal stance of members of the filmmaking community in Brazil was not new. Indeed, the inauguration of the Truth Commission came after years of work done in cinema to analyze the dictatorial past and reveal the nation's recent history. Between 1994 and 2014, nearly fifty feature-length fiction and documentary films were released that reflect on Brazil's military dictatorship. Films released during the rebirth (*retomada*) of filmmaking from approximately 1995 to 2002 differ significantly from those works produced during the dictatorship. Allegory and other tangential modes of critique found in films from the 1960s and 1970s (Xavier 1997; Johnson and Stam 1995) are relatively absent.

The goal of this chapter is to explore the particular investments in the past found in select films of the contemporary dictatorship film cycle, which exist alongside state and nonstate initiatives and demands for an accounting of the dictatorship. The period of film production in question is one that coincides with significant economic growth, as well as the goal to solidify democracy in Brazil. The Brazilian government demonstrated a keen interest in the nation's external image, and evaluating the recent authoritarian past while emphasizing contemporary democratic practices and progressive social policies was part of the larger narrative of its emergence as a new global player. These works engage in a process of making claims on the past but contribute to (re)defining

Brazil as a stable, modern, democratic nation poised for a much-heralded new role as an economic power and global political leader. I argue that at the same time that these films emerge at the intersection of mediated nationhood, sociopolitical reconciliation, and the memory market, they are also engaged in a broader process of constructing a new nation brand for Brazil.

This corpus of films reflecting on the authoritarian past forms a dictatorship film cycle consisting of three phases. The first phase begins around 1994 and ends in 2002. A second phase begins in 2002 and concludes around 2009. Finally, a third phase begins around 2009 and the cycle comes to a gradual closure around 2014. In the first section of this chapter, I map key tendencies of the dictatorship film cycle, noting how the past was made distant from the present and how films celebrate past heroes and current democratic accomplishments. These works engage in a negotiation with the past that seeks various profits—social, political, and economic—and most notably an investment in the idea of a new Brazil. I then offer close readings of films from the second phase, focusing on *Zuzu Angel* (Sérgio Rezende, 2006), *Quase dois irmãos* (*Almost Brothers*, Lúcia Murat, 2004), *O ano em que meus pais saíram de férias* (*The Year My Parents Went on Vacation*, Cao Hamburger, 2006; hereafter referred to as *O ano em que*), and *Os Desafinados* (*Out of Tune*, Walter Lima Jr., 2008). The final section of this chapter discusses the closure to the film cycle and provides a brief overview of the tendencies of films released between 2009 and 2014. Unlike films from the first two phases, works in the final period of the dictatorship cycle offer more reflective, intimate considerations of the past. Notably, films such as *A memória que me contam* (*Memories They Told Me*, Lúcia Murat, 2012) and *Hoje* (*Today*, Tata Amaral, 2011) suggest that the past haunts a present that must live with rather than reject history.

The Dictatorship Film Cycle Begins

A film cycle is generally defined as a set of films that repeat settings and character types, are released during a given time period, and often respond to social problems or political situations (A. Klein 2011; A. Klein and Palmer 2016, 6–14; Verevis 2016, 97–98; Doles 2016, 80–81). Film scholars have theorized the lifespan of a film cycle and note that cycles are frequently initiated by the success of one production. In this instance, the 1992 television miniseries *Anos rebeldes* (Rebel years, Globo Network, 20 episodes) establishes a beginning point to the dictatorship cycle of films in Brazil. Its narrative foregrounds the romance of two young people with different degrees of political interest against the backdrop of the authoritarian regime and the first signs of the restoration of democracy. Rebecca Atencio notes that *Anos rebeldes* is considered to be the first serial drama to provide an unprecedented examination of the nation's violent political past and observes that the Globo Network, which had been an authoritarian ally, used *Anos rebeldes* as a tool to make over its image as a "champion for democracy and model corporate citizen" (2011, 41–44). As discussed later, Globo Filmes, the ostensibly independent film company founded in 1998, has extended its "good corporate citizen" status and participated as a coproducer and distributor of several films of the dictatorship film cycle.

That a television show can be seen as the starting point for a film cycle can be attributed largely to the fact that the Brazilian film industry in the early 1990s had been virtually shut down following the closure of the state film agency Embrafilme under President Fernando Affonso Collor de Mello (1990–1992). During the *retomada*, filmmakers and related industry professionals, eager to regenerate the industry and looking for box office successes, took note of the interest displayed by national audiences in *Anos rebeldes* and were motivated to tap into the zeitgeist and examine the authoritarian past as well. Notably, the resurgence of filmmaking coincided with the democratic consolidation of the country after a complicated democratic transition (Stampa and Rodrigues 2016; D'Araujo 2014; Teles and Safatle 2010).

I turn now to describe briefly the salient trends of the three phases of the dictatorship film cycle. The early films from the cycle join other works from the *retomada* in a broad critique of the nation's social and political history. For instance, *Carlota Joaquina, princesa do Brazil* (*Carlota Joaquina, Princess of Brazil*, Carla Camurati, 1995), *O quatrilho* (*The Quartet*, Fábio Barreto, 1995), and *Guerra de Canudos* (*The Battle of Canudos*, Sérgio Rezende, 1997) take up the colonial period to reflect on the nation during a critical transition point in Brazil's political, cultural, and social trajectory. Still other films from the *retomada* period suggest that there were lingering political issues from more recent history to work through and a desire for significant change. Fernão Pessoa Ramos (2003, 65–67) observes a tendency in the films from the early 1990s to reveal a deep dissatisfaction with an "unviable nation," which comes through in various films' critiques of the sordid aspects of life and incompetent figures. Others observe a tendency to portray resentful characters focused on exacting revenge (Xavier 2003, 55–62) or existential angst toward the social, political, and cultural structures of Brazil as a nation (Vieira 2003, 85–86). These critics observe, through the medium of cinema, that there were social and political issues from the past that demanded reconciliation at the same time that there were concerns regarding the future direction of the nation, marked by authoritarian violence and inequality.

Films from the first and second phases of the dictatorship cycle are notable for focusing on individuals who engaged in armed resistance against the military regime. *Lamarca* (Sérgio Rezende, 1994), which is one of the first films of the *retomada* and one of the first feature-length films of the dictatorship cycle, portrays the defection of Carlos Lamarca, an army officer who turns against the military and joins a leftist group to fight against the regime. Cinematic reflection on the authoritarian past was further stimulated with the commercially successful, international coproduction and 1998 Oscar nominee for the Best Foreign Language Film *O que é isso, companheiro?* (*Four Days in September*, Bruno Barreto, 1997). The film treats transnational subject matter—the 1969 kidnapping of the American ambassador Charles Burke Elbrick by members of an armed group opposing the dictatorship. These works were followed by *Ação entre amigos* (*Friendly Fire*, Beto Brant, 1998) and *Dois Córregos—verdades submersas no tempo* (*Two Streams*, Carlos Reichenbach, 1999). These first four films were followed by additional films featuring protagonists who fought against the dictatorship, including *Araguaya—a conspiração do silêncio* (Ronaldo Duque, 2004), *Cabra-Cega* (Toni Venturi, 2004), and *Batismo de sangue* (*Baptism of Blood*, Helvécio Ratton, 2006).

The second phase of the dictatorship cycle begins around 2002, the year when the *retomada* is generally understood as ending. As discussed in chapter 1, a new national film agency (the Agência Nacional do Cinema, ANCINE) was established in late 2001 as a regulatory agency to develop and manage the audiovisual industry. New funding programs for filmmaking brought renewed investment. Consequently, this period of film production brought bigger budgets and encouraged a commercial orientation to reclaim a market share for Brazilian productions vis-à-vis foreign imports (mostly from Hollywood). From 2002 to 2008, Globo Filmes played a key role in the ANCINE-era growth strategy for Brazilian cinema, consolidated its presence in the film industry, and coproduced several films of the dictatorship cycle, including *Zuzu Angel*, *O ano em que*, and *Os Desafinados*, discussed later.

The third phase emerges at a time when the new middle class became a target audience for film productions and producers sought to dialogue with the public. Consequently, broader tendencies in Brazilian cinema include an increasing focus on quotidian life and issues like urban marginality, social inclusion, and urban security. With a strengthening economy and increasing international attention serving as backdrops, cinematic portrayals of Brazil's dictatorial past shifted focus before coming to a gradual closure. Unlike films from the first two phases, films from the dictatorship cycle at this time do not aim to contain the past. As noted earlier, films from the third phase like *Hoje* and *A memória que me contam* address more coherently the process of reconciliation with the lingering effects of the authoritarian regime on the present.

Film cycles tend to be very topical, addressing an issue that broader society is working through or trying to resolve. Indeed, film scholars have illustrated how film cycles, sequels, and remakes gain traction at particular moments in time (Loock 2016; Verevis 2016; A. Klein 2011; Jess-Cooke 2009). The cultural moment concerned evolving notions of government and citizenship, as well as new ideas about Brazil and its place in the global order. The first and second phases of the dictatorship cycle include several anniversaries and historic landmarks. The year 1994 marked the thirtieth anniversary of the military coup d'état and, as noted earlier, marked the release of the film *Lamarca*. One year later, the Law of the Disappeared (Lei dos Desaparecidos Políticos do Brasil, Lei 9.410) was ratified. The 1995 law documented the first time the state acknowledged illegal actions during the military regime, and it permitted the creation of the Comissão Especial sobre Mortos e Desaparecidos Políticos (Special Commission on the Dead and Disappeared, CEMDP), whose research over a period of eleven years culminated in 2007 with the publication of *Direito à memória e à verdade* (The right to memory and the truth) (Brazil 2007).[2] Reflections on Brazil as a nation and its place in the world were also further stimulated in 2000 by the five hundredth anniversary of the discovery of Brazil by the Portuguese sailor Pedro Alvares Cabral. This monumental anniversary prompted reflection on myths of the nation and piqued interested in Brazil's history.

The second phase of the dictatorship film cycle appeared during a relatively intense period of reflection on the past. The year 2000 certainly prompted review of Brazil's history, yet 2004 was a particularly important year for further stimulating debate, as it was the fortieth anniversary of the military coup d'état and the twentieth anniversary of the Diretas Já movement, a mass movement of civil society that demanded direct free elections and the return to democracy. Benito Bisso Schmidt (2008, 127–130) observes that although a "memory culture" had formed in Brazil at the end of the 1980s, the fortieth anniversary of the military coup d'état prompted a keen interest in memory work. Schmidt (142, 151) also notes that debates about history were waged by journalists and the media, countering official gestures to try to turn the page. For instance, in 2004 the newspaper *Correio Braziliense* published photographs of Vladimir Herzog, a journalist who was tortured and killed during the dictatorship and whose suspicious death (a forged suicide) while in custody had prompted widespread protests in 1975. His death was and continues to be a touchstone for civil society's demand for democracy and justice.[3] These important anniversary dates prompted remembrance of the past. However, some directors draw attention to the arrival of the Partido dos Trabalhadores (Workers' Party) to the federal government in 2003, as it inspired and allowed for reflections on the dictatorship by creating financial conditions for film production and by opening important archives (Cunha 2006, 90).

The period is also marked by tensions concerning what to reveal and when and how to define the authoritarian past. In addition to films, other notable efforts to acknowledge the past include public memorials titled Pessoas indispensáveis (Indispensable people) that were erected in 2007 throughout Brazil. In 2009, the federal government launched the online site Memórias Reveladas (Memories revealed).[4] Contrasting these efforts to acknowledge Brazil's violent, authoritarian past, the newspaper *Folha de São Paulo* published a text in

2009 that referred to the military regime as a *ditabranda* (soft dictatorship), which prompted public outrage. Demands for greater political transparency and accountability of the government to its citizens eventually led to two landmark laws in 2011. The first law (12.527) revoked legislation from 2005 that allowed for eternal nondisclosure of documents from the period of the military regime. A second law (12.528) called for the creation of the Truth Commission, described earlier. During the approximately twenty-year period briefly sketched here, the political culture of the nation underwent an intense period of review and reflection during which human rights programs were established and citizens demanded greater accountability and transparency from their government.

The cycle of films that reflect on the military regime enter into this heightened moment of memory work. In addition to factors allowing a cycle to gain traction, it is also important to consider how cycles operate in a given period. Whereas a film genre may be defined by its semantics or syntax, Amanda Ann Klein (2011, 3–4) asserts that film cycles are primarily defined by how they are used (or their pragmatics). As noted earlier, the concept of the future state of democracy and citizenship stood out in the inauguration of the Truth Commission. For Ksenija Bilbija and Leigh A. Payne (2011), the circulation and exchange of reflections on the past to seek sociopolitical progress in the present and future constitutes a memory market with multiple profits. In a memory market, "profit" should be thought of in terms of its Latin root, *profectus*, which implies progress. For Bilbija and Payne, the recollection of the past "means progress towards human rights goals, acknowledgement of events in the past, justice, and deterrence" (3). The cycle of films treating the military dictatorship sought profit in the form of social and political progress, especially efforts to promote a new political culture. In this way, the cycle can be seen as contributing to conceptualizing a more ideal nation and supporting a belief in the systematic transformation of Brazil to become a rightful voice as an alternative policy formulator from the developing world and champion of democracy.

The Past Has Passed

Common to the films from the first two phases of the dictatorship cycle are aesthetic strategies that contain or bind discussion of the past. In his study of postdictatorial Latin American literature, Idelber Avelar (1999) asserts that the neoliberalism that was installed by Latin American dictatorships demands forgetting partly because of its violent, repressive origins and partly because of the free market's demands to live in the perpetual present. He further notes that "the erasure of the past as past is the cornerstone of all commodification, even when the past becomes yet another commodity for sale" (2). The films of the dictatorship cycle do not aim to fully erase the past, such as through forgetting. Rather, they contain the past as a way to package understanding of the dictatorship for contemporary exchange and to emphasize a new cultural, political, and economic period in Brazil's history. This, in fact, is the concept of profit that Bilbija and Payne reference. The dictatorial past in the films from the first two phases of the cycle in particular becomes commodified most notably in the ways that they emphasize the past as *having passed* and convey that social and political progress has brought a new era.

With few exceptions, the historical period of the dictatorship is seen as part of a sociopolitical period from which the current era differs in terms of political sensibilities. This distancing involves historical concentration by focusing on high-profile figures or by setting films predominantly in the late 1960s to early 1970s. The majority of the recent cycle of films that reflect on the authoritarian past do not consider the full period of the dictatorship (1964–1985). Rather, nearly all focus on the most repressive period (*anos de chumbo*, the lead years) of the regime from approximately 1969 to 1974, which spans from the declaration of the Ato Institucional Número Cinco (Fifth Institutional Act, AI-5) to the end of General Emílio Garrastazú Médici's government in 1974. Among other acts, the AI-5 called for censorship of the press, suspended habeas corpus, temporarily closed the National Congress, and suspended the voting rights of people suspected of subversive political activity for up to ten years. Most of the provisions of the AI-5 remained in effect until 1978, concluding the slow process of political relaxation (*distensão*) that General Ernesto Geisel began after assuming power in 1974. This historical concentration results in a focus on those who fought against authoritarianism and injustice. For example, several films focus on the years surrounding the declaration of the AI-5 and armed militant resistance to the dictatorship undertaken by groups such as the Vanguarda Popular Revolucionária (Popular Revolutionary Vanguard) (*Lamarca*) and MR-8 (*O que é isso, companheiro?*; *Zuzu Angel*), and Communist-led armed struggle in the Amazon region (*Araguaya*; *Dois Córregos*). Notably, *Zuzu Angel* shows the sustained struggle the protagonist undertakes to confirm the death of her missing son at the hands of military officials and demand accountability until her own death (by murder) in 1976.

These films tend to make the past more distant also through their use of found and faded photographs or scenes that replicate the aesthetics and iconography of historical images. That is, these films draw on the codes of realism to make authenticity claims regarding their historical re-creation. Notwithstanding creative interventions made by directors and producers, these films can be seen as extensions of historical documents given that their screenplays adapt testimonial works of former militants.[5] Notably, these films fill gaps in understandings of history at a time when archives were still closed and documents remained sealed. For instance, the protagonist of *Dois Córregos* finds weathered photographs from her youth buried in a time capsule on a family property she is preparing to sell. The protagonist's point of view (as an adult) located in the late 1990s is partly nostalgic but also obscures the dictatorial past with innocence and uncertainty in a way that resembles *O ano em que* (discussed later). Meanwhile, the final moments of *Lamarca* and *O que é isso, companheiro?* appear as frozen images as if they were still photographs. Subsequent shifts from color to black and white indicate the end of the diegetic moment of the film and that the story now belongs to a faded, weathered, black-and-white past. Whereas the final image of *O que é isso, companheiro?* re-creates (with poetic license) the photograph of political prisoners released in exchange for the release of the U.S. ambassador Charles Elbrick,[6] *Lamarca*'s final image of the dying Lamarca includes intertitles that state the date and location. Both images effectively create temporal distance and archive cinematic events in the past.

If films from the first two phases of the dictatorship cycle concentrated on the more distant past, they also frequently focused on armed resistance to the regime. Yet another way to mark a separation from the past is the frequent portrayal of leftist militants and political activists as defeated, debilitated, or isolated. Perhaps paradoxically, portrayals of defeated militants help celebrate reconstructed heroes whose actions are framed as sacrifices leading to a stable present. For instance, participants in armed resistance to the dictatorship are injured and struggle to survive, such as in the climactic scenes of *Lamarca, O que é isso, companheiro?*, and *Cabra-Cega*. Similarly, the former armed militant and uncle to the young protagonist in *Dois Córregos* disappears, referencing metaphorically the silenced deaths and disappearance of those who actively opposed the authoritarian regime. The graphic, spectacular portrayals of the tortured bodies of political prisoners and the suicide of Frei Tito in *Batismo de sangue* not only underscore just how systematically violent the military was but also emphasize how bright, young people were physically and psychologically broken by the regime.

These images of defeated, debilitated, and isolated individuals can be understood as part of what Maria Rita Kehl calls an "aesthetics of resentment." According to Kehl (2000), cinema frequently mobilizes resentment through the way characters are constructed or developed. The resentful character is frequently portrayed as morally superior but quieter or passive against a more vocal, powerful opponent. What is more, an aesthetics of resentment creates characters who are victims of others or their circumstances and, subsequently, motivate feelings of sympathy (as cited in Cunha 2006, 112–113). The aesthetic choices in the portrayal of injured or isolated individuals in dictatorship-cycle films mourn those who died and suffered. Yet these films emphasize that the circumstances that brought about these social and political conflicts have been resolved and belong to the past.

Another result of the aesthetics of resentment in these films is that leftist ideology is not portrayed critically. For instance, in a memorable scene from *O que é isso, companheiro?*, the U.S. ambassador Charles Elbrick (played by American actor Alan Arkin) remarks calmly to his captor Paulo/Fernando Gabeira (played by Brazilian actor Pedro Cardoso) that the approach they are taking has historically not succeeded. Establishing a similar tone, the ending of *Cabra-Cega* closes with a poetic dedication to all Brazilians, or *cabras-cegas* (blinded players), who tried to "atravessar a escuridão para tomar os céus de assalto" (cross through the darkness to take the skies by force). As much as the final quote aims to pay homage to these young people who fought for what they believed in, the tone also suggests they were not fully aware of the political actions they were undertaking. In fact, the title of the film, *Cabra-Cega*, and a salient moment when a character escapes confinement on a rooftop of a building refer to a game whereby a child is blindfolded and must try to find playmates without the benefit of sight. In this way, these films tend to present the ideals that drove individuals to take extreme measures to defend their beliefs as innocent and noble but misguided.

In their politics of remembering, the past is reconstructed in these films for the purposes of the present. The actions and ideas of the past are not just displaced but contemporary audiences are encouraged to develop new interpretations of history and its relationship to the present. Fernando Seliprandy (2013, 59) observes that reflections on the defeat of armed militants and the logic of taking up arms are frequently followed by contemporary statements of participants in armed resistance that Brazil is better off today than it was twenty to thirty years ago, suggesting that there has been progress and that the struggle was "worth it." Similarly, others observe a strategic rewriting of revolutionary struggle as democratic resistance despite the fact that armed militants were not seeking a democratic order but were, rather, inspired by Cuban- and Chinese-style socialist and communist revolutions (Ridenti 2004, 58). What these authors observe is not just the telos of a nation that is "better off today" but practices of nation branding whereby past conflicts are resolved, a break from the past is established, and a "new and improved" version of the nation is celebrated.

Seeking Known Truths in *Zuzu Angel*

Several of the feature-length fiction films from the dictatorship cycle feature male protagonists and call on the generic codes of the thriller. This is true of the films *Lamarca*, *Ação entre amigos*, *O que é isso, companheiro?*, *Cabra-Cega*, *Batismo de sangue*, and *Zuzu Angel*. However, *Zuzu Angel* stands out as a film that foregrounds the story of a woman who fought against human rights violations committed during the dictatorship. It is also notable that the film does not focus on conflicts between agents of the military and armed militants who opposed the regime. Rather, it highlights how otherwise apolitical citizens gained greater political awareness and how they were affected by the authoritarian regime, whose oppressive reach extended more broadly into civil society. Like other films of the dictatorship cycle, *Zuzu Angel* mourns past heroes and, despite the death of the film's protagonist, celebrates current democratic achievements.

Zuzu Angel centers on the life of Zuleika "Zuzu" Angel Jones, who was assassinated by the military regime in 1976. In the 1960s and early 1970s, Zuzu rose to international prominence as a fashion designer. Her son, Stuart Edgard Angel Jones, a member of the revolutionary leftist organization MR-8, was detained, tortured, and killed by agents of the military in 1971. After his disappearance, Zuzu sought information about her son and became a vocal opponent of the military dictatorship. To narrate this story, the film deploys several elements common to the thriller, as well as elements of the melodramatic mode, including the persecution of the innocent by the powerful, female self-sacrifice for a (presumably) greater good, and, especially associated with melodramas in Latin America, the juxtaposition of a family drama to national issues (Sadlier 2009, 2–8). From the crime or mystery thriller, *Zuzu Angel* includes secretive phone calls, anonymous meetings, and suspenseful situations in which characters must escape or hide. A divorced mother raising her children, Zuzu is an innocent, vulnerable figure who comes to a new consciousness about the criminal activities of the authoritarian regime. She assumes a heroic position to find answers after being thrust into the midst of political subterfuge. The film underscores that remembering the past is a process, but it engages in an ambivalent logic. *Zuzu Angel* creates a desire to know more about the past and, in the end, offers a resolution of conflicts, suggesting that the search for truth and justice has been successful.

The narrative structure offers closure on the past. In the opening scene, Zuzu takes pen to paper to write a personal declaration stating that if she dies by accident or by attack, it will have been retribution for her activities looking into the facts concerning her son's disappearance. Moments later she makes a call from a pay phone to Ray Bunker, a representative of Amnesty International. She informs him she has the last piece of evidence needed for the dossier and implores him to come to Brazil to get the documents to proceed with investigations of human rights violations. Zuzu rushes to a hotel, where she begins to record herself as if in a legal deposition, offering her name and biographical information. Thus, suspense is established and an in media res structure becomes an extended flashback where events before the opening diegetic moment unfold.

The flashback structure also frames the protagonist's heroic quest to discover the truth about her son's disappearance. Common to the mystery thriller in film is an ordinary individual as protagonist who must deal with an impending problem whose resolution demands an investigation. Zuzu's collection of information about her son's disappearance is central to the plot and lends an episodic structure to the film's narrative. She assumes the moral authority of a concerned mother and perseveres in finding and demanding information regarding her son's disappearance. In this way, she takes on the role of militant mother as other women have to make human rights claims on military dictatorships in Latin America (Álvarez 1990; Cooper and Phelan 2014; Maier and Lebon 2010). What is more, the film redefines militant struggle against the military regime, which Zuzu undertakes not by kidnapping or taking up arms but by wielding a pen, collecting documents, and making a persistent, vocal demand for justice.

It is through the eyes of the protagonist Zuzu that the past is portrayed. The melodramatic matrix of the film shows Zuzu's son and other leftist revolutionaries in a more benevolent way than characters affiliated with the military regime. That is, a dichotomy of good versus bad is established. Moments after a military general claims he is being unfairly accused of committing acts of torture, a Catholic priest hypocritically minimizes the use of torture on political prisoners when he dismissively informs Zuzu that the electrical shocks they administer are light and not so bad. Meanwhile, Stuart is portrayed as innocent and idealistic. Viewers do not see him engage in kidnapping or the armed robbery of banks. Rather, he is portrayed as a young, idealistic man in love with his girlfriend. His naïveté and virtue are particularly evident when Zuzu reads aloud to her daughter a letter Stuart had written her, in which he reflects on the existence of God. His words express his belief in the power of individuals to bring about change, noting that each and every one has the ability to influence the nature of the future and change the course of history.[7] The statement seems at once to define Zuzu's actions and inspire her while also reflecting a contemporary vision of empowered citizenship in which individuals demand accountability from the government. The touching moment between mother and daughter operates as an exoneration for Stuart and his unseen actions as a revolutionary activist and, by extension, makes Zuzu more heroic in her efforts to understand and locate him. Yet the scene of her mourning the loss of her son repeats a tendency of the dictatorship cycle films and overlooks the leftist ideology that his letter conveys. Stuart's posthumous words are touching, but they are also presented as idealistic and with nostalgia.

It is the combination of melodramatic mournful remembrance and thrilling investigative process that redefines an understanding of the past in *Zuzu Angel*. In his study of the thriller as a genre, Martin Rubin (1999, 5) asserts that the thriller mobilizes visceral, gut-level feelings more than sensitive, cerebral feelings such as pity, pathos, love, or nostalgia. Yet, from Laura Podalsky, we gain an understanding of the importance of affect in mainstream film genres such as the thriller. Podalsky (2011, 59–80) asserts that the thriller not only mobilizes sensibilities such as pathos or nostalgia but also holds the politicizing potential of demanding reconsideration of established knowledge about the dictatorial past in Latin America. It is through the actions of the morally superior mother that *Zuzu Angel*, alongside other films of the dictatorship film cycle, contributes to further resignifying a narrative about armed resistance and opposition to the dictatorship. Those who fought against the military regime—directly as militants and indirectly as self-sacrificing mothers—held admirable goals that eventually led to a contemporary democracy headed by empowered citizens.

Zuzu's efforts reveal the absurd and arbitrary machinations of the military regime, and audiences become aware of the ways the dictatorship fabricated the appearance of legality. Indeed, scholars have noted that the Brazilian military was exceptional in its ability to appear to follow legal procedures (Teles and Safatle 2010, 9–12). Zuzu gains access to a prison at the military air base (where her son had been detained), but she is given a sanitized visit of empty jail cells. Crosscutting images show military officials stating that Stuart was not a prisoner in their facilities; some get his name wrong, illustrating how little the truth concerns them. An egregious moment of duplicity occurs when Stuart is called to appear before a court for criminal prosecution despite the fact that he is dead. Before the courtroom scene, Zuzu had received a handwritten letter from Alex Polari de Alvarenga, who witnessed Stuart's torture and death while also detained by the military. Spectators as well as Zuzu are positioned to suspect the official acts as well-crafted deception.

A false past is countered by truths revealed in a presumably more authentic, cinematic present. The 2006 film emerges from multiple layers and modalities of knowing about and understanding the past—memory, personal declaration, confession, official documentation from the past, and contemporary resources. Zuzu's writings, letters, and documents, whose preparation is dramatized in the film, formed part of the text *Eu, Zuzu Angel, procuro meu filho* (1986) compiled by Virginia Valli, who published it a year after the end of the dictatorship and the same year the archdiocese of São Paulo published the text *Brasil, nunca mais* (*Torture in Brazil: A Report*). Notably, the process of seeking and collecting textual evidence allowed Zuzu to reclaim what was lost. According to Hildegard Angel, her mother collected fragments of information and memories about her son as if it were a way to form the body she was never able to bury and mourn.[8] The material included in the edited text by Valli and portrayed on-screen was later corroborated by contemporary findings. Notably, Zuzu's death was declared an accident in 1976, but research officially revealed in 1998 that she had been assassinated by agents of the military regime.

The investigative process Zuzu undertakes drives the episodic nature of the film and creates suspense, which is established in the opening scene. For viewers, suspense involves being caught "between question and answer, between anticipation and resolution, between alternative answers to the question posed, and sometimes ambivalent emotions and sympathies" (Rubin 1999, 35). As a thriller, *Zuzu Angel* certainly creates a desire to know whether the protagonist will succeed in her efforts and motivates curiosity: What information has she uncovered that she must share immediately? Will she reach Amnesty International in time? Will human rights violations committed by the regime be revealed? In his work on suspense in film, Aaron Smuts examines "the paradox of suspense" whereby a viewer has knowledge that could save a character and offers a desire-frustration theory to explain the experience and mechanisms of suspense in film. Smut's theory poses that viewers feel suspense because they know something that could save a character but, regardless of how strongly they desire to help, they can do nothing with their knowledge (2008, 289). Viewers' hoping the protagonist will succeed is one way the mystery thriller creates suspense. However, contemporary Brazilian viewers are likely aware that Zuzu Angel died in a car crash, which closes the film's action.

In the case of *Zuzu Angel*, viewers are motivated to want to help Zuzu succeed in her mission and they are ultimately relieved to know that knowledge of pasts events has been acted upon. The final scene shows a military official, with whom Zuzu had spoken earlier, remove from the vehicle the envelope containing evidence she had planned to submit to Amnesty International while the song "Apesar de você" by Zuzu's friend and famous musician Chico Buarque de Hollanda plays on the cassette deck.[9] The central element of the thriller here is not whether a character will get caught but whether the truth will be revealed. The closing intertitles inform viewers that Zuzu's declaration was distributed by Chico Buarque to sixty celebrities and the press.

The narrative of the film foments a demand for knowledge and establishes questions whose answers are offered at the end. The film is ambivalent, however, concerning the emotional sequelae of the past. Closing intertitles state that Hildegard and Ana Cristina Angel were never able to bury their brother, suggesting that the emotional traumas of the past remain unresolved. Still, the film's ending satisfies a suspense-filled need for information. The film appeared after two National Programs for Human Rights during the Cardoso administration (1996 and 2002) and the creation of the CEMDP (discussed earlier). And, *Zuzu Angel* appeared before the publication of the book *Direito à memória e à verdade* (The right to memory and the truth, 2007). The final intertitles, which refer to the work of the CEMDP, suggest that the right to memory and the truth is upheld and government programs are revealing the past and fostering reconciliation. In sum, *Zuzu Angel* draws on the codes of melodrama to cultivate pathos for individuals who suffered at the hands of the dictatorship while mobilizing the codes of the thriller to underscore that the conflicts of the past have been resolved in a stable, democratic Brazil committed to truth and transparency.

Recalibrating Geopolitical Imaginaries

The dictatorship cycle of films circulated in a contemporary memory market in Brazil and contributed to developing new notions of the nation and citizenship. While scholars of film cycles underscore the need to consider how film cycles operate in a given context, Alice A. Nelson, who writes from the perspective of the political economy of memory, asserts that "any gesture toward recuperating historical memory is always simultaneously about *two* moments and contexts: the moment remembered as well as the moment of remembering, the context of past events and the present context of their recollection" (2011, 340–341). The fortieth anniversary in 2004 of the military coup d'état of 1964 occurred at the beginning of the first Lula administration (2003–2006). This political moment can be characterized as a time of fervent belief in the possibility of greater social, economic, and political equality both at home and internationally. Whereas the films discussed in previous sections contained the past as having passed (by engaging in historical concentration, isolating leftist ideas and activists, and resolving the contradictions of the past), other films draw on the codes of melodrama and circular narratives to recalibrate geopolitical imaginaries. That is, they examine the past but emphasize the political present, revise myths of national identity, and celebrate contemporary cosmopolitanism.

Films such as *Quase dois irmãos*, *O ano em que*, and *Os Desafinados* adjust a portrayal of the past for the purposes of the present to imagine a different, new future for Brazil. These films address the violence and repression of the period, but they are invested in strengthening (as well as celebrating) contemporary democratic accomplishments and the potential of Brazil. While *O ano em que* emphasizes the inability to know or understand the past and portrays the early 1970s in accordance with ideas of a new Brazil cultivated during the Lula administration, *Quase dois irmãos* locates contemporary problems in the political failures of the past and urges new political approaches to seek greater socioeconomic equality and inclusion in the present and future. Similar to *O que é isso, companheiro?* and *Zuzu Angel*, *Os Desafinados* seeks to make Brazilian history part of global history while displacing violence at home and foregrounding the cultural richness of Brazilian music. Each film contributes to a broader process of recalibrating geopolitical imaginaries of Brazil, aiming to see Brazilian society on new terms at home and as part of an international landscape. This reconfiguration of political identities and geographic imaginaries is central to nation branding. Presenting Brazil as a stable democracy was fundamental to the political and economic goals of the Lula and Rousseff administrations. Yet this place-making effort is not without its tensions and inconsistencies.

Moving toward a New Brazil in *Quase dois irmãos*

Quase dois irmãos was first screened in 2004 at the Rio de Janeiro International Film Festival, where Lúcia Murat won the awards for Best Director and Best Latin American Film. Murat had previously addressed sequelae of the military regime. Her 1989 film *Que bom te ver viva* (*How Nice to See You Alive*) is a landmark documentary in Brazilian cinema for its combination of fictional and documentary modes, as well as the poignant testimonials of women who were tortured by military officials and their experiences of survival. This docudrama is particularly important as, according to Murat, in the late 1980s there was little desire to reflect on the recent past or talk about the long-term effects of political repression (Marsh 2012, 34–35, 88–96, 106). In more recent works, Murat has further developed her interest in memory and the relationship between the present and the past, including in the fiction film *A memória que me contam* and the documentary *Uma longa viagem* (*A Long Journey*, 2011).

In terms of structure and thematics, *Quase dois irmãos* coincides with other films of the dictatorship cycle but differs in its intent to overcome current and past failures to rethink a new future. It shares a circular narrative structure (similar to *Zuzu Angel, Dois Córregos, Cidade de Deus, Batismo de sangue*, and *Os Desafinados*) and, like other films, explores leftist militant activists who protested against the military regime. Beginning and ending in 2004, the film contains cuts to sepia-colored images of 1957 and darker blue-and-gray images of 1970. Additional cuts on matching graphics and action between 2004, 1957, and 1970 weave the three moments together, making causal claims that current sociopolitical problems are linked to past periods of authoritarianism and ongoing discrimination. The film largely focuses on the story of two men, one White (Miguel) and one Black (Jorginho), who are first shown as childhood friends in 1957 and then prison inmates in 1970—Miguel is jailed for political activities and Jorginho for bank robbery. In 2004, they reunite in prison, where Miguel (now a lawyer) approaches Jorginho (now a convicted drug lord) for permission to start an outreach project in Jorginho's community. The film's circular structure is completed when viewers again see Miguel from the opening scene rushing to a hospital to attend to his daughter Julia, who has been attacked in a favela after visiting a boyfriend. The opening and closing scenes of Miguel racing through traffic serve as a metaphor that Brazil must urgently work through its own social and cultural blockades en route to becoming a more inclusive, peaceful, and democratic society.

Murat's film may repeat a circular narrative frequent in the dictatorship film cycle, but it does not aim to contain the past. The circular structure frames an episodic narrative that moves from past to present, and the overall movement of the film is forward and pointing toward the future. Scholars of the politics of memory in the Southern Cone of Latin American have asserted that remembering the past can serve various purposes, such as countering official versions of history, acknowledging those who were killed or disappeared, continuing to fight for human rights, finding the truth, or making sense of the past (Druliolle 2011; Salvi 2011, 47–56; Lazzara 2011, 88–93). While these objectives are found in other films of the dictatorship film cycle, those operations are not emphasized in *Quase dois irmãos*. Rather, Murat's film is engaged in what Vikki Bell refers to as pressing forward. For Bell (2011, 209–211), memory works should be seen as a politics of the present to imagine the nation in terms of its difference from its own past in order to construct a viable, shared future. Indeed, the circular structure of *Quase dois irmãos* is completed in the penultimate scene, in which Miguel confesses in voiceover that there is a rift in the imagined nation whereby what is dreamed or desired differs from what is lived.

Unlike other films of the dictatorship cycle, *Quase dois irmãos* does not celebrate past or present heroes. Both Jorginho and Miguel are portrayed as having good intentions and being driven by base motivations. What is more, the portrayal of moments of the past vis-à-vis the contemporary moment undertakes an investigative process that focuses not on isolated individuals or moments (as in *Zuzu Angel*) but rather on otherwise known truths (concerning urban violence, drug trafficking, and racial and class divisions) in a broader diagnostic view of Brazilian society. In a society that frequently identifies (until more recently) other Western nations (in Europe and the United States especially) for being racist but continues believing it is a racial democracy (despite evidence to the contrary), crosscutting between temporal moments in the film analyzes the replication of violence as well as a structured history of racial and class divisions.

Indeed, the film portrays a history of racial and class discrimination as existing before the dictatorship, becoming exacerbated during the military regime and entrenched in the present. Miguel's father and Jorginho's father (Seu Jorge) played samba music together either at Miguel's middle-class home or in the favela where Jorginho's family lived. The fathers ostensibly bond over their music, but their wives reveal racial and class tensions. Dona Rosa chastises Seu Jorge for being lazy and being taken advantage of by a White man, while Miguel's mother complains about the *feijoadas*[10] they hold on Sundays, which are getting them into trouble with the apartment building management and neighbors. Immediately following the women's critiques, a flash-forward to 2004 shows Miguel, now a lawyer, visiting Jorginho in jail. Additional cuts between scenes of both children playing soccer and the present create a dialectic to reveal how they began at similar points in time but their lives were structured to be lived in different ways.

The possibility of cross-class and racial solidarity was, as suggested by the film's portrayal of these men's lives, destroyed during and by the military dictatorship. The dictatorships of Latin America are generally understood as imposing a neoliberal economic order and fomenting social divisions. Murat's film suggests people have made choices that have exacerbated social divisions. Shortly after arriving to the penitentiary on Ilha Grande, Jorginho joins Miguel and the other political prisoners. He consoles Miguel at low moments; joins the political prisoners' hunger strike, which earns him a brutal beating from the prison guards; and tries to ease tensions between a group of common (mostly Black) prisoners and the political (mostly White) prisoners. Jorginho maintains his solidarity with Miguel until political prisoners reveal themselves to be intolerant of difference and use violence as retribution for an alleged act of incivility—the theft of Miguel's watch. When Miguel demands construction of a wall to separate political and common prisoners, he declares his choice for separation and segregation of social groups. The military regime was an abomination, but leftist groups were also inconsistent, intractable, and discriminatory despite claiming idealistic goals to better society. Jorginho eventually also turns to violence to ascend to the leadership of the group of common prisoners.

Scenes from 1970 are intercut with scenes from 2004 where members of the gang Jorginho controls from jail engage in a violent struggle for power of the drug trafficking syndicate and domination of the favela. The juxtaposition of periods suggests a structure and history of violence whereby problems of the past continue to negatively affect the lives of citizens in the present. It also underscores inegalitarian attitudes transmitted between generations. Julia confronts her father, calling him racist, and rejects his stories about the past. Yet she fails to see how she is equally idealistic and does not consider the structurally differentiated lives of others, assuming she can, in an uncomplicated fashion, live in the world of her Black drug-trafficking boyfriend in the favela and vice versa. She seems unaware of her upper-middle-class White privilege when she instructs a maid to make her coffee and takes for granted that she was released by the police in one instance rather than being charged and detained. In scenes from 1970, Miguel shares his belief that the life one dreams of determines the life one lives ("a vida que sonhamos determina a vida que vivemos"). In 2004, he rephrases this idea to accept a division between what is imagined and what is lived in reality ("Temos todos duas vidas. Uma a que sonhamos. Outra a que vivemos"). This shift in perspective is a call for change. In *Quase dois irmãos*, there are no mourned heroes or strategic redefinitions of militant struggle. Rather, Murat's film calls for not repeating past political failures in order to unite a desired imaginary of a new Brazil with lived reality.

Celebrating Diversity and Inclusion in *O ano em que meus pais saíram de férias*

Whereas *Zuzu Angel* suggests that the past can be known and resolved through official means, the historical melodrama *O ano em que* presents the past as mostly unknowable through the eyes of the young protagonist in a way that resembles the vague memories of the teenage protagonist, Ana Paula, in *Dois Córregos*. Not only does *O ano em que* reiterate the youthful point of view that started the cycle (with *Anos rebeldes*), but it also returns to the genre of the historical melodrama. Whereas other films of this cycle include young protagonists, they are generally teenagers or on the verge of young adulthood. The point of view of these characters emphasizes their growing awareness and political consciousness, which often presents more idealistic political views of the 1960s and 1970s and their participation in political activities. By contrast, *O ano em que* supplants coming to greater critical awareness for the possibility of (re)discovering Brazil.

O ano em que largely displaces discussion of political militants and leftist ideologies to develop a coming-of-age story. In a bildungsroman, the protagonist experiences a loss, undergoes a journey that frequently symbolizes a quest for identity, and, ultimately, moves from alienation to integration into society (Sammons 1991; Boes 2012). It is a form that has been developed in Latin American film to address the region's history (Bost 2009; Kushigian 2003). In *O ano em que*, a young Mauro is dropped off to stay with his grandfather in the predominantly Italian and Jewish neighborhood of Bom Retiro in São Paulo in 1970, while his parents make an unsuccessful run from the military regime. Largely unaware of political events taking place around him, Mauro focuses on the upcoming World Cup championship matches and befriends the local kids while his grandfather's neighbor Shlomo, a Jewish immigrant from Poland who escaped the Holocaust, takes Mauro in after his grandfather unexpectedly passes away. Mauro's life is bittersweet while staying with Shlomo. The joy he experiences in the multicultural and multiethnic enclave of Bom Retiro is met with frustration and longing for his parents. Shlomo investigates the disappearance of Mauro's parents, eventually reuniting Mauro with his mother, who had been beaten and presumably tortured by the military regime. In the closing scene, Mauro and his mother sit in the backseat of a car while Mauro explains with great naïveté in voiceover that his father is permanently "atrasado" (running late) and that he, without wanting to or understanding exactly, ended up becoming "uma coisa chamada exiliado" (something called an exile).

The narrative culmination of a bildungsroman generally involves a child protagonist who reaches maturity and adopts society's values in order to be accepted by a given community. What is more, the bildungsroman is a novel of emergence that frequently promotes the performance of ideals (Boes 2012, 11–71). The ending of *O ano em que* suggests a relatively acritical acceptance of tragedy. Whereas other films of the cycle, such as *Zuzu Angel, Batismo de sangue*, and *Quase dois irmãos*, include characters who come to new levels of political consciousness, the protagonist in *O ano em que* moves on with life largely in guileless denial of violence.

Viewers take up the youthful point of view of the innocent outsider and experience history as not fully understandable. This reiterates a tendency to include young protagonists in films treating darker political or historical moments in world cinemas and Spanish and Latin Americans in particular (Marsh 2017a).[11] The young subject is not yet fully included in the adult world and embodies a fundamental "otherness" (K. Lury 2010, 2). In *O ano em que*, Mauro offers an innocent perspective and he is an outsider in three distinct ways. First, his voiceover narration is located in time outside the diegesis of the film. Although we hear the voice of a child, he speaks from the present looking back. Second, he is an outsider to an adult world and as an abandoned child made temporary visitor to the neighborhood of Bom Retiro. Viewers see Mauro eating alone in his grandfather's apartment and his inexperience when he tries to cook eggs for himself. His awkwardness and vulnerability are emphasized further when he tries on his grandfather's clothes, donning a pair of large gloves to practice his future role as a goalie. Lastly, Mauro is a cultural outsider both in terms of not being raised Jewish but also because he is from Minas Gerais, a different region of Brazil.

Mauro creates sympathy and his perspective allows for overlooking historical details. A child's feelings of loneliness, joy, and curiosity substitute for fears of repression and violence committed by an authoritarian regime. Uglier facts of the past are generally elided. Indeed, images of and references to violence are relatively limited or minimized, emphasizing a lack of understanding or knowledge about the past. For instance, when Shlomo tells Mauro what he discovered from his investigations in Belo Horizonte, the sound fades when the two talk and a rack focus distances viewers from knowing what was learned. Thus, the film frames the portrayal of the dictatorial period with silence. Mauro witnesses acts of violence (armed forces beating and detaining street protesters), but his voiceover narration is notably absent in these moments. He does not explain his observations as in other moments. Mauro is relatively oblivious to the stress his parents experience as they smoke nervously when facing the impending threat of being found by agents of the state. Heavy symbolism and use of euphemisms (e.g., "being on vacation") not only reflect a child's way of understanding but also address a difficulty of capturing the past clearly.

If the past is not fully comprehensible in this film and the narrative ends with another traumatic event (going into exile), then what is the role of the past (as represented in the present) in shaping contemporary individual and collective identities? Scholars of memory and violence have debated the generational transmission of memory. Marianne Hirsch has coined the term "postmemory" to describe a "*structure* of inter- and trans-generational transmission of traumatic knowledge and experience" that is a "*consequence* of traumatic recall" (2008, 106). The concept of postmemory has become an important framework for understanding Latin American dictatorships (Lessa and Druliolle 2011; Maguire 2017; Jara 2016). Yet Mauro seems to recall the past with few traumatic memories. Indeed, his euphemistic understanding suggests few real *consequences* of traumatic events. Rather than transmitting trauma, the film transmits hope and optimism. The Jewish community reinterprets Mauro's arrival as the story of Moses, who was abandoned by his mother in the Nile River and later became a prophet of the Jews. Shlomo eventually refers to Mauro as "Moishele" (little Moses) and Mauro inadvertently becomes a Judeo-Christian symbol of hope for the future.

The youthful point of view offers a presumed innocent, universal, ideologically neutral position easily adaptable to transhistorical identification. Historical events or knowledge of the past are displaced as a nodal point for subjectivity in the present. Rather, the past serves as a context for renewing myths to celebrate the present and future of Brazil. Despite the longing for his parents, Mauro's perspective helps to depoliticize the past while reviving myths of Brazilian cultural identity. Via Mauro, *O ano em que* emphasizes a jubilant "melting pot" nationalism and society-unifying zeal for soccer. Crosscut scenes show Jewish men adjusting their television antennas while university student political activists gather around a television set. Still others gather at a neighborhood sandwich shop while Shlomo watches the game with Mauro at home. In addition to providing social common ground, *O ano em que* suggests that racial democracy and cross-class, ethnic harmony can be achieved regardless of political circumstances. Mauro cheers for a local soccer team and comments from the stands in voiceover with celebratory naïveté how large and diverse São Paulo is. He marvels at how Shlomo is a Polish Jew, Irene is Greek, Ítalo is Italian, and Irene's boyfriend, Edgar, is the grandson of an African. When Edgar blocks a shot on goal, Mauro reveals his epiphany that when he grows up he wants to be Black and to be able to fly. His identification with a political activist father who has disappeared is displaced by a larger multicultural myth of racial and cross-class harmony, which upholds long-standing ideas promoted by official and unofficial actors about Brazilians' cultural identity as people who are friendly, peaceful, and gregarious.

Notwithstanding a few scenes that juxtapose celebration and references to authoritarian repression, the film replicates the idea that society at large was generally unaware of and unaffected by the machinations of the dictatorship.

In her work on children in film, Vicky Lebeau (2008) asserts that representations of children in film are a valuable resource for reflecting on cultural histories. Acknowledging that myths of childhood shape ways of understanding, Lebeau suggests thinking about how the child in film operates, and asks, What does cinema *want* of the child? (12). In the case of *O ano em que*, the child protagonist is the innocent outsider who discovers a peaceful, diverse, and inclusive nation. In this way, *O ano em que* de-emphasizes critical examination of the dictatorship or its long-term consequences and celebrates cultural diversity and inclusion, consistent with ideas of the new Brazil promoted at the time.

Brazilian History as International History

Several films from the dictatorship cycle make Brazilian history part of international history. Whereas *Os Desafinados* draws on the historical melodrama to foreground Brazil's rich cultural history vis-à-vis political history, *Zuzu Angel* replays strategies found in *O que é isso, companheiro?*, developing codes of the thriller and production choices that prime it for broad commercial appeal. All three films feature Globo TV actors in lead roles and enjoyed coproduction support from Globo Filmes as well as international agencies (Warner Brothers, Columbia, and Sony). These films also include international talent and several scenes whereby Brazil's dictatorial past is linked to international stakeholders (especially the U.S. government and its officials), thus priming cinematic reflections on Brazil's past to enter the global memory market. Critics note that *O que é isso, companheiro?* aimed to be a universal, internationally understandable film (Cunha 2006, 102–103) that would reach, especially, a North American audience (M. Santos 2010, 148). Indeed, *O que é isso, companheiro?* seems to confirm the observation of Alice A. Nelson that national memory processes are bound up in transnational flows. More specifically, Nelson states that "memory formation is never innocent of the intersecting local and global power relationships it simultaneously enacts and rebuts, invokes and potentially rewrites" (2011, 340).

Zuzu Angel aims for a cosmopolitan view of the past and acknowledges local and global power relations. Characters speak English and travel to Europe and North America. The use of English, the thriller, and international coproduction with Warner Brothers seemed to prime the film for an international audience. In his work on the transnational memory film, Russell Kilbourn asserts that easily identifiable film genres (such as the thriller or action adventure film) afford the possibility to lure international audiences and create "the matrix within which transnational identities are generated, appropriated, recontextualized and resignified" (2010, 207). Zuzu uses her celebrity status as well as her personal and professional connections to make claims to international figures to demand that the Brazilian government be held accountable by international standards of civil and human rights. She speaks with lawyers, Amnesty

International, and a U.S. senator, given that her ex-husband was an American. Viewers also see her confront Henry Kissinger during a visit to Brazil, imploring him to investigate human rights violations in Brazil.

Yet her interactions with international figures are generally unsatisfactory. They are hesitant to act, unable to do so without proper documents, kept at a protective distance, or, in the case of Zuzu's American ex-husband, disconnected and effete by comparison with the determined Zuzu. Similar to *O que é isso, companheiro?*, *Zuzu Angel* aims to establish Brazilian history as belonging to and participating in world history. However, the U.S. agent in *O que é isso, companheiro?* was a victim of Brazilian kidnappers, while U.S. agents in *Zuzu Angel* are ineffectual, disengaged, or hesitant to get involved. Rather than present past violence as a shared and equally suffered international crisis, *Zuzu Angel* is more successful in suggesting a complicity of international actors.

Like *O que é isso, companheiro?* and *Zuzu Angel*, *Os Desafinados* aims to situate Brazilian history, people, and culture as part of the global landscape and a shared (inter)national history. However, the film *Os Desafinados* represents a point of exhaustion in the second phase of the dictatorship cycle that contributes to a narrative of a new Brazil. It reiterates several tendencies of the dictatorship cycle (e.g., a youthful point of view, a circular structure, a past framed by the viewpoint of the present), but the film's disjointed plot, displacement of the past, and nostalgia neutralize meaningful engagement with the dictatorial period. The investment in the past by *Os Desafinados* is one that mostly displaces authoritarian violence and commercializes the past en route to promoting a cosmopolitan future.

Os Desafinados develops a circular framing device, opening with an older man viewing black-and-white footage on an editing deck in a contemporary moment. Indeed, the opening resembles the review of photographs on a microfiche reader in *Ação entre amigos*, but unlike in this previous film, the older men do not seek revenge. Theirs is a nostalgic reunion prompted by the death of a bandmate. A close-up image then transports viewers to the 1960s and a group of young musicians entering Copacabana Palace—a landmark hotel in Rio de Janeiro—to try out for a bossa nova talent show. The narrative of *Os Desafinados* revolves around the experiences of the musical group (Joaquim, Glória, Davi, Geraldo, and Paulo) and an aspiring filmmaker friend (Dico), who strive to succeed in their artistic endeavors. An American music agent offers the group $1,000 for the rights to the song, and the group makes their way to New York City to pursue their dreams.

As if taking a cue from Lula-era cultural policies that supported the creative economy, scenes show members of the band working on their music and, despite some challenges, enjoying social mobility and fortune from their music. By way of their creative productions and artistic talent, they become global citizens on an international stage. Numerous shots of characters walking down New York

City streets, purchasing desired items (e.g., a camera, an electric guitar)—fulfilling fantasies of consumption and success—and wandering through Central Park further affirm their status as global citizens. Brazilian music is rich and varied, but bossa nova, in particular, is a genre of Brazilian music that is arguably the most well known outside Brazil. Thus, *Os Desafinados* repackages the past as a backdrop to one of Brazil's most recognizable exported cultural products. The focus on bossa nova in this film selectively emphasizes (or remembers) celebrated music and largely deemphasizes (or forgets) authoritarianism.

If forgetting the past is one of the goals of postdictatorial neoliberalism, the film achieves this in one way by making the violent past (almost literally) another country. The film primarily offers a U.S. setting and U.S. history as the social and historical context. Save for a brief shot of a newspaper referring to the 1964 military coup d'état, the stratagems needed to get Dico's film out of the country past censorship boards, and a scene when the police stop an unauthorized concert, violence and repression are displaced geographically. Martin Luther King Jr.'s famous "I Have a Dream" speech plays on a television in a bedroom where Geraldo, who is Black, snuggles in bed with his White, French girlfriend, Catherine. The romantic scene suggests that class and racial strife exist in the United States but Brazilians are unaffected by racial animus regardless of geopolitical context. Lastly, the lead character Joaquim is abducted by agents of the military regime in Argentina but not Brazil, thus indirectly reiterating the idea that violent repression took place under other dictatorships of the region (especially Argentina) but Brazil's military regime was far less authoritarian.

Besides geographic displacement, the aesthetics and structure of the film emphasize a cosmopolitan present and future. The film draws on the codes of melodrama, including binary tensions between good, innocent characters who are persecuted and exploited by the powerful. Crestfallen characters solicit an emotional response from viewers in the course of developing themes of self-sacrifice and impossible passion. However, *Os Desafinados* dilutes meaningful discussion of the dictatorial past by ineffectively combining the historical epic (consisting of the adventures of a group of young musicians) with the nostalgic testimonial reflections of the four older characters on their youth.

The episodic structure of flashbacks between the present and the past eventually culminates in an uncanny supplanting of the past by the present. After short sequences that consider Joaquim's disappearance in Argentina and relatively brief acknowledgments of efforts to protest the authoritarian regime, the final scenes are located in the diegetic present in a bar where the older members of the band are interviewed for a television program. Reflections on the past end when Glória's son, Antonio Goldfarb, enters the bar, speaking in

English and seeking help to spread his recently deceased mother's ashes in Rio de Janeiro. The well-known actor Rodrigo Santoro plays Joaquim and Antonio. The doppelgänger effect in this instance underscores the notion of rebirth or renewal in the present. The articulation of memory in the present (about the past) concerns literally putting the past (Joaquim, Glória) to rest and ultimately emphasizes a future, cosmopolitan Brazil (as embodied in the Brazilian American, English-speaking Antonio). In this way, *Os Desafinados* offers an optimistic resolution of the past more than critical analysis. The final message is that Brazil is a new, cosmopolitan nation that metaphorically does not even speak the same language as the past.

Os Desafinados had the potential to be a commercially successful film, especially in light of the backing of coproducer Globo Filmes and talent from the Globo star system. However, it was a box office disappointment. By contrast, the remarkable success of the family comedy *Se eu fosse você* (*If I Were You*, Daniel Filho, 2006), the favela action film *Tropa de elite* (*Elite Squad*, José Padilha, 2007; discussed in chapter 5), and the historic biopic *Dois filhos de Francisco* (*Two Sons of Francisco*, Breno Silveira, 2005) signaled the arrival of a new trend in the Brazilian film industry toward commercially successful genre films that followed Hollywood-style blockbuster production strategies. Although the Globo TV network prompted the dictatorship film cycle with the 1992 miniseries *Anos rebeldes*, Globo Filmes did not fully participate in the cycle until 2006 with the coproduction of *Zuzu Angel* and *O ano em que*; however, it has, overall, coproduced or supported the production of six films from the cycle—more than any other production company.[12] This prompts a question: How can the role of Globo Filmes in the dictatorship cycle be best understood?

If the Globo TV network engaged in "memory merchandising" in the early 1990s to promote alternative understandings of history as much as to market itself as a champion of a new democratic order (Atencio 2011, 46), similar reflections can be made regarding the films coproduced by Globo Filmes. Globo Filmes, which was founded in 1998, did not lend support to the military regime as had the Globo Network and did not need to improve its image. However, like the network, Globo Filmes productions are attuned to its audience base, whose outlook was increasingly shaped by changing demographics and evolving concepts of citizenship. The dictatorial past is confronted in these films, but contradictions are mostly resolved and violence is largely neutralized. Taking into account *when* Globo Filmes got into the dictatorship cycle and *what* these productions suggest, Globo Filmes showed an investment in a new democratic order and supported the developing narrative of a new Brazil. As will be discussed in the next chapter, the Globo conglomerate also became a champion for commerce and the new middle class.

The Cycle Closes

As noted earlier, film cycles tend to be very topical, addressing an issue that society is working through and trying to resolve. Cycles frequently begin as a response to a social problem or political situation, and they tend to end with a shift in cultural logic, as well as when their commercial potential wanes vis-à-vis other productions and trends. In the years following the fortieth anniversary of the military coup d'état, additional films of the dictatorship cycle were released. However, the cycle gradually closed after 2008. During the third phase of the dictatorship cycle, from approximately 2009 to 2014, films tended to engage less in rewriting the past for the purposes of the present. Broadly speaking, films from the third phase offer more personal engagement with the authoritarian past than films of the first two phases.

In her work on film sequels, Carolyn Jess-Cooke (2009, 22) asserts that repetition is rooted in an endeavor to "capitalize on popular trends" as well as articulate an experience of change. Films from the first two phases of the dictatorship cycle reflected on the contemporary political status of Brazil. After 2008, reflections on the dictatorial past began to not harmonize with the contemporary moment in terms of the sociopolitical context, the development of the Brazilian film industry, and moviegoing preferences of middle-class spectators. Growth in the national economy resulted in a marked increase in the number of Brazilians who could be classified as belonging to the new middle class. With new disposable income and, consequently, a new political and cultural role, members of the new middle class were eager to see their lives on-screen.

The dictatorship cycle continued, but it took new directions. During the last phase, documentary and feature-length fiction films expanded treatment of the issues, experiences, and events linked to the dictatorship. Some works investigated the regime and its practices, especially following the opening of archives (discussed earlier). For instance, the documentary *Cidadão Boilesen* (*Citizen Boilesen*, Chaim Litewski, 2009) reveals how business executive and civilian Henning Albert Boilesen supported the military, including the torture of political prisoners. Still other works locate the regime as a political backdrop to an otherwise vibrant cultural milieu and ongoing struggle for civil rights. Hilton Lacerda's feature film *Tatuagem* (*Tattoo*, 2013) includes brilliant performances by Irandhir Santos and Jesuita Barbosa as lovers Clécio (a cabaret singer) and Arlindo (a soldier), whose lives are upended by the military regime. Similarly, the documentary films *Dzi Croquetes* (Tatiana Issa and Raphael Alvarez, 2009) and *Uma noite em 67* (Renato Terra and Ricardo Calil, 2010) consider countercultural movements during the dictatorship. The portrayal in these films of official repression and social discrimination of nonheteronormative behavior during the dictatorship leads to consideration of how LGBTQ individuals continue to experience discrimination in the contemporary moment. Similar to *Quase dois irmãos*, Lacerda's film suggests that current intolerance can find historical roots in the dictatorship.

The most significant tendency of films from the last phase is a shift to more personal reflections on the past. This "cinema of intimacy" is characterized by an introspective and reflective consideration of individual dramas supported by portrayals of interior spaces and the use of close-ups that bring spectators into proximity with characters and their conflicts (Seliprandy 2013, 64–69; Távora 2011, 41–47). Central to a cinema of intimacy, several films explore how to live in the present with the experiences of the past. In contrast to *O ano em que*, the documentary *Diário de uma busca* (Flávia Castro, 2010) explores the suspicious death of the director's father, who was a political militant and exile. Castro's exploration of the past resembles the Argentine documentary *Los rubios* (*The Blonds*, Albertina Carri, 2003), in which the director similarly searches for information about her parents, who disappeared. Indeed, in its willingness to dialogue with different interpretations of the past, Castro's film shows a tendency more common in Argentina's cinematic reflections on its dictatorial past (M. Souza 2007).

Many films from the dictatorship cycle portray interior spaces and personal dramas, but *Hoje* and *A memória que me contam* develop these aesthetic strategies to emphasize the haunting emotional experiences of an authoritarian regime responsible for the loss of friends and beloved family members. In *Hoje*, Amaral develops a narrative around a woman, Vera, who buys an apartment with government indemnification funds—made possible by federal law in 1995, discussed earlier—that she claimed for her partner, Luis, who disappeared after being detained and tortured by agents of the military regime. Moving into the apartment serves as a metaphor for negotiating how to inhabit the present when the past still causes emotional pain. Tight framing and handheld camera work draw viewers into the exchanges between Luis and Vera, whose dialogues possess a theatrical quality that seems to break with reality and the temporal moment.[13] Multiple perspectives and creative use of projected images on blank walls play with visual planes and underscore the difficulties of determining the truth. When Luis asks Vera when she determined he was dead, she eventually responds, under pressure, "Hoje" (Today), declaring her need to live in the present while accepting her past.

Murat's *A memória que me contam* also develops an intimate portrayal of reconciliation with the past. Numerous close-up shots, reflections off glass, and shots framed by windows and doorways capture a group of friends recalling their memories, prompted by the impending death of their friend and former political militant, Ana. *A memória que me contam* reprises an autobiographical and metacritical quality found in Murat's previous work. The actress Irene Ravache, who embodied Murat in *Que bom te ver viva*, plays the role of Irene, a filmmaker and another thinly veiled reference to the director. Frequent flash-backs between the past and the present, as well as sound bridges and matching graphics, link temporal moments. Like Luis in *Hoje*, Ana reappears to her friends in the present as if transported from the 1960s. These uncanny moments emphasize an intense and conflicted process of remembering the past. Similar to films from the first two phases of the cycle, *A memória que me contam* focuses on an injured and isolated political militant—Ana in this case—but the emphasis is on mourning her passing and not monumentalizing her actions as a mythical national hero. Unlike films from the first and second phase of the dictatorship cycle, *A memória que me contam* does not aim to contain history or create a break from the past. Rather, Murat explores a question she has raised in previous works: How does one live with the past in the present?

The dictatorial past continued to be addressed by official and unofficial practices, but the nation began developing a new profile at home and abroad. Brazil repaid its International Monetary Fund loans in 2005 and survived the 2007–2008 global economic crisis, and its unique status among nations was further emphasized by being selected to host several international mega-events (such as the 2014 World Cup and the 2016 Olympic Games). In celebration of being asked to host the 2016 Olympic Games and underscoring a new view of Brazil, then-president Lula asserted that it was Brazil's opportunity to show to the world that it had transformed into a developed nation and that Brazil had begun a "nova fase da sua história" (new phase of its history) (P. Fonseca 2009). Brazil and its apparent new international role meant shifting attention away from an authoritarian past to celebrate a vibrant present and capitalize on its more profitable traits. In terms of Jess-Cooke's observations discussed earlier, films addressing the dictatorship began to no longer articulate the change that was being experienced more broadly in society. That is, following the apparent solidification of democracy, the experience of change was the nation's remarkable economic development, the unprecedented growth of the new middle class, and Brazil's more prominent international presence. Whether exploring the past in ways that support the politics of the present or offering more reflective engagements with the authoritarian past, it must be emphasized that films from the dictatorship cycle have contributed to developing a new political culture in Brazil. In their negotiation of the past, the films discussed in this chapter reproduce history to make claims for human rights and democracy, but they also seek a break from the past to celebrate Brazil's new geopolitical profile.

3

Courting the New Middle Class on Primetime TV

■■■■■■■■■■■■■■■■■■■■■■■

From 2003 to 2014, the levels of optimism in Brazil seemed to follow the trajectory of the nation's rising gross domestic product. The months toward the end of 2012 and early 2013, however, punctuated this period as protests concerning World Cup and Olympic preparations, rising costs of living, and government corruption boiled over into the streets. Yet before popular protests and flaws in government policies were fully revealed, a remarkable series of programs aired on the Globo TV network (or Rede Globo) that explored the nation's shifting cultural identity through the lens of gender, race, and class. Brazilian women in urban settings took center stage in two miniseries. First, Globo aired *As cariocas* (2010), an adaptation of the homonymous 1967 literary work by Sérgio Porto. Its sequel, *As brasileiras* (2012), expanded the beauty pageant parade of female stock characters found within the nation's borders. Joining both miniseries is the television trifecta of the primetime shows (*novelas*) *Cheias de charme* (2012), *Avenida Brasil* (2012), and *Salve Jorge* (2012–2013), in which the emerging middle class played a leading role. The programs share several points in common. The plots largely revolve around strong female characters, feature female domestic workers, and explore issues of social mobility and self-reinvention. The narrative tensions, modes of speech and dress, humble and lower-middle-class interior spaces represented, and portrayal of suburban communities[1] clearly appealed to a popular audience by celebrating their lifestyles and casting their lived experiences on-screen.

These television programs captured a phenomenal moment that celebrated an emerging middle class in Brazil, and they reveal how the Globo Network was mapping its brand onto the techno-cultural zeitgeist. What is of particular interest is the focus on women and their portrayed social roles as a way to think through changing cross-class relations and an increasingly market-driven citizenship in Brazil at a time of significant socioeconomic and political change. To that end, this chapter focuses on selected episodes from the two miniseries *As cariocas* and *As brasileiras*, as well as the cross-media, engagement marketing practices of *Cheias de charme*, to consider how television attracted (or, "courted") viewers to ostensibly new ideas about belonging in Brazil. In my discussion, I examine the contemporary cultural economy of stardom in Brazil, aiming to understand developments in television at this time and their relation to desired, broader economic and political outcomes.

Branding involves cultivating buy-in. In programs discussed here, the Globo Network mobilized its star system to garner support for the notion of a "new Brazil." I approach the idea of the star in two ways. First, a preeminent star of the moment was the new middle class. Programming sought to connect with middle-class audiences whose new purchasing power was of keen interest to advertisers. Second, "stardom" refers to the pantheon of Globo actresses who portray the women of Rio de Janeiro and Brazil on television in *As cariocas* and *As brasileiras*. (Notably, the titles of these programs loosely translate as "The women of Rio" and "The Brazilian women"). It is through the celebration of female stars—both actresses and members of the new middle class—that these shows cultivated buy-in to the idea of a new, emergent Brazil. However, analysis of these programs shows that transformation in citizenship at this time was ambivalent concerning sociopolitical and economic inclusion. These programs reveal tensions concerning aspirational citizenship that seemed to move toward greater equality despite ongoing social, economic, and political exclusion.

The Emerging Middle Class and Emergent Citizenship

The growth of the middle class during the period in question was remarkable. Income inequality steadily decreased from 2001 to 2009 and nearly 40 million people entered the ranks of the middle class in Brazil between 2003 and 2011 (Neri 2011, 25–27). This demographic shift meant that by 2011 nearly 106 million Brazilians were members of the middle class, which in turn constituted about 55 percent of the total population (Neri 2011, 28). A significant number also left extreme poverty, referred to as the "ascensão da classe E" (rise of the E class) (Neri 2011, 163). The number of Brazilians newly designated as middle class was a significant factor stimulating international interest in Brazil as an emerging nation and a factor that was greatly celebrated by politicians as evidence that their policies were successful. It appeared that the nation was moving toward greater equality and shedding its status as a nation with one of the world's greatest income disparities. Yet this interest and celebration were also motivated by the possibilities offered to the local and global economy by this new group of consumers. As Marcelo Cortes Neri (2011, 28–29) points out, the new middle class not only became the dominant political and economic class and thus able to decide elections but also held the majority of the purchasing power in Brazil. Notably, the market research agency Associação de Empresas de Pesquisa developed the "critério Brasil" (Brazil criteria) to define categories (A, B, C, etc.) widely used in Brazil to describe class status. Hopes were high that the Brazilian economy could move away from its dependence on the export of commodities and develop a more independent economy sustained by internal consumption.

Contrary to Neri, economist Marcio Pochmann (2012, 2014) refers to the idea of a large middle class as a myth and argues that one does not really find the rise of a middle class at this time but, rather, an increase in the number of Brazilians belonging to the lower-income working class. Others urge us to consider factors in addition to income and assert that a minority of the new middle class actually belongs to the middle class if we also consider occupational status, which reflects a broader range of life opportunities and social positions (Cardoso and Préteceille 2017).

What is clear is that during this time period, the income levels of the poorest members of Brazilian society rose and they were encouraged to embrace their new consumer potential. Indeed, the new middle class (*classe C*) has been referred to as the "consumption class" (*classe de consumo*), with the letter *C* referring to cars, computers, cable television, credit, *casa própria* (home ownership), and, most importantly, *carteira de trabalho* (a signed work card or official employment status). Formulas for defining economic class generally rely on consumption potential. However, the "critério Brasil" takes into consideration other symbolic aspects that define middle-classness, including access to and ownership of durable goods (e.g., television sets, washing machines, and refrigerators), number of bathrooms, and type of housing (Neri 2011, 79).

Yet how did these economic changes affect women specifically? In relative terms, women's incomes rose by 38 percent while men gained 16 percent between 2001 and 2009. What is more, incomes for those who self-identified as *preto* (black) or *pardo* (brown) rose by 43 percent and 48.5 percent, respectively, while those who identified as *branco* (white) saw their salaries rise by 20.1 percent (Neri 2011, 33). These numbers suggest that Afro-Brazilian women experienced the most significant improvement in their economic status during the Lula and Rousseff administrations. Notwithstanding government efforts to reduce gender and racial inequality,[2] significant gaps in formal employment remain and wage disparities reflect persistent discriminatory practices (Agénor and Canuto 2013, 6–7). Although women as a broad demographic group may have seen some economic improvements during this period, the relationship between gender and race in the domains of labor and citizenship remains unequal.

Historically, citizenship in Brazil has been markedly uneven in its development. James Holston (2008) describes practices of "insurgent citizenship" where social movements in the 1970s and 1980s in urban peripheries gradually eroded entrenched regimes of inegalitarian citizenship. The economic boom in Brazil during the first decade of the twenty-first century established new parameters of inclusion and exclusion. Celebrated economic improvements joined a broader sociopolitical tone set by government administrations whose policies sought greater social inclusion. In their evaluation of the transformation of citizenship after years of neoliberal economic policy, Jürgen Mackert and Bryan Turner (2017) underscore the importance of analyzing the practices of citizenship in the midst of fundamentally transformed conditions. They note that neoliberalism has evolved from a policy paradigm to a social imaginary, and they call attention to the intrusion of market principles into the private sphere and the marketization of citizenship. Whereas the idea of insurgency aptly describes the practices and experiences of citizenship in the late twentieth century, during the branding period from 2003 to 2014 we find a modality of citizenship that can best be described as *emergent*.

In their study of the new middle classes (and the state of being middle class) in emerging nations, Leslie Marsh and Hongmei Li (2016) propose the concept of emergent citizenship as a framework for theorizing the experiences of people whose economic status has (ostensibly) improved. The emergent citizen is one whose "transformed economic status leads to new modalities of sociopolitical participation and new pressure points for belonging" (Marsh and Li 2016, 8–9). The authors note that emergent citizenship is shaped by new modes of consumption, the occupation of new spaces, tensions between classes, and new lifestyle practices in a process of developing new identities (9). The cultural moment discussed here celebrated new modes of belonging. Yet, drawing on Mackert and Turner, it was also a neoliberal moment when market principles intruded upon the social imaginary, which becomes evident in the programs discussed next.

Mobilizing Desire in *As cariocas* and *As brasileiras*

Both miniseries find their point of departure with the 1967 collection of humorous narratives *As cariocas*, by Brazilian author Sérgio Porto (1923–1978).[3] The author, also known by the pen name Stanislaw Ponte Preta, had a varied literary career, publishing newspaper columns as well as scripts for theater and television. The urban chronicle has a rich history in Brazil, and Porto's columns, alongside others, helped invent the *carioca* (native resident of Rio de Janeiro) in the 1950s (Mesquita 2008, 39–42). Bryan McCann (2012, 512–513) observes that the greatest strengths of Porto's chronicles were their use of earthy humor to critique politics of the day and their mass appeal, especially for readers of Rio's lower-middle and working classes of the urban periphery. At a time when the growing new middle class was celebrated for its newfound political and economic power, the television miniseries *As cariocas* adapted the work of Porto to once again define what it means to be *carioca* from a popular perspective.

Both programs inherit the spirit of Porto's urban chronicle, with a voyeuristic gaze and male voiceover narration that guide viewers' exploration of geographic locations. The omniscient narrator intervenes on occasion during episodes to provide commentary on the actions and thoughts of the female protagonists. In keeping with key characteristics of the chronicle, the historical and social information shared by the narrator suggests journalistic authenticity and objectivity while the fictional narratives about Brazilian women's lives emphasize cultural life and commonly lived experiences. In the opening sequence that begins each episode of *As cariocas*, establishing shots show postcard-style images of the city's landscape before a montage shifts focus to a specific neighborhood of Rio de Janeiro. The upbeat narrator provides basic information about the history of the locale, its inhabitants, its most important landmarks, and other salient details about the urban community. Not only does this opening sequence anticipate a humorous tone, but the introductory comments also align each episode with the role of the chronicle to historicize and establish an order of events. A cut transports viewers to an all-white backdrop and actresses featured in the series parade forth in full makeup, wearing high heels and formal evening gowns. Finally, the actress who plays the protagonist of a given episode steps toward the camera and the male narrator introduces the character at the center of the story. The city of Rio de Janeiro and Brazil as a nation are explored and become knowable from a gendered perspective that emphasizes female sexuality and women's roles in society.

Indeed, both programs make gender an important part of a place-making strategy. The titles ("The women of Rio" and "The Brazilian women") make overt claims on local and national as well as gendered identity. The marketing language found on the DVD cover for *As cariocas* explains that the contours of women's bodies enjoy the backdrop of the beautiful landscape of Rio de Janeiro and illustrate that being a *carioca* is a unique way of being and state of spirit. Similarly, the marketing materials for *As brasileiras* claims that the miniseries comprises a series of "microdocumentários" (micro-documentaries) with a touch of humor on women and their temperaments from the four corners of the country. Thus, viewers are encouraged to partake in a pseudo-ethnographic exploration of the city of Rio de Janeiro and the entire nation, accompanied by the leading female actresses in the Globo Network's star system.

The procession of well-coiffed, famous Globo actresses in formal attire that opens each episode of both miniseries resembles a parade of beauty contestants.

Sarah Banet-Weiser (1999) asserts that beauty pageants offer insights into the complicated, evolving stories about a nation and reveal claims on national and feminine identity as well as who counts as part of the nation and on what terms. What is more, pageants are highly visible performances of gender and (typically heteronormative) sexuality where women are positioned as highly desirable (Banet-Weiser 1999, 2). Banet-Weiser asserts that idealized concepts of the nation need women to sustain their cultural and political currency and, thus, she argues, "any concept of the nation must incite particular desires in its public to remain a legitimate institutionalized system of beliefs and practices" (8).

Drawing on Banet-Weiser, desire is mobilized in both programs as a way to think through shifting notions of belonging, and it frequently frames narratives that address social mobility. Whereas the episodes in *As cariocas* more clearly revolve around sexual desire for the female character and her desires for others, the majority of the episodes of *As brasileiras* feature protagonists who are overtly sexualized or wanting (be it affection, status, or even revenge). Both series use humor to make fun of prevailing social values and interactions while celebrating the idiosyncrasies of regional and national identity. In both programs, famous actresses play largely comic stock characters, which balances new and old cultural models and helps cultivate buy-in for the notion of a new Brazil. These shows intervene in understanding emergent citizenship and what it means to be middle class in contemporary Brazil.

Spectacles of Self-Reinvention and the Urban Erotic in *As cariocas*

The first episode of *As cariocas*, "A noiva do Catete" (The engaged woman of Catete), introduces the theme of self-reinvention and can be squarely placed in the tradition of the erotic urban comedy. The narrator explains that Catete was once home to the nation's elite and the site of government institutions before the capital was transferred to Brasília. A cut introduces Nadia (Alinne Moraes), a young woman who changes her demeanor and personality to be with three different men. With the young surfer Nelson, she is a glamorous, sexually free-spirited, uncommitted lover. With Fagundes, an older businessman from São Paulo, she is an obsequious, childlike lover who receives a monthly stipend and gifts. With the paraplegic Carlos, who was injured protecting her one night from thieves, she is a seemingly angelic, self-sacrificing fiancée committed to being by his side and providing for his every need (food, fellatio, friendship).

For Nadia, playing different roles and conducting her own self-reinvention are just part of daily living. Adopting different identities gains romantic rewards, but this role-play is limited in terms of reflecting a deeper change in citizenship for women. In fact, Nadia's identities—sexually liberated, obsequious, or doting caregiver—all replicate to varying degrees sexist, patriarchal roles for women. The episode closes with Nelson agreeing to accept Nadia's two other relationships but insisting that no other men be allowed into their romantic arrangement. As they embrace to settle their agreement, Nadia winks directly at the camera, suggesting she has no intention of limiting the number of her sexual partners and affirming a complicity with the viewing audience.[4]

In the 1967 story, the female character has to behave in ways that secure a future for herself, but the wink by Nadia in the television episode suggests freedom and playfulness. The contemporary character makes fun of the traditional expectations of women in a patriarchal society yet ultimately uses those stereotypes to her personal advantage. The wink also cheekily suggests not just the possibility of future encounters with a sexually vivacious woman on the streets of Rio de Janeiro but also that the urban landscape of Rio de Janeiro is an erotic playground where women's sexuality is mobile and adaptable to different desires.

Similar to the urban chronicle of the early twentieth century, *As cariocas* humanizes the city, albeit in this instance through women's bodies and sexual behaviors. The urban sphere is taken up as a space for discovery as well as a subject of inquiry. Indeed, social relations are conceptualized in terms of sexual desire that transcends the neighborhoods of Rio de Janeiro and socioeconomic classes. Scholars of the chronicle in Brazil have analyzed its social history, asserting that the form has played an important role in influencing attitudes and illustrating models of urban social relations and identities (Nery 2005; Brayner 1992; G. Bastos 1992). The chronicle in Brazil has also been an important form for imagining the nation's political future (A. Ramos 2005; Lopez 1992) and for critiquing class divisions (Chalmers 1992). Lastly, it has been a very immediate (or ephemeral) and complicit form, critiquing contemporary events and seeking to connect with the masses (Chalhoub, Neves, and Pereira 2005). This proximity to the public has often been achieved through the chronicle's use of humor.

In *As cariocas*, traditional social values and gendered behaviors associated with different classes in the neighborhoods of Rio de Janeiro are portrayed onscreen in a mocking way. A carnivalesque sense of humor questions social hierarchies and norms.[5] That is, no neighborhood or demographic group is free in this series from the equalizing force of humor. This becomes particularly apparent in the episode "A invejosa de Ipanema" (The envious woman from Ipanema), which targets the upper-class living in one of the most prestigious areas of Rio de Janeiro and lampoons its residents' base motivations and behaviors. The episode stars Fernanda Torres as Cris, a woman married to an older, wealthy Gustavo. Cris has an ongoing affair with Luis Felipe, a plastic surgeon married to another woman. When Cris discovers that Luis Felipe has given his wife an expensive necklace and a yellow Ferrari, her avarice overcomes her and she strives to manipulate both men to obtain the objects she covets. Her machinations ultimately fail and Gustavo ends up buying the prized sports car for his lover. Humor in this instance allows for an evaluation of the elite, portrayed

as greedy and failed exemplars of morality. In a society historically characterized by marked inequality, social hierarchies are briefly reversed in this episode.
Making fun of social norms and behaviors—especially those of the upper
classes—is a type of humor that appeals to the popular classes and prevails in
both Globo programs.

If the protagonist of the first episode, Nadia, embodies various traditional
patriarchal fantasies of women while also seeking her own pleasure, then Clarisa
(Paola Oliveira) in "A atormentada da Tijuca" (The tormented woman from
Tijuca) tries to start a new life as an independent, separated woman after leaving
her abusive husband. The narrator presents the neighborhood of Tijuca, offering similar information about the location as in other episodes. Yet in this
instance, he remarks that Tijuca is a middle-class neighborhood and, unlike
other areas of Rio, Tijuca "não é um ponto turístico" (isn't a tourist destination). Consequently, the narrator not only suggests that other locations featured
in the series are commercially spectacular but also admits to some complicity
in presenting the landscape of Rio de Janeiro as a consumable space for leisure.
The narrator asserts that Tijuca residents are humble, honest, and hardworking, which is affirmed by the protagonist Clarisa, who is also described as shy,
timid, quiet, and newly separated. With this introduction, social relations are
clearly conceptualized in this urban setting in terms of gender and middle-class
status.

The television adaptation of Porto's "A desquitada da Tijuca"[6] closely follows the original text. Clarisa is harassed in public spaces and at her workplace.
Although Clarisa claims she was never bothered at work when she was married, once it becomes known she is separated, her male colleagues cannot seem
to leave her alone. The narrative suggests that Clarisa may be an independent,
white-collar working woman and have the right to leave her husband, but she
still needs the protection of a man in the public sphere. In Porto's original text,
Clarisa's childhood friend and neighbor, Gilberto, suggests that she is harassed
because a single, separated woman is seen as a woman without a "dono" (owner,
overseer, protector) (Porto 2010, 112). After she complains about her predicament, Gilberto, who is widely believed to be gay because he is a ballroom dance
instructor and uses some effeminate gestures, suggests they invent a fake lover
named Rodolfo Sarné. The two craft their ruse and convince Clarisa's office-
mates she has a wealthy, powerful boyfriend, and she consequently earns respect
from her male colleagues and admiration from her female coworkers.

If the episode portrays the single woman as professional and independent,
she is also stressed and isolated. It would seem that women's status in society
has not improved much since the original text was published, despite financial
and legal advances. A new civil code, which was ratified in 2002 and went into
effect in 2003, granted women greater autonomy and equal rights in relation
to men in Brazilian society.[7] As noted earlier, women's economic status appeared

to improve during the economic boom period. Notwithstanding these advances, the female protagonist Clarisa needs male protection in the public sphere and must engage in social subterfuge to secure her peace and respect. The professional working middle-class woman is one caught between progress and traditional value systems. The pretense of having a wealthy lover gains Clarisa freedom from harassment at work. That is, an upper-class status grants the nonexistent Rodolfo Sarné power over Clarisa's male colleagues. The joke may be humorous, but it also normalizes harassment in the workplace, as it does not question abusive, sexist behavior.

When Gilberto, who had been an ally in Clarisa's ruse, reveals that he has been secretly in love with her, their closing embrace suggests that true romance can be found between individuals from the same community and social class. Traditional, patriarchal values, whereby a single woman needs to be linked to a male partner to be respected, are mocked but eventually upheld. A modern, middle-class Brazilian woman may seek her independence and pursue a career, but she will not be liberated from an abusive situation unless she is happily united with a male companion.

The episodes of *As cariocas* and *As brasileiras* make clear gendered claims to national and cultural identity in terms of female sexuality and women's roles in society. They also investigate male heteronormative sexuality and men's social roles. That Gilberto reveals himself to not be gay is a twist in the contemporary television episode and a divergence from the original text by Porto. The mother of Clarisa, who does not exist in Porto's text, declares her belief that Gilberto is a closeted gay man and makes a reference to herself as a former muse of the *pornochanchada* (Brazilian sex comedy films). In fact, the playful eroticism found in the original narratives by Porto, which is transferred to the television miniseries, was common in the *pornochanchada* of the 1960s and 1970s. In the case of the early *pornochanchada*, male sexuality was under evaluation and insecurities regarding heteronormative male sexuality and social impotence were exercised on screen (Dennison and Shaw 2004, 161). What is more, norms were briefly inverted but narratives eventually returned to the status quo (170). The role of Gilberto offers a slightly more progressive view of masculinity in that he demonstrates that nonnormative male sexuality should be recognized and suggests that there are difficulties accepting homosexuality in contemporary Brazil. Gilberto's role as a seemingly gay man who gains female affection through subterfuge does little to advance gay rights in Brazil. But his interactions with Clarisa suggest that sexist, patriarchal ways of being are not acceptable in the new context.

The narratives of self-reinvention have relatively happy conclusions in the episodes just discussed. By contrast, the episode "A internauta da Mangueira" (The web-surfer of Mangueira) combines a discussion of the eroticized female body, women's labor, and the intersection of gender, race, and class that coincides with prevailing development policies. The episode revolves around the relationship between Gleicy (Cintia Rosa) and her husband, Armando, who live in an apartment in Mangueira. As with other opening sequences, the voiceover introduces viewers to Mangueira, which originally formed as a favela built on a hillside in the mid-nineteenth century. The location is famous for its samba music and the narrator notes that the neighborhood is the former residence of the renowned samba composer Cartola. Rather than refer to needed infrastructure or greater access to education and health care, the narrator also describes Mangueira in a way that celebrates the beautiful landscape *around* it. The narrator references the neighborhood's ideal location *near* Maracanã soccer stadium and its *proximity* to the imperial home of Quinta da Boa Vista. This presentation of Mangueira engages in a practice of invisibility politics that promoted Rio de Janeiro's landscape but hid or overlooked issues of inequality in favor of spectacular beauty. What is more, this portrayal of Mangueira resonates with security policies before a series of international mega-events that aimed to eliminate the control of drug gangs in favelas near important touristic and cultural sites (such as the Maracanã stadium), introduce the state into formerly neglected areas, and reimagine these areas as safe, vital spheres of Rio's landscape. It is in this former favela in the North Zone of Rio de Janeiro that the couple ostensibly enjoys a modest but comfortable middle-class lifestyle. Armando works as a small shopkeeper, while Gleicy uses her computer skills in a home office.

In a series that makes claims on defining all women of Rio de Janeiro, it is notable that Rosa is the only actress of evident Afro-Brazilian heritage to play a protagonist in the program. What is more, Gleicy is one of very few phenotypically darker-skinned characters in all ten episodes of the miniseries. Whereas the phenotypically white Clarisa in the episode discussed earlier works in a typical office environment, Gleicy appears to engage in independent, contract labor on projects. This is consonant with flexible "gig" employment promoted by neoliberal economic development. That is, Gleicy does not find stable employment in an office environment (like Clarisa) or enjoy the benefits to which formal employees are entitled. As discussed in chapter 1, cultural and economic policies that embraced the creative economy were viewed as particularly important in integrating formerly excluded groups into a mainstream economy. Given the relatively nice furnishings in the apartment where Gleicy lives with her husband in the lower-income neighborhood of Mangueira, she apparently helps sustain a comfortable lifestyle through her freelance work at home.

Gleicy's flexible participation in the workforce appears to help reinvent a role for Black Brazilian women in the contemporary economy. However, this participation involves unresolved cultural tensions around the Black female body and labor. Similar to anxieties with regard to single women's participation in the workplace revealed in the episode "A atormentada da Tijuca," Gleicy's digital skills are presented as a threat to her husband despite her openly professed, ardent commitment to him. The introduction to the character shows Gleicy walking down a street in Mangueira, licking an ice cream, when she is approached by a former lover, Leleco, who notices she is wearing a wedding ring, which prompts him to say that she now has a "dono" (an owner or husband). The episode supports several stereotypes about Black women's bodies. For instance, Black women are frequently viewed as hypersexual and available (E. Williams 2013; Goldstein 2014). The episode emphasizes the conception that women without a male guardian are easily threatened or threatening. Nonetheless, Gleicy affirms her love for her husband. Yet her professed commitment to him does not assuage his patriarchal fears of her infidelity. It is, in fact, Armando who requires that she work at home and not Gleicy's preference. She can enter the digital economy, but her body and her labor do not seem to escape the configuration of the Black female as a *domestic* worker.

The episode further supports the stereotype of the sexually available Black female body. Patriarchal fears and racist beliefs concerning Black Brazilian women are revealed again when Gleicy appears partially disguised (with a face mask) and mostly nude before a webcam late at night. (It is not revealed whether she participates in digital voyeurism for financial gain.) Emilson, a neighbor and friend, informs Armando he is a cuckold by technology because Gleicy is cheating on him digitally without leaving the home. Thus, the episode expresses an anxiety about gendered roles in contemporary Brazil and the redrawing of the boundaries between the public and private spheres. Regardless of where they participate in the paid labor force, women's sexuality is a potential disruptor of established gendered and socioeconomic boundaries.

Physical violence expressed as an honor killing aims to restore a threatened patriarchal social order. Yet the episode is socially tone-deaf regarding institutionalized violence against women. Scholars and activists have fought since the 1970s against the so-called legitimate defense of honor used as a legal defense by men accused of killing their female partners. In 2006, President Lula da Silva signed the Maria da Penha law (Lei 11.340/06). In addition to providing mechanisms to prevent, punish, and eradicate violence against women, the law defined domestic violence and it characterized violence against women as a violation of human rights (Andrade and Almeida 2017; Campos 2015; Machado 2015). Armando confronts Gleicy for her cyber infidelities and threatens to kill her. Her murder is preempted by a championship soccer match in which Armando's favorite team, Flamengo, is playing. While cheering, Armando observes a fearful Gleicy, whom he has forced to accompany him to the stadium while knowing she is under threat of being killed. His erotic desires for her, a realization that he is fortunate to have her in his life, and the success of his soccer team save her from premeditated murder. The closing scene shows

Armando celebrating his team's win with gunfire out the window of their apartment while a naked Gleicy wraps her arms around him. The voiceover explains that Armando realized he was only a cuckold in the virtual world. In the apparently real (or analog) world, he retains his virility and power over Gleicy.

The episode joins others from *As cariocas* in attempting to bridge spatial and social segregation in Rio de Janeiro. The episode also examines how members of the community are positioned in the context of development and how understandings of place are fashioned that are productive and profitable. Black Brazilian women's social mobility and their potential as participants in a digital workforce are celebrated as much as seen as a threat. The episode addresses the intersection of technology, race, class, and gender, but it upholds broader, unequal social relations. The "symbolic capital" of the eroticized Black Brazilian female body is further institutionalized to support contemporary economic development plans. Indeed, it is an erotic desire for the Black female body that manages to overcome patriarchal, physical violence (i.e., honor killing) and allows for thinking about how the favela and emerging middle-class women's labor may participate in a transitional Brazil. That Gleicy possesses some degree of digital literacy while Armando is relatively ignorant of computer-based work serves as a threat to the working-class male character and an impetus for him to become more informed of digital technology to protect and defend his patriarchal social status.

Aspirational Claims in *As brasileiras*

The opening sequences of *As brasileiras* expand the geographic scope of the humorous, gendered explorations of contemporary Brazilian culture in *As cariocas* and situate Brazil as part of the global order. Viewers first see an image of planet Earth and a glowing Brazil in South America before a camera (ostensibly) swoops down to view the natural beauty of Brazil (its waterfalls, green forests, and winding rivers) and modern urban landscapes (skyscrapers, busy avenues, and maritime ports). Thus, the sequence underscores a notion of diversity that forms a celebrated cornerstone of Brazilian cultural identity. Once again, high-heeled and well-coiffed actresses parade forth against an all-white backdrop and a male voiceover provides pertinent details about a given city, region, and its culture before introducing viewers to the episode's main female character. It is in this diverse landscape that women are "explored" in a negotiation of established and new cultural identities and practices. A male voiceover then announces where viewers will travel to in the episode. As if flying in from outer space, viewers land in the midst of a situational comedy with one of twenty-two well-known Globo actresses who populate this sequel's pantheon of idealized Brazilian women.

That the sequel miniseries broadens its geopolitical scale and continues the beauty pageant parade of famous actresses demands thinking about idealized local and global citizenship in *As brasileiras*. The shift in viewpoint from the regional, urban focus of *As cariocas* to a broader, international view of Brazil marks an expanded understanding of Brazil's belonging in the global landscape and affirms a long-held belief in Brazil's global potential as an economic and cultural powerhouse. In his account of modern citizenship, T. H. Marshall suggests that societies where citizenship is developing as an institution "create an image of an ideal citizenship against which achievement can be measured and towards which aspiration can be directed" (1950, 29). The idealized citizenship promoted at this time was greatly aspirational and celebratory of the new middle class. Furthermore, the ideals proposed during this period—as reflected in cultural policies discussed in chapter 1—greatly emphasized integrating the previously excluded into the national and global economy. Considering the changing politico-economic context at this time, how are female characters in these episodes portrayed as emergent citizens? How are women presented as new consumers with access to financial credit? What new spaces do they occupy? And how are cross-class tensions and social mobility addressed? These are key questions I examine in the discussion of two selected episodes from *As brasileiras*.

The episode "A desastrada de Salvador" (The clumsy woman from Salvador) opens similarly to other episodes in the series but includes elements to indicate that viewers have arrived in Bahia, a state in the Northeast of Brazil. The samba song "O que a baiana tem?," whose lyrics refer to the traditional clothing worn by women of African descent in Bahia, plays over images before a narrator intervenes to describe Bahia as the most carnivalesque state of the union. This observation upholds some racist and classist beliefs that the North and Northeast, home to a significant population of African descent, are less industrious relative to the southern and southeastern regions of the country, home to sizable populations of European (Italian, Spanish, German, and Portuguese) and Asian (Japanese) ancestry. The voiceover describes the capital city, Salvador, as a happy place and evokes the image of Bahians running after a *trio elétrico* (a music float during Carnaval), albeit slowly, furthering a stereotype of people from the Northeast as having an indolent nature. This geopolitical presentation of Salvador and the region cultivates existing myths of cultural identity that seem more appropriate for a foreign viewer and not an intended audience of national, local viewers who are likely familiar with the city and state.

Indeed, the presentation offers a propagandistic blend of stereotypical content and celebratory tone before introducing the protagonist, Raquel (Ivete Sangalo), who works at home as a translator. As the title of the episode indicates, viewers discover that Raquel is a slightly irresponsible, maladroit figure. The irony that she translates self-help books becomes evident when the power goes out and she does not know how to retrieve her autosaved documents. Although Raquel works at home (like Gleicy in the *As cariocas* episode just discussed), she generally lacks the understanding of technology that Gleicy demonstrates. Her momentary crisis becomes gendered in a traditional way as she calls on her muscular, unemployed brother, Pedro, for help. Technological skill is further shifted to the masculine figure when Pedro manages to get a job helping a gym set up their technology. Thus, traditional masculine brawn is met with contemporary, working-class digital savoir faire. Meanwhile, female characters are associated with more traditional expectations to be beautiful and charming.

It is the protagonist's desire to impress her social circle that creates a context for chaos and misguided consumerism. Among the envelopes piled on her desk at home, there are a number of bills, which the narrator informs viewers are overdue. Raquel also finds an invitation to the wedding of an old friend from school and her focus shifts to gathering the items she needs to wear. Raquel, who viewers surmise has a history of destroying or losing items, manages to borrow a dress from her sister, Telma, a pair of expensive earrings from her mother, and a designer purse from her sister-in-law Úrsula. Female solidarity in this instance revolves around helping one another become appreciated spectacles in public. At the wedding reception, Raquel gains desired attention. The episode suggests social mobility can be attained through acquiring objects that support (or improve) female beauty.

Yet the afterglow from impressing her social circle and reconnecting with her former love interest, Mauro, does not last as a comedy of errors is set in motion. Home from the wedding reception, Raquel tosses the borrowed bag on the sofa. Since she has not fed her dog, he eats it while she rushes to the bathroom, where an earring falls down the drain. She then dismantles the sink but ruins the dress by getting it wet and dirty. Raquel then confesses her woes and consults with her sister, Telma, and her mother. Both tell her she must resolve the problem with Úrsula on her own.

The humor found in this episode largely rests on physical mistakes, but it is also related to questions of social class. The predicament Raquel makes for herself resembles the unexpected challenges people with fewer financial resources encounter in their daily lives, where they are exposed to and suffer the consequences of small mistakes without the financial buffers and protections the upper classes enjoy. That is, wealthier individuals can buy or finance their way out of difficult situations, while those of fewer means must find creative solutions to solve problems.

Humor is mobilized in this episode to reflect on negotiating socioeconomic status and new behaviors. Scholars of comedy have emphasized how humor addresses social relations, especially related to hierarchies and incongruity (Hokenson 2006, 127–140; Vandaele 2002; Morreall 1987; Clark 1987). Female comics and actresses in the U.S. have frequently used humor to upend norms and ideals surrounding women's bodies and expected behaviors (Mizejewski 2015; Mizejewski, Sturtevant, and Karlyn 2017). In Latin American cinemas, Juan Poblete (2016) asserts that humor has contributed to a critical understanding of the nation and film comedy has been one of the most popular forms (alongside melodrama). What is more, comedy has been particularly prevalent at moments of economic and political transition (12–20). Regarding Brazil specifically, popular cinema has consistently used humor to mock urban elites, expose the contradictions of modernity, and question social integration (Dennison and Shaw 2004; M. Bastos 2001). The contemporary *globochanchada* (film comedies produced by Globo Filmes) and the romantic comedy have provided a key venue for critique of cross-class relations and gender (Marsh 2017b, c). And humor was key in the urban chronicle—the inspiration for the Globo series—to reach the masses and imagine a new political future for the country (A. Ramos 2005, 89), as well as addressing class divisions and ethnic identities (Chalmers 1992, 198–201).

In this episode, Raquel is portrayed as being out of place with new consumer behaviors, which offers a critique of contemporary citizenship. Raquel attempts to purchase a replacement purse at an upscale designer shop, but her credit card is rejected because she has exceeded her spending limit. This and other traits cue the shopkeepers to be condescending to Raquel. The disrespectful scene in the shop reflects a broader tendency to associate discrimination in Brazil with class and not race. James Holston has described citizenship in Brazil as "differentiated," meaning that social rights are distributed in an inegalitarian way. Individuals may identify as Brazilian, but they "occupy very different places within the hierarchy of powers and privileges that the inegalitarian dimension maintains" (Holston 2008, 197). Less courteous behavior reminds Raquel of her lower socioeconomic status.

The scene reveals one way in which individuals experience quotidian acts of discrimination. However, it makes race a largely invisible factor. It is remarkable that an episode set in Bahia, which is purportedly the region with the highest percentage of people of African descent in Brazil, has no darker-skinned characters with significant speaking parts. The protagonist, Raquel, is phenotypically white—as are, notably, the other characters in this episode with significant speaking parts. The arrogance and differentiated treatment (e.g., being offered water and not wine at the upscale shop) are apparently due to a class difference. It is the clothing that Raquel wears, the way she carries herself, or other cues, but not her skin tone, that earn her less respect.

Yet humor is mobilized to lend support to new consumers. When Raquel later returns to purchase a replacement bag, the shopkeepers initially mock her, assuming she will attempt another purchase with an invalid credit card. They are silenced when she presents cash, which she obtained through an informal loan. Thus, the ability to purchase desired items is presented as a social equalizer that can upend discrimination. When it is later revealed that Raquel inadvertently returned a counterfeit bag to the store, humor is further mobilized to critique the foibles of the upper class. In this way a comedy of errors critiques class-based discrimination but also provides a theme of revindication for new middle-class consumers, affirming a place for them in the booming economy.

Raquel's awkwardness reflects a transitional politico-economic state. Comedic situations help inform less savvy or inexperienced consumers how to participate in the economy using credit cards and personal loans. After her credit card is declined, Raquel consults Mauro, whom she reconnected with at the wedding and who works at a credit agency. He offers Raquel a low-interest personal loan, but he discovers her name on a "negative list" of the SPC, a large credit bureau in Brazil. Notably, consumer lines of credit improved under the Real Plan, which began in 1994 (de Oliveira and Nakatani 2000, 16–28). During the Lula administration, access to personal credit increased significantly alongside increased household financial stress (International Monetary Fund 2013). Raquel demonstrates new consumer behaviors that have been possible since the mid-1990s. Her experiences inform viewers with newfound disposable income of credit opportunities but also educate them about the necessity of having a good credit record to be able to participate as responsible consumers in the booming economy.

In her attempt to find a solution to her situation, Raquel reveals new consumption behaviors. Old ways of purchasing items on the street or negotiating in an informal way are presented as leading to numerous problems. In contrast, being a careful, responsible consumer with good credit will allow for the purchase of desired items to have a better life. This is one of the utopic promises of neoliberal capitalism—happiness and social harmony through individual consumption. In the closing scene, viewers see Raquel having a romantic evening out with Mauro. She looks at the camera, breaking the fourth wall and establishing complicity with the audience, as if to affirm playfully that the viewer can enjoy the parameters of new consumerism and everything will work out successfully and pleasurably in the end.

Seeking a harmonious, happy ending is common for the characters of the program and is repeated in the episode "A doméstica da Vitória" (The maid from Vitória). Following the narrative of a modern Cinderella, this episode develops a narrative of cross-class relationships, social mobility, and women's labor. Cleonice (Dira Paes) works as a maid in the home of a famous writer, dona Muriel. The narrator's introduction first comments on Cleonice's attractive, well-formed body before viewers see her writing in a small notebook. She is humble, hardworking, and thoughtful while also being sexually desirable.

Like Cinderella, Cleonice possesses unrecognized potential, as an author who works as a maid for an unjust, self-centered *patroa* (employer), dona Muriel, who, in a desperate attempt to retain her youthful vigor, undergoes a bizarre beauty treatment. When dona Muriel suffers an allergic reaction to the skin treatment, she is horrified in part by the red patches on her face but mostly because she will not be able to attend a gala event to celebrate her as an author. Maria José, Cleonice's workmate and ad hoc fairy godmother, encourages Cleonice to go to the event as dona Muriel. Cleonice dons a borrowed dress and attends the gala in the place of her *patroa*, which includes an impromptu reading of dona Muriel's new work (i.e., passages from Cleonice's notebook). Cleonice meets and falls in love with a modern-day Prince Charming named Fernando, who believes her to be the famous reclusive writer. Additional tropes nod to the Cinderella narrative, including a moment when Cleonice's gold stiletto shoe falls off while she quickly descends a stairwell to join the wealthy Fernando in a romantic rendezvous at his apartment.

The trope of mistaken identity in this episode operates as a way to think about social mobility and the aspirations of the working class. Cleonice's true identity is revealed and serves as a turning point. Dona Muriel, who finds and reads Cleonice's notebook, blackmails her to hand over her writings so she can publish them under her name. Fernando, who initially rejects Cleonice when he realizes her deception, works in publishing and recognizes the notebook dona Muriel submits to be published. He approaches Cleonice to apologize and acknowledge her true talent. That is, the oppression and rejection by the upper class of the lower class is deemed illegitimate and the intelligence and creativity of the lower class is celebrated as authentic and honorable.

Mistaken identities eventually lead to the revelation of true identities. The theme is further developed when Fernando locates Cleonice's daughter, whom she had lost years earlier and had written about. The final scene shows the happily married couple joined by the daughter, cementing a positive message of cross-class heteronormative romance brought about by destiny and recognition of one's abilities. Notably, the trope of mistaken identity is common in Brazilian cinema and appears in numerous film comedies (*chanchadas*) of the 1940s and 1950s, where temporary role reversals and instances of crossing over class lines served as a way to critique a culture that has historically been sharply divided between the haves and the have-nots (Dennison and Shaw 2004, 19). Unlike the *chanchadas*, this episode does not present the act of changing one's class status as temporary. Cleonice's social mobility is attributed to recognition of her talent as a writer. The idea that a domestic worker could liberate herself from oppressive, poorly paid work and improve her social and economic status through her artistic abilities lends further support to cultural policies that embraced the creative economy.

The Articulation of Stardom: Promoting *Femotypes*

Several elements from this episode, "A doméstica da Vitória," find resonance in future novelas produced by the Globo Network as well as the sociopolitical moment. For instance, actress Dira Paes again plays the role of a domestic worker (Lucimar) who has lost her daughter, who became a victim of human trafficking in the show *Salve Jorge* (2012–2013). Roles are repeated in other ways as well that demand consideration of the broader significance of this articulation of stardom in both miniseries. Actresses cast in the episodes of *As brasileiras* frequently play characters that are close to their brand either in terms of roles they have previously played (as with Dira Paes) or in terms of their ethnic or geographic origins. Juliana Paes, who portrays a jealous woman from the northeastern state of Pernambuco in the episode "A justiceira de Olinda," (The vigilante from Olinda) frequently portrays women from the Northeast of Brazil and followed her appearance in *As brasileiras* by starring as the protagonist in the 2012 Globo novela *Gabriela*, based on the novel by Jorge Amado. Other actresses play roles close to their geographic origins. For instance, Xuxa, who is from the state of Rio Grande do Sul, plays a gossipy woman from Porto Alegre, the capital of the state. And Ivete Sangalo, who is originally from Bahia, plays Raquel from Salvador in the episode just discussed. Actresses also play roles that are linked to their ethnic backgrounds. Giovanna Antonelli, who is of Italian ancestry, plays a woman from São Paulo, home to a significant number of Italian immigrants in the twentieth century. Suyane Moreira, whose physical features suggest Amerindian ancestry, plays an indigenous woman at the edge of the Amazon. Notably, Moreira also played a role in the 2007 television miniseries *Amazônia*.

The casting of actresses aims to achieve a high degree of proximity to roles and types associated with these actresses. This is not entirely unusual in casting individuals for specific roles, but casting purposefully creates a connection in *As brasileiras* between an actress and a geographic region or ethnicity. In his foundational study of acting, James Naremore (1988) examines the relationship between stars, actors, and the characters they play. He notes that contemporary naturalist acting in Hollywood films frequently merges star, performer, and character such that audiences tend to regard people in movies as "spectacular human beings" (157). Naremore provides a model for distinguishing among these three roles, noting a distinction between role (fictional character), actor (person), and star image (intertextual phenomenon born out of an actor's previous roles) (158). In *As brasileiras*, these distinctions are especially reduced.

Yet what is significant about the fact that actresses are cast in recognizable roles and that there is reduced differentiation between actress and character? These roles introduce new traits, practices, and values that are profitable for the cultural moment. Scholars of stars and stardom have noted that stars frequently model behavior that fans imitate, and embody culturally desired characteristics (Dyer 2012; Gledhill 1991; Meeuf and Raphael 2013). What is key to the cultural economy of stardom here is that both shows develop what can best be understood as *femotypes*, defined as geopolitically and socioeconomically favorable portraits of women that uphold the idea of a new Brazil. What is more, these portraits of women negotiate established cultural expectations or practices alongside change. Women may work with new technologies, enjoy newfound social mobility, cultivate their independence, and pursue careers, but they remain eroticized and nonthreatening to gendered hierarchies, and they ultimately demand (and enjoy) the protection of their male companions. A recognizable balance of what is known and what is new structures an ambivalence found in the portrayal of female characters in these shows that facilitates introducing and accepting new cultural narratives.

Acting style cultivates buy-in to the idea of a new Brazil. Naremore has proposed thinking about ostensiveness and frames as well as representational and presentational performances. Whereas a representational style of acting refers to those performances that create a sense of a fictional character rather than the performer, a presentational style refers to those performances in which the performer's performance overshadows a sense of the character (Naremore 1988, 28–30). Additionally, Naremore presents the concept of frames to think about the ways in which performers are demarcated in some ways to call attention to them as something to be looked at, and to think about how performers' actions are identified as performances by noting the performative qualities of their gestures (poses, movements, etc.) (14–17, 34–40). With *As cariocas* and *As brasileiras*, we find a framing device whereby actresses parade in front of a camera before approaching the camera in direct address to be identified as the star who will play the leading role in a given episode. This direct address breaks the fourth wall, acknowledges they are to be looked at, and draws attention to the idea that they are going to perform a role. The fact that the actresses play roles that approximate their own backgrounds further suggests that playing with identities can still be relatively authentic. In this way, the acting style, the roles developed by these stars, and the presentation of the actresses encourage viewers to also play and try on new, different identities. As discussed in the next section, this overt presentation of identities also appears in engagement marketing practices for *Cheias de charme*.

Cheias de charme and Appeals to Authenticity

Both *As cariocas* and *As brasileiras* formed part of the Globo Network's programming that focused on the emerging middle class and shifting cross-class relations. As a miniseries, *As brasileiras* aired once a week as late-night programming after the highly successful *Avenida Brasil* and *Cheias de charme*.[8] The show *Salve Jorge* replaced *Avenida Brasil* in October 2012 at the coveted primetime slot. The three novelas share a number of points in common with the miniseries. In a broader sense, several episodes of *As cariocas* and *As brasileiras* as well as the novelas resonate with a larger preoccupation with social mobility and shifting class relations. The narratives of these programs also revolve around strong female characters whose economic success and social mobility are celebrated. But their social mobility is threatened by ill-willed bosses (*Cheias de charme, Avenida Brasil*) or the exploitation of their bodies and labor on an international scale (*Salve Jorge*). Indeed, the phenomenal success of *Avenida Brasil*, which can be understood in part as a curiosity about the portrayal of the emerging middle class, can also be attributed to the fact that the show effectively took the pulse of the aspirations and anxieties surrounding changing class status and social structures.

Cheias de charme provides a relevant context to reflect on the cultural economy of stardom and on how the Globo Network mapped its brand onto the techno-cultural zeitgeist. Against the backdrop of changing labor regulations for domestic workers and an alleged maid crisis, *Cheias de charme* celebrated working-class women. Yet the maid appears as a focal point for thinking through shifting sociopolitical relations and efforts to (re)establish a new cultural authenticity. I examine how, in the case of *Cheias de charme*, the Globo Network appealed to the emerging middle class through social merchandising as well as cross-media, online engagement marketing. Although individuals were induced to participate in new social and economic relations as part of a contemporary praxis of citizenship, the program and related marketing practices reveal little challenge to existing social hierarchies.

The Maid as Zeitgeist Star

If the new lower-middle class was celebrated on-screen at this time, its most prominent zeitgeist star was the female domestic worker. Although the figure of the maid appears in other programs aired at this time (*Avenida Brasil, Salve Jorge*), the narrative of *Cheias de charme* centers squarely on the lives of three domestic workers, Maria da Penha (Penha), Maria Aparecida (Cida), and Maria do Rosario (Rosario). Rosario is a cook who dreams of being a famous singer and has an obsession with a famous singer named Fabian. Cida is a young woman who lives with her godmother, Valda, in her employer's mansion. Penha works as a maid for Chayene, a famous *electroforró technobrega*[9] diva who mistreats her employees, including Penha. After being physically assaulted by Chayene, Penha goes to the police to report her employer. There Penha meets Cida and Rosario. Although they arrive at the police station under different circumstances, the three are eventually detained for contempt. They befriend one another and, reiterating a trope from Cinderella, make a pact to be working-class employees by day and upper-class ladies by night. In this way, the novela addresses the theme of social mobility and desires to be recognized and respected in society.

The novela includes several other common tropes, including mistaken identities and role reversals, the hardworking and humble woman who confronts and overcomes unfair situations and oppressive authority figures, and a critique of cross-class relations and social hierarchies. One day while Chayene is away, the three women gather at her mansion, where they decide to dress up in her clothes. With the assistance of a friend, they make a video clip of them singing "Vida de empreguete" (The life of a little maid), which playfully critiques the oppressive situations maids must deal with daily. The video is accidentally released online—in the narrative of the novela—and becomes a viral sensation in the diegesis of the show as well as in real life. Soon the three form a band and become increasingly successful. Inspired by the upbeat rhythm of the song and lyrics celebrating individual resilience in the face of adversity, fans made and posted hundreds of imitations of the viral video online, changing the lyrics to suit the scenarios of different social groups (such as students, nurses, teachers, and so forth).

If maids play an important role on-screen in *Cheias de charme*, they play an even more important role in the socioeconomic structures of Brazilian society. In addition to income, it is important to note that the employment of domestic workers figures into the calculations of whether an individual belongs to the middle class. As noted earlier, the "critério Brasil" for defining class status includes whether an individual employs a domestic worker (Neri 2011, 78). This reminds us that class is a socioeconomic status where lifestyle practices, taste, educational level, occupation, and other factors play a role alongside consumption potential. Employing a maid signifies more than paying someone with more time or skill to perform household tasks. Notably, Thorstein Veblen (1918, 53), who analyzed the master-servant relationship at the end of the Victorian era in the United Kingdom, asserts that having a servant reveals the employer's "propensity for dominance" and serves as a public display of their prowess.

Cheias de charme appeared not only at a time of economic change but also when women's labor rights were being debated. National and international media reported on a maid crisis in Brazil. Discussion largely revolved around the passage of new labor laws and their (mostly negative) impact on middle-class households as well as domestic workers themselves. In April 2013, a proposed constitutional amendment (Proposta de Emenda Constitucional, PEC) was ratified in the Brazilian Congress that granted various rights, including an eight-hour workday, overtime pay, and benefits enjoyed by other workers such as social security. Given that wages for domestic workers had nearly doubled since 2006, news outlets anxiously celebrated the conquest of workers' rights but questioned the real benefits of the new labor laws, noting how increased wages would inadvertently result in greater unemployment as middle- and upper-class households fired their maids and nannies because they could no longer afford them (Goodman 2013; *Economist* 2011; Rapoza 2013).

Women's employment as domestic workers fluctuates with economic opportunities. With the most recent recession, the number of women employed as domestic workers has increased (*Veja* 2015). Yet a drop in the number of women engaged in domestic labor during the period in question further fueled fears of the disappearance of readily available, affordable domestic workers. Notwithstanding the fact that the International Labour Organization reported in 2013 (25–26) that Brazil had the greatest number of domestic workers of the 117 nations surveyed, there had been a demographic shift in the number of domestic workers as record-low unemployment encouraged the poor to find better-paying and higher-skilled jobs. In this sense, fears of the disappearing domestic were not entirely unwarranted. Those members of the middle and upper classes in Brazil who "lost" a domestic worker to better work and life opportunities or the inability to pay legal wages faced the possibility of experiencing a lowering of their own socioeconomic status.

The disappearance of the maid threatened established social relations in terms of class as well as gender. Educated, professional women have relied on domestic labor to help manage their households and child-rearing, allowing them time to pursue their own careers. Meanwhile, the possibility of losing access to low-wage, female-dominant domestic labor upset traditional gender roles. Just after Congress approved the PEC, the April 3, 2013, cover of *Veja*, a newsmagazine read by middle- and upper-class Brazilians, featured a man in a button-down shirt and tie wearing an apron while washing dishes. The cover caption stated (or warned?), "Você amanhã" (You tomorrow). Smaller text celebrated the new civilizing labor laws but also noted that the laws signaled (or threatened?) that domestic chores would have to become a shared responsibility. The *Veja* cover captured doubts about how middle-class households would operate in the future, and the presentation of the man—ostensibly a white-collar professional—wearing an apron suggested some social incongruity with the new labor laws.

With a looming maid crisis and ongoing debates surrounding the PEC, *Cheias de charme* countered an alleged disappearance of the female domestic worker with increased visibility and regressive fantasies. Indeed, there are several inconsistencies in the portrayal of maids in *Cheias de charme* that reflect certain conservative fictions. It bears repeating that middle- and upper-class households have historically relied on domestic workers. Modest apartments have been built to include closet-size maids' quarters—frequently near the kitchen—and generations of children have been raised by nannies. In *Cheias de charme*, the young, fair-skinned Cida lives with her Black godmother, Valda, in the mansion of their employer, Sonia. However, since the early 1990s, increasingly fewer domestic workers have lived with their employers. According to a study conducted in São Paulo, only 1.7 percent of maids lived where they worked in 2014 (Barros 2015). Also, the fact that Cida is a very young woman replicates past trends. Notwithstanding the fact that the booming economy provided other, more lucrative job opportunities, social programs like Fome Zero and Bolsa Família required teen girls in poor families, who had been a historical pool for exploitable domestic labor, to stay in school in order not to lose out on receiving welfare program benefits.

Cheias de charme also largely misrepresents the racial demographics of domestic labor. Of the three protagonists, only Penha (Taís Araújo) possesses a darker skin tone, identifying her as being of Afro-Brazilian descent. Meanwhile, both Cida and Rosario are very fair-skinned. Race, gender, and domestic labor cannot be separated in Brazil, where 93 percent of domestic workers in Brazil are women (International Labour Organization 2013) and 61 percent are Black (C. Nogueira 2012). These inconsistencies with contemporary facts reveal that countering the feared disappearance of the maid by making her more visible also meant reiterating past fantasies regarding female domestic labor. In turn, this portrayal largely erased the realities of domestic labor in terms of race and age and sustained a social hierarchy for middle- and upper-class households.

Social Merchandising in *Cheias de charme*

Although the show is regressive in its conservative imaginings of domestic labor in Brazil, it ostensibly lends support to social progress and new labor relations through the practice of social merchandising. Whereas merchandising (or product placement) promotes consumer products or experiences, social merchandising consists of a type of promotional discourse wherein contemporary (and occasionally sensitive) social topics are addressed in the program through either specific scenes or the broader context of a show's narrative. Novelas have generally played a vital role in forging national identity, but social merchandising on them has been cited as playing a particularly important role in the transformation of Brazilian society, especially in terms of attitudes and behaviors (Joyce and Martinez 2017; Joyce 2012; Hamburger 2005; Rosas-Moreno 2014, 2017).[10] What is more, the Globo Network has acknowledged its role in social mobilization and defined itself as a pioneer in the use of social merchandising as a way to educate and contribute to social development (Schiavo 2006). Indeed, novelas in Brazil are noted for playing a consistently important role in addressing contemporary topics such as human trafficking, bone marrow donation, alcoholism, religious tolerance, and attitudes concerning gender and sexuality.

In the case of *Cheias de charme*, the show addresses new labor rights and recognizes the importance of domestic workers in Brazil. Penha, who is assaulted by her employer, Chayene, seeks justice and eventually begins work with Lygia (Malu Galli), a lawyer who advocates for labor rights. As part of her collaboration and emerging friendship with Lygia, Penha acts as a consultant and maintains a website with information on the rights and responsibilities of workers and employers. In this way the *novela* models cross-class solidarity (between Lygia and Penha) and consciousness-raising.

The show also extends social merchandising outside the diegesis of the novela. Penha and Lygia headlined a campaign in collaboration with the Globo Network, the United Nations, and the International Labour Organization. In the campaign, the two female characters sought to bring greater awareness to domestic workers of their rights and encouraged employers to follow new labor regulations. If product placement in a show seeks economic profits, social merchandising seeks less obvious benefits. One effect of extending the social merchandising campaign into the world outside the programs is a blurring of the lines between fact and fiction or between real life and the imagined world of the novela. A sense of cultural authenticity and legitimacy is subsequently associated with the campaign and the show. Social merchandising functions as a way to practice social responsibility and provides other modes of profit such as attracting and sustaining audiences. By celebrating working-class women, Globo raised its profile as a legitimate promoter of new rights, connected with audiences, and contributed to redefining new parameters of citizenship for the previously marginalized. Through social merchandising, the Globo Network (re)established itself as a good corporate citizen and as a cultural platform for social activism.

Social merchandising is an increasingly common promotional discourse central to branding that aims to connect commerce and culture. It bears repeating that branding involves cultivating profitable exchanges between marketing (or promotional practices like social merchandising), a product, and consumers. Branding also involves telling stories that create affective links to consumers. In the case of the social merchandising campaign for *Cheias de charme*, the characters clearly take the practices of branding outside the corporate realm of a Globo Network program, enter into the broader culture, and connect to new progressive politics. In her study of contemporary branding, Sarah Banet-Weiser (2012) questions the perspective that corporate culture exists outside—or even in opposition to—a presumed authentic culture. She asserts that brands are "about *culture* as much as they are about economics," and as brands become increasingly enmeshed in our social and cultural relations, she encourages scholars to examine ways in which economic exchanges enter arenas of life—especially those cultural contexts where individuals craft their identities—that are otherwise thought to be generally free of commercialization (4–7). The social merchandising campaign in *Cheias de charme* was one effort at intervening in understanding how women and female domestic labor belong in Brazil. Another key practice that did this was the development of a cross-media, online engagement marketing campaign that celebrated the figure of the maid in

Brazilian society but also revealed tensions in terms of race, class, and gender surrounding new ideals of citizenship.

Searching for the Most Charming Maid in All of Brazil

Recognizing the culture of the emerging middle class and celebrating its political and consumer strength was certainly important. But what was also central was to cultivate new experiences around the TV Globo brand. Whereas it had once been the dominant media conglomerate in Brazil, the Globo Network had lost a modest percentage of its market share to other networks in recent years (Brittos and Bolaño 2005). What is more, the significant increase in internet access in Brazil during this time posed the possibility that middle-class audiences could drift toward streamed content.[11] Indeed, Netflix entered Brazil in 2011 and the country quickly became one of the company's major markets (Moreira de Sá 2016). The Globo Network's programming engaged with the political and cultural moment, but it also faced an emerging digital landscape.

Cheias de charme clearly addressed the increasing importance of the internet for traditional broadcast television by extending the narrative of the show into the online digital sphere. Yet a significant aspect of the show's intermedial engagement with audiences was a competition sponsored on *Fantástico*, a weekly newsmagazine broadcast on Sunday nights. In addition to its usual telejournalism pieces, *Fantástico* included brief segments featuring the show *Cheias de charme* to cultivate interest in Globo's primetime novela airing during the week. On the heels of the unprecedented success of the viral "empreguetes" video accidentally released on the internet—in the narrative of *Cheias de charme*—and numerous real-life fan imitations posted to YouTube, *Fantástico* held a competition to find the most charming maid in all of Brazil. The competition was an engagement marketing campaign, understood as "a firm's deliberate effort to motivate ... a customer's voluntary contribution to a firm's marketing functions beyond the core, economic transaction" (Harmeling et al. 2016, 317). In the case of *Cheias de charme*, viewers were enticed to participate in a competition to help cultivate interest in the show and increase the size of the viewing audience.

The competition supported ideals regarding women's domestic labor. Participation was limited to women over eighteen years of age who were officially employed (i.e., had signed work cards [*carteira assinada*]) and residents of Brazil. To enter, contestants had to submit a one-minute video made in their workplace in which they creatively demonstrated their artistic abilities (by dancing, singing, reciting poetry, telling jokes, etc.). That is, contestants demonstrated how charming they were. In this way, the competition further supported the social merchandising campaign found in *Cheias de charme* and new labor requirements by limiting the contest to those who were legally employed.

Similar to the social merchandising campaign, the competition on *Fantástico* extended the narrative of the show outside the realm of the novela and into the broader culture.

From over 1,400 videos submitted, sixteen semifinalists were selected. Each week for four weeks, the videos of four semifinalists were featured on *Fantástico* and the viewing public voted to select the eventual four finalists. The three actresses who played the main roles in *Cheias de charme* (Taís Araújo, Isabelle Drummond, and Leandra Leal) formed the jury to select the winning contestant, who received an all-expenses paid trip to Rio de Janeiro to make an appearance on an episode of *Cheias de charme*.[12] In late July 2012, the unanimous winner, Marilene Machado de Jesus of Salvador, Bahia, experienced her first trip on a plane and joined her fellow actress–domestic workers on set, where she was a star for a day. The competition on *Fantástico* was both a well-practiced strategy of cross-media marketing for which Globo is well known and a timely engagement marketing strategy to cultivate buy-in to its programming. In this way, the network sought to foster and sustain relations with its audience base as well as to promote ideals of the new Brazil, a nation in which achieving social mobility and overcoming entrenched class hierarchies was possible. Real maids and real employers of maids participated in the recognition of domestic labor and celebration of social change.

If *Cheias de charme* succeeds in celebrating domestic workers' rights and the aspirations of working-class women, it falls short in terms of a more nuanced discussion of race, class, and women's labor. The competition on *Fantástico* provides a lens through which we can evaluate *Cheias de charme* and prompts questions regarding the intersection of race, region, gender, and class in a deeply inegalitarian society. For instance, what can we make of the fact that a Black woman, Marilene Machado de Jesus, from Salvador, Bahia, was the winner of this competition while the majority of the cast members of the show *Cheias de charme* are White? And what tensions exist surrounding new ideals of female labor?

Notably, the passage of the PEC in 2013 was celebrated by some as being almost as significant as the abolition of slavery in Brazil in 1888. This equation is not entirely inappropriate. Historically, middle- and upper-class households in the more industrialized South and Southeast have employed women from the North and Northeast who have migrated to find work to support themselves and their families. Marilene Machado de Jesus is a phenotypically Black woman from a region (Bahia) known for having a high population of people of African descent owing to the history of slavery. And her traveling to the South repeated a historical trajectory of Black Brazilian women's labor and internal migration. At the turn of the twentieth century, newly freed slaves were forced to take low-paying jobs as manual laborers. A lack of educational opportunities largely prevented members and descendants of this demographic group from leaving manual labor (J. Souza 2017). That is, the fact that the majority of female domestic workers today identify as Black has a history in racism, slavery, and discrimination (de Santana Pinho and Silva 2010; de Souza 1980). However, there is a notable tension regarding labor and race when the novela and competition are juxtaposed. Whereas the majority of the cast members are White in *Cheias de charme*, only one of the finalists of the *Fantástico* competition was phenotypically White. Consequently, the novela may promote a broader view of domestic labor as a job that employs Brazilian women of any regional, racial, or ethnic background, but the competition reaffirmed the idea that the domestic worker is imagined as a Black female from the Northeast.

Indeed, the image of the Black maid taking care of children, cleaning, and cooking is ingrained in the Brazilian social imaginary (Cleveland 2019). Less common is the image of the Black Brazilian woman engaging in leisure activities. This demands thinking about the significance of portraying such a woman—and asking her to portray herself voluntarily—in a curious combination of work and leisure activities (e.g., dancing while dusting, singing while sweeping) to her own delight and that of audiences. That is, what does it mean to ask domestic workers to present themselves as *charming*? Jesus and the other finalists danced and lip-synced to popular songs.[13] In their videos, they wear typical work clothes as well as more elegant or festive attire, thereby replicating elements of the "empreguetes" video from *Cheias de charme*. Notably, this also repeats a trope of flexible or mutable identities seen in *Cheias de charme* as well as episodes of *As cariocas* and *As brasileiras*. The contestants also directly address the camera, breaking the fourth wall in a way that is similar to how the actresses highlighted in each episode of *As cariocas* and *As brasileiras* do. Here, we find a conscious presentation or presentational style of acting, as described by Naremore, of an idealized role: the gracious, happy, well-mannered domestic worker.

The search for charm, grace, and happiness conceals tensions between developing cross-class solidarity and sustaining social inequality. In his analysis of class hierarchies, labor, and economic development, Veblen (1918) describes the performance of conspicuous leisure not on the part of the primary or legitimate leisure class but by a subsidiary or derivative leisure class. He defines this type of leisure, performed by a servant class, as a vicarious leisure and asserts plainly that "the leisure of the servant is not his own leisure" (59–60). Rather, the performance of leisure by the servant class serves to benefit the reputation and life of the master (60). Although there is a celebration and recognition of female domestic labor and support for new labor laws in both Globo programs, the competition directly asks domestic workers to portray the proper spiritual disposition that preserves social inequality and sustains what Veblen calls "conspicuous subservience" (60).

Indeed, the competition sponsored by *Fantástico* revealed a particular gendered and cross-class solidarity. In interviews, Jesus explained that her employer (*patroa*), dona Vitória, encouraged her to enter the competition and helped her make the video (Zuazo 2012). Meanwhile, the broadcast of the competition showed the *patroa* excited about Jesus becoming selected as a semifinalist and cheering for her to be chosen as the final winner.[14] When it was announced that Jesus was the winner, dona Vitória celebrated alongside her as if she, too, had won. What is more, the hosts of *Fantástico* and the actresses from *Cheias de charme* who cast the final vote praised Jesus's *patroa*, dona Vitória, for supporting Jesus and for employing her legally (i.e., providing her with an official work status and a *carteira assinada*). Thus, the competition offered a positive model of cross-class solidarity between women, which echoed the cross-class solidarity that develops between Penha and Lygia in the novela.

However, as a practice of engagement marketing, we must consider how people are encouraged to participate in supporting larger institutions and proposed values. In other words, how were people being encouraged in this instance to cultivate buy-in to the ideas of a new Brazil? Jesus was asked to be jovial and charming and demonstrate a proper disposition that did little to undermine existing social inequality. She was presented in interviews as being content with being a domestic worker (Zuazo 2012). She was not quoted making any references to new labor regulations or her labor conditions, nor did she refer to employment opportunities outside manual domestic labor. By contrast, she was quoted as being excited about her first trip on a plane and the chance to meet the celebrity Marcos Palmeira. That is, Jesus did not contest existing social roles or seek attention. Indeed, it was Jesus's employer who asked her whether she would like to enter the competition—perhaps as a show of her own class prowess, described by Veblen. Jesus may have celebrated her position as a manual laborer and her ability to dance and sing (or lip-sync), but her citizenship—in terms of labor rights and recognition—was still bestowed on her by her upperclass *patroa*. The charming disposition for which Jesus was celebrated upheld the role of the benevolent, upper-class woman and affirmed that Jesus was a content working-class woman with little desire to disrupt social hierarchies.

The development of social merchandising in *Cheias de charme* and the crossmedia engagement marketing campaign of *Fantástico* cultivate relationships between media and viewers while also presenting new (but sometimes conflicting) ideas about contemporary social identities. Jesus may have won the prize as the most charming maid in all of Brazil, but who else benefits from this practice of branding and how? Returning to Banet-Weiser's suggestion to consider how branding enters arenas of life previously considered separate from commercial interests, we see that there is a clear commercialization of not only the figure of the domestic worker but also the maid-employer relationship. Indeed, the figure of the maid became a flexible commodity for exchange. Specifically, the maid became a concept around which women—and society generally—could celebrate their social identities and affirm the boundaries of their belonging in contemporary Brazilian society. Working-class women could cultivate an idealized, aspirational identity while their employers could generally maintain their middle- and upper-class status. The Globo Network operated within the cultural context of the maid-employer relationship, which had been firmly entrenched in Brazilian society and culture and was now under threat of transformation. Furthermore, the network positioned itself between state-sponsored social transformation and its own market imperatives to support the narrative of a new, progressive Brazil. Promotional discourses (i.e., social merchandising and engagement marketing) developed in *Cheias de charme* and *Fantástico* linked commerce and culture and lent support to a new regime of citizenship.

4

Selling Citizenship
in Alternative Media

■■■■■■■■■■■■■■■■■■■■■

The city of Rio de Janeiro is often celebrated for its beautiful landscape, including the iconic Sugarloaf Mountain and the Christ the Redeemer statue towering over postcard-perfect neighborhoods like Copacabana and Ipanema nestled between the Atlantic Ocean and hilly tropical rainforests. Yet this is a visual fraction of the urban landscape of Rio de Janeiro—and, by extension, most urban centers in Brazil. Most Brazilians do not live in refined neighborhoods flanked by extensive beaches and promenades. Rather, a significant portion of the Brazilian population resides in favelas, frequently composed of terracotta brick houses perched on hillsides, stretched out on tracts of land distant from urban infrastructure, or squeezed into spaces between, behind, or around "official" spaces.

Until recently, these urban territories were known to exist but did not appear on government maps and were not considered part of the real, official, established city. This invisibility has contributed to these areas being largely overlooked for the development and improvement of infrastructure, such as connections to sewer systems or access to clean drinking water. The undeniable existence of favelas has been met with an imposed absence, and the space and its residents have been associated with lack, disharmony, and existence outside the norm. As residents of a "noncity," they became stigmatized as "noncitizens." During the period in question, the regime of (in)visibility began to shift and favelas became simultaneously sites of threat and opportunity. If these urban territories were violent, chaotic, "no-go" zones that undermined plans for massive urban development projects—especially those related to a series of international mega-events—these same spaces were prime locations for economic development and sites to be celebrated for their cultural richness.

A central tension of the narrative of the new Brazil concerned how to incorporate previously marginalized people and urban territories. And on whose terms? This chapter further explores the theme of cultivating buy-in to realize the ideals of a new Brazil. Whereas chapter 3 discussed how audiences are solicited to participate in a new consumer society and adopt neoliberal attitudes and behaviors, here I consider how two popular media projects promote a new regime of visibility and a new urban sociability. Specifically, I consider two alternative popular media projects sponsored by the Observatório de Favelas (Slum Observatory), a nonprofit organization located in the North Zone of Rio de Janeiro: a photography project, Imagens do Povo (Images of the People), and the Juventude Marcada Pra Viver (Youth Marked to Live, JMV) affirmative publicity campaign developed by the Escola Popular de Comunicação Crítica (Popular School of Critical Communication, ESPOCC).

Both alternative media projects are examples of efforts to rebrand the favelas, but they offer a different understanding of buy-in to ideas of a new Brazil that is premised on greater socio-spatial inclusion. Consonant with the goals of the creative economy (discussed in chapter 1), the Images of the People program aims to train photographers to enter the for-profit marketplace. It has also maintained an archive for commercial and nonprofit use. Photographs from the program emphasize the representation of the quotidian. Thus, my discussion of selected photographs considers how an aesthetics of the everyday is mobilized as a way to include favelas and their residents in the new Brazil and, by extension, expand an understanding of contemporary citizenship in Brazil. The JMV affirmative publicity campaign, which includes several photos of the Images of the People project, draws attention to the rights of young, Black men and violence committed against them. My discussion of this campaign, which borrows from the U.S.-based idea of affirmative action as well as marketing, explores the significance of using the practices and language of branding as tools for social advocacy.

Between Ordinary and Extraordinary: Images of the People

The Images of the People program was created in 2004 as part of the Slum Observatory's social-pedagogical outreach and sought to align photography with social questions. The program consists of several initiatives: an agency (Agência Escola), a school that provides training in photography (Escola de Fotógrafos Populares) to people primarily from favelas, an image archive (Banco de Imagens), a course that trains educators in photography (Curso de Formação em Educadores da Fotografia), workshops on pinhole photography (Oficinas de

Fotografia Artesanal), and an exhibition gallery (Galeria 535). One of the goals of the Images of the People program was to include photographers from favelas and other popular spheres in the labor market. In this way, the program emerges from a shift in cultural policy influenced by a belief in the potential of the creative economy to help "leapfrog" in development while also fostering social and cultural integration. Indeed, the Images of the People program received funds from the Secretary of Culture for the State of Rio de Janeiro, which established a grant program for the visual arts to stimulate diverse artistic creation.[1] Notably, the archive of images was intended to be a resource for commercial interests as well as nonprofit organizations. Several photos from the Images of the People program have been used in the affirmative publicity campaigns developed by the ESPOCC (discussed later), and the program has also partnered with the nonprofit advertising agency Diálogos. Yet the photographs produced as part of the program were also clearly intended to foster artistic and cultural production as a mode to revindicate political rights and foster a sense of cultural identity emerging from the favelas. Images taken in the program have been exhibited to the public in Galeria 535. And in 2012, a collection of 102 photographs was published in book form.[2] The Images of the People program continues to sponsor exhibitions of photographs that reflect on the everyday lived experiences of those in the favelas.[3]

Overall, the program has sought to register daily life in the favelas with a critical perspective in a way that respects human rights and the local culture. In her excellent analysis of several photographs of the program, Kátia da Costa Bezerra (2018, 13–42) offers that these works intervened in rethinking the relationships between individuals and urban spaces to advocate for a sense of belonging. The program also fostered the production of images that would intervene in the way favelas and residents of favela spaces were imagined in society, seeking justice and countering a history of symbolic violence. In this sense, the program was part of an unprecedented cultural effervescence in which the relationship between who produced and consumed media dramatically changed (Hamburger 2007, 124). Of particular interest is how the program emphasized representations of daily life (or the everyday). The discussion that follows aims to explore the emphasis on the quotidian and its relation to the transformation of citizenship in a group of selected photographs from the Images of the People program.

Scholars working in the emerging field of everyday aesthetics have advocated for expanding an understanding of aesthetic experience and domains that we have not generally contemplated in aesthetic terms. A central question for scholars of everyday aesthetics concerns relationality. This line of enquiry deemphasizes the formal properties that may make an object beautiful and emphasizes instead the relation between a subject and object that makes a given experience beautiful (Smith 2005, ix–xii). Approaches to understanding the experience of the everyday take diverging viewpoints. Thomas Leddy (2012, 128–133) proposes thinking about aesthetic qualities that have been neglected in contemporary discussion and the way artists can convert the ordinary into something extraordinary. Arto Haapala (2005) thinks through the problems of the everyday in terms of place, suggesting that place is a sphere (or "area") in which the everyday is realized. In his theorizing of responses to everyday things and activities, Haapala objects to an aesthetic model of "strangeness" and advocates for the concept of familiarity. Central to the experience of familiarity is the concept of attachment, whereby an individual develops an affective relation with that which is perceived (51). Meanwhile, Jane Forsey (2013, 237–238) asks whether we can appreciate the ordinary *as ordinary* without making it unusual or extraordinary.

Theorizing the aesthetics of the everyday and thinking about photographs that aim to capture the everyday would benefit from Jacques Rancière's discussion of images. In *The Future of the Image*, Rancière proposes that images are not just something that you see but "are . . . operations: relations between a whole and parts; between a visibility and a power of signification and affect associated with it; between expectations and what happens to meet them" (2007, 3). Taking into consideration these different viewpoints, in my discussion of representations of the everyday in photos taken as part of the Images of the People program, I wish to foreground the operations at play. In other words, is there an emphasis on the ordinary *as ordinary* or the ordinary *as extraordinary*? Ultimately, I assert that the aesthetic relevance of the everyday in these photos concerns seeking social justice and incorporating the favela as well as favela residents into the socioeconomic and political imaginary on their own terms. On the one hand, the photos of the everyday counter a spectacular, hyperrealist representation of the favela frequent in mainstream media (discussed in chapters 5 and 6). On the other hand, portraits of the everyday counter notions of the favela as chaotic, unrelatable, or disconnected from the "official" city.

Affirming the Aesthetics of the Favela

One of the fundamental ways in which the photos from the Images of the People program makes the ordinary extraordinary is by celebrating an aesthetic of the favela space. Notwithstanding the fact that approximately one-third of the population of Rio de Janeiro lives in favelas, these urban communities are referred to as subnormal agglomerations by the Instituto Brasileiro de Geografia e Estatística (Brazilian Institute of Geography and Statistics). This terminology is fed by a perception of the favelas as existing outside or separate from real or official urban areas and is related to a perception of these spaces as being irregular, precarious, unorganized, unfinished, and unsafe. What is more, this perception is an evaluation informed by dominant, homogenizing aesthetic models. A repudiation of the aesthetics of the favela further isolates these spaces as not forming part of the city as a whole and excludes the nearly two million people who live in these communities. An appreciation of the aesthetics of the favela is, thus, a political act of inclusion. Indeed, the production of new viewpoints on these territories and their diverse range of cultural activities is at the heart of the Images of the People project.

One of the main goals of everyday aesthetics is to think of aesthetic issues that are not already connected with well-established domains such as the fine arts or the natural environment. Leddy acknowledges that qualities like "ordered" and "right" have been fundamental in traditional (or dominant) aesthetics and precede more complicated concepts like "symmetrical," "proportional," "balanced," "integrated," and "harmonious" (2005, 9). However, emphasis on qualities like "ordered" or "right" have been at the heart of categorizing favelas as "subnormal agglomerations" and the cultural practices that emerge from them as "disordered" and an affront to security and progress. When considering the aesthetics of the everyday, Leddy suggests thinking about a quality of "rightness" (such as "sounds right" or "looks right"). What is more, some qualities will be more prominent in other domains and some less so (2005, 8–9). Leddy's approach suggests both the expansion of an understanding of aesthetic domains and a flexible appreciation of aesthetic qualities that may introduce new patterns.

Several photos from the Images of the People program feature graffiti and their artists as well as murals painted on walls. These are clear examples where the aesthetic experience of the favela differs from that found in the "official" city landscape. What is of particular interest are those photos that transmit or call attention to aesthetic qualities that are unexpectedly evident in the subject matter. For instance, a photo taken by Edmilson de Lima of a child running in front of two marked doors in the Morro da Providência reveals a sense of balance between the rectangular shapes of the doors and the square tiles, whose blue color matches the color of the spray paint marking the walls of the buildings for demolition.[4] The overall color palette—blue, off-white, turquoise—is harmonious, but in a way that does not reiterate more prized and classic aesthetic models of symmetry found in wealthier spaces. The photo demonstrates that qualities of neatness or orderliness can appear in nontraditional ways and that these qualities are dependent on socioeconomic class status and access to resources.

In other instances, photos register an everyday moment in the favela space that celebrates objects or characteristics that have been used to denigrate the favela. Several photos show children playing (running, swimming, playing soccer, jumping rope, flying kites). A notable photograph by Léo Lima captures a child playing with a kite on a slab rooftop.[5] It is an image that needs to be understood in terms of layers. A blurred image of a yellow kite floats in the foreground, covering the upper body and face of a young child standing on a flat cement roof. Brick and concrete walls and rooflines intersect, connecting at irregular angles. A cloudy sky covers the glow of a bright sun. The buildings and the young child are in clear focus, which contrasts with the blurred lines of the yellow kite and white strips of material, ostensibly blowing in the wind. The kite blocks the view of the child's upper torso and head and emphasizes movement and play. This and other photographs of children playing with kites reinterpret these moments as innocent play. The kite has become associated with young men in favelas who use them to signal the approach of police or rival gangs to the drug lords who recruit them, but here it is an object for leisure. Thus, the photo provides a different interpretation of everyday experience. Specifically, the image prompts a different understanding of cultural practices in the favela whereby both the kite and the child are decriminalized.

Lima's photo and several others in the collection are reminiscent of surrealist paintings that draws upon everyday objects, offering unexpected or irregular combinations that seek to liberate the imagination and suggest the possibility of other (potentially superior) realities. In these instances, incompleteness, irregularity, and what is ostensibly disordered are traits that are not used to critique the favela. Rather, they become suggestive of different ways of living. Photos from the Images of the People collection do not deny the existence of poverty but reflect an understanding of different lived experiences based on a relationship to an environment (e.g., a child seeking joy and happiness in playtime).

Converting Strangeness into Familiarity: People and Urban Space

Several photos reveal how the ordinary becomes extraordinary by expanding an understanding of the relation of people to the urban sphere. Streets, passageways, and stairwells are frequent locations for photos. Groups play cards, watch a soccer match together, and carry items to celebrate the city's patron saint (see figure 4.1). Other images capture musical ensembles playing in the street, adults and children dancing in open venues, and devotees attending religious ceremonies. Although the urban spaces featured are designated officially as "irregular areas of construction," these images emphasize how they are culturally diverse and vibrant. Rather than define these locations as empty, anonymous places to neglect or despise, these photos invite viewers to participate and interact with these spaces. They also illustrate how people's everyday lives are closely linked to their urban environments. This is particularly evident in a photo by Marcos (Ratão) Diniz[6] (see figure 4.2). Taken with a fish-eye lens, the image is divided into two halves by the wall of a home in Maré. On the

FIG. 4.1 Flamengo fans watching TV. (Marcos [Ratão] Diniz da Silva.)

FIG. 4.2 Nevinha at home. (Marcos [Ratão] Diniz da Silva.)

right side, we see the narrow street of the favela and two blurred images of children running. On the left, we see an elderly woman sitting in her living room watching television. The image emphasizes a familiar everyday experience of an older woman relaxing in her home. It also illustrates the remarkable way in which residents of favelas are closely integrated into their urban environments, in contrast to other urban territories where people often live distant from streets in high-rise apartments.

Just as it is important to reclaim the aesthetics of the favela by reinterpreting everyday objects, spaces, and people with a perspective that imbues new significance, it is equally important to challenge hegemonic aesthetic models and practices that have framed the everyday existence of the favela as outside the norm. To make the ordinary extraordinary is as important as redefining the extraordinary. That is, it is important to define what constitutes preconceived norms as well as established practices and the degree to which they create strangeness or are extraordinary themselves. In this last sense, it is particularly important to question how favelas have become sites for official policies to make them familiar, knowable, and controllable.

Favelas have been understood as areas that members of wealthier classes generally do not enter (or "no-go" zones). Consequently, they have been excluded historically from officially recognized urban neighborhoods. In the mid-1990s, acclaimed journalist Zuenir Ventura proposed that Rio de Janeiro was a *cidade partida* (divided city), drawing on Pierre Lambert's influential notion of "two Brazils" and referring to the markedly different lived experiences of the city's inhabitants (Ventura 1994).[7] Yet this view of Rio de Janeiro tacitly accepts social segregation, does not recognize how those who live in the presumably excluded zones have historically participated in urban life, and fails to place responsibility with a state that has exacerbated inequality (J. Silva 2012a). Conversely, photos from the Images of the People program emphasize the connections between favela spaces and other urban territories as well as challenging notions that the favela space and its residents are sources of social and cultural chaos. In his approach to the aesthetics of the everyday, Haapala analyzes the concept of place, which he considers an area in which the everyday is realized. For Haapala, the process of making sense of places can be framed in terms of strangeness and familiarity whereby individuals construe a sense of place by creating familiarity (2005, 43–46; 1998).

Several photos challenge the prevailing notions of the favela as strange or outside aesthetic models and present recognizable points of reference (see figures 4.3 and 4.4). Most of the photographs in the edited collection focus on the streets, plazas, stairwells, and houses of favelas. A few capture views from favelas of iconic locations and landmarks such as the well-lit beaches of Copacabana or the Christ the Redeemer statute.

FIG. 4.3 A view of Corcovado from a favela. (Marcos [Ratão] Diniz da Silva.)

FIG. 4.4 View of Copacabana at night from Vidigal. (Marcos [Ratão] Diniz da Silva.)

These images may show some of the city's iconic landscapes, but they are more concerned with revealing how the favela is connected visually and physically to more celebrated spaces. In the case of several images taken at night, the issue of seeing and being seen comes to the foreground. The intensity of light reveals and questions what have been considered priorities in urban development (i.e., iconic tourist spots and middle-class neighborhoods). Meanwhile, the subtle light that shines within the favelas creates layered, visual planes and denies their invisibility despite the relative darkness. Rather, the trajectory of the gaze moving outward from the favela and nighttime lights shining bright in the distance reveal how these locations are integrated into the urban landscape. These photographs reject past notions that favelas are not constitutive of the city and question a history of territorial segregation.

Another set of photographs questions the increasing visibility of the favela in terms of the control and commodification of geographic spaces. These works consider how the favelas have been sites of official policies and efforts to recreate the city of Rio de Janeiro on the heels of several international megaevents. At the turn of the millennium, the favela became a site for reinvention in multiple senses. On the one hand, a shift in cultural policies and the political landscape that sought the democratization of culture following the election of Lula in 2002 prompted greater interest in favelas as fertile spheres of cultural production. Yet favelas also became viewed as sites for development and areas that demanded state intervention to normalize their cultures and spaces.

The case of a gondola in the Complexo do Alemão[8] demands consideration of the process of imposing order, making visible previously neglected urban territories, and commercially developing the favelas in Rio de Janeiro. Opened in 2011, the multimillion-dollar project was one of several expensive projects before the 2014 World Cup and 2016 Olympic Games. Ostensibly, the gondola was intended to provide public transportation to residents and connect areas of the hilly area of the Complexo do Alemão with other regions of the city. However, the cable car was of limited use to residents, who had called for improved sanitation. By contrast, tourists were more likely than residents to ride the gondola and turn the favela into a spectacle.[9]

A photograph by A. F. Rodrigues in the Images of the People collection reflects on the gondola in the Complexo do Alemão, drawing attention to how space is organized and understood.[10] The image, which appears to have been taken from another cable car or a hilltop station, looks over the urban landscape of homes. It references a curious contradiction between the gondola as a state-sponsored transportation project with massive investment and the extensive population and neglected communities below that it does not reach. Whereas the favelas appear integrated into the broader landscape with the mountains stretching out on the horizon, the gondola appears out of place. The aesthetic appreciation of the gondola is an experience of curiosity. It hangs from steel cables like a question mark, asking viewers to consider how the favela forms part of the urban landscape. State intervention is recognized, but it is cited as an incongruous way to undertake development.

Before becoming sites of development during the economic boom period, favelas were associated with chaos, violence, and urban insecurity. During the application process for its bid to host the Olympic Games, the city of Rio de Janeiro implemented the Operação Choque de Ordem (Operation Shock and Order). The program was intended to combat small crimes, improve the overall quality of life in the city, and increase economic activity in urban areas that would otherwise be unoccupied because of fears of violence. The poor were the most affected by the plan to impose "law and order" in the city. Although the program sought to provide shelter to homeless people, street vendors had their materials confiscated, irregularly constructed buildings were demolished, and unofficial neighborhood bars were closed. This effort to reorganize the city joined the controversial program of Unidades de Polícia Pacificadora (Police Pacification Units, UPPs), which intended to reclaim the favelas from the control of drug gangs that had established quasi-parallel states in these territories that had been neglected by the government. As discussed further in chapter 5, the UPPs were part of extensive state investment in urban security, but they did not alter social structures that lead to urban insecurity, such as economic inequality, unequal access to quality public education, and so forth.[11]

This is the case of a poignant photograph taken by Rodrigues during the military occupation of the Complexo do Alemão in 2010.[12] The photo shows a man hunched over, protecting an infant in his arms and apparently rushing to seek shelter while looking to the street, where a police officer rides on a motorcycle. Behind the father and infant, a police officer passes by a fruit and vegetable stand with weapons drawn. The moment is captured with natural lighting and registers an intense, unforeseen experience. The fact that the man is carrying an infant in his arms and that people are gathered at a grocery stand suggests that the day was anticipated by people living in this location to be calm, peaceful, or routine. The movement of the police—on foot and motorcycle—who approach the man from behind is suggestive of the way in which programs to ostensibly improve the quality of life in the city were an imposed order that not only shocked favela residents but also instilled great fear.

Images of police action in favelas are far more frequently depicted in mainstream press in a celebratory fashion without consideration of how these state-sponsored actions affect the vast majority of innocent but poor citizens. If Haapala is correct that a moment of "strangeness" commands attention, then it is the way in which agents of an official order are present that is unusual. The sidewalk, the man clutching the infant, and the men at the vegetable stand represent familiar, recognizable people and experiences of quotidian life. Their everyday experience has been made extraordinary by external agents, who bear the responsibility for chaos and disorder in this instance.

What profits do these photos seek? One of the profits sought in this instance is inclusion. These photos cultivate buy-in to the ideals promoted at the time of a new Brazil by conveying aesthetic experiences not usually associated with the favelas or their residents. These images do not deny class, racial, ethnic, or territorial differences and they underscore common human experiences—children at play, watching television with friends, or moments of celebration. These images cultivate a sense of order, harmony, or peacefulness where it is not stereotypically expected. They also ask viewers to reconsider aesthetic qualities and experiences present in these spaces.

As noted earlier, aesthetic appreciation is linked to inclusion. Indeed, Leddy asserts that efforts to improve society should "take into account the role that aesthetics plays in everyday choices" (2012, 13). Similarly, Jailson de Souza (2012b, 13–14) asserts that several areas of work overseen by the Slum Observatory are mobilized around the idea that aesthetic interpretation of favelas correlates with how these urban territories (and their residents, by association) become excluded or marginalized. A significant body of photographs works against the sense of the extraordinary to emphasize what is ordinary or to question policies, programs, and a history of development that has been extreme. That is, these photographs counter past processes that have made favelas and their residents "strange." It is in this way that these photographs intervene in a place-making strategy that emphasizes what is familiar and accessible. And in emphasizing the familiar, a sense of relationality is created that draws onlookers into the favela spaces while also placing the favela and its residents in communion with outsiders.

One of the concerns raised by scholars interested in the aesthetics of the everyday revolves around the commercial aestheticization of the everyday. There is an undeniable backdrop to these images that is commercial in nature. As noted earlier, the photography program Images of the People emerged from a context in which cultural policies supported the notion of a creative economy. The training of photographers was part of a program that was intended to incorporate residents of favelas into the creative economy. What is important to reiterate is that these images are taken from the perspective of people who are from the favelas and they emphasize everyday objects and aesthetic experiences. These works intervene to change the dynamics of visibility and prompt new socio-spatial connections. The collection of photos may celebrate certain aspects of the favela with positive perspectives familiar in promotional discourses, but they are rarely one-sided. These images do not deny poverty, infrastructure problems, or imbalances of power. They also do not participate in the reiteration of symbolic violence committed against the favelas as a community and their residents. In the next section, I discuss a more overt use of promotional discourses as a mode to sell citizenship.

Affirmative Publicity and a New Urban Sociability

The Slum Observatory coordinates its work around five overlapping areas of action: communication, culture, human rights, education, and urban policy. In the area of communication, the observatory has become one of the most active leaders in alternative popular media in Brazil in recent decades. Communication practices in the observatory are largely framed by an understanding of the link between racial justice and human rights. That is, a right to communication supports a fight for racial justice whereby alternative media participates in an ongoing, democratic struggle to demand full citizenship. In the discussion that follows, I explore how the work of the observatory recognizes the relationship between symbolic and physical violence committed against favelas and their residents. My discussion focuses on the ESPOCC and its program on affirmative publicity. What is of particular interest is thinking about how the language of marketing is mobilized to advocate for a new urban sociability.

In 2005, the observatory founded the ESPOCC and developed partnerships with two federal universities (the Universidade Federal do Rio de Janeiro [Federal University of Rio de Janeiro] and the Universidade Federal Fluminense [Federal Fluminense University]), Canal Futura, and a diverse range of agencies in the area of communication. Although the ESPOCC emphasizes training residents of Rio's favelas, students from other regions of the city are welcomed to participate in its programs, thus fostering exchanges among individuals of different social backgrounds. Initially, students were offered training in journalism, photography, and audiovisual production. The ESPOCC was founded in a particular moment when the expansion of digital technologies facilitated alternative communication practices. That said, Brazil has historically been home to relatively strong expressions of popular video groups and alternative media.[13] Since its founding, the ESPOCC has become one of the most important examples of alternative communication in Brazil in recent history. Students of the school have produced a series titled *Crônicas urbanas* for Canal Futura and participated in workshops led by esteemed film director Carlos (Cacá) Diegues, which resulted in the film *5x favela—agora por nós mesmos* (*5x Favela, Now by Ourselves*, 2010). Alumni of the school have contributed to the magazine *AfroReggae*, the website Viva Favela, and the small-circulation, independently published magazine (or zine) *Tangolomango* and formed independent collectives.

The year 2012 marked an important shift in the operations of the ESPOCC. First, the school received financial support from the state-controlled oil company Petrobras, which had been a significant funder of cultural projects in Brazil until the revelation of the Lava Jato (Car Wash) corruption scandal of 2014. The year 2012 was also when the school announced that it would guide its work based on the language, tools, and planning of affirmative publicity and would offer the first course on the subject in the nation. In recent years, decreases of funding exacerbated by the corruption investigations and a prolonged economic recession have demanded that nonprofit organizations seek funding from other resources. The ESPOCC continues to operate with financial support from the Brazil Foundation and the global nonprofit organization ICCO.

The idea of affirmative publicity was conceptualized by leaders of the ESPOCC and emerged at a time when social movements were strong and there was a belief in the viability of inventing a "new Brazil" that was more inclusive and just. Similar to the Images of the People program, the ESPOCC sought to offer professional training to young people who would be able to enter the professional labor market and introduce innovative and transformative ideas about society. In a broader sense, affirmative publicity aims to rethink the role of publicity in society. As a communicative practice, it refers to a type of publicity that is not concerned directly with seeking profits in a marketplace. According to those who proposed the idea and shaped the practice of affirmative publicity, the goal is to work with the language of publicity to advocate for civil and human rights and promote new modes of social interaction that respect differences of gender, race, urban territories, and sexual orientation (J. Silva, Nascimento, and Salles 2012; Nascimento 2012; Luis Henrique Nascimento, interview by the author, Rio de Janeiro, June 29, 2012). In this way, the ESPOCC's goal to orient its work by the concept of affirmative publicity affirms the belief that contemporary political and community action takes place through communication.

Social marketing bears some resemblance to affirmative publicity.[14] Social marketing is a multifaceted practice that generally aims to influence individual behaviors for the social good, such as improving health, protecting the environment, or preventing injuries (Andreasen 1994, 2006; Lee and Kotler 2011). It has also become a strategy for effecting changes in social policy (French and Gordon 2015). By contrast, affirmative publicity may result in taking new actions—especially the development of effective race-conscious public policies and legal practices—but it prioritizes intervening in belief systems, especially those regarding race and class, that sustain inequality. Similar to other marketing practices, affirmative publicity draws on the major interventions of the marketer's toolbox (or "marketing mix"), including the well-known "four Ps" (product, price, place, and promotion). However, affirmative publicity does not concern itself with profit potential (of products or prices), substituting commercial imperatives with progressive social gains and increased democratic values. Affirmative publicity considers place in the broader sense of the public sphere and in the specific sense of different urban territories. In terms of pro-motion, affirmative publicity encompasses different modes of communicative strategies, including various materials, events, and platforms, to reach differ-ent publics, such as groups that marketers commonly refer to as "upstream," "midstream," and "downstream" audiences.

In addition to promoting new modes of social interaction, affirmative pub-licity seeks to intervene in the language of publicity to not simply address mem-bers of the new middle class as targets of traditional marketing practices such as the engagement marketing scheme discussed in chapter 3. Indeed, the con-cept emerged at a moment when there was a keen interest in the new middle class and favelas as sites for reinventing the city of Rio de Janeiro. As a communicative practice, affirmative publicity aims for a different strategy of inclusion. Rather than convert members of the new middle class, especially those located in favelas, into mere consumers, the goals of affirmative public-ity include redefining how people think about the favelas and social relations. On the one hand, affirmative publicity aims for countering a historically neg-ative representation of favelas and residents of these urban territories. On the other hand, it eschews consumption and ostentation as modes of superficial eco-nomic inclusion of previously marginalized peoples and spaces (J. Silva, Nas-cimento, and Salles 2012; Nascimento 2012).

The JMV Campaign

One of the first manifestations of affirmative publicity was the JMV campaign. The goal of the campaign was to address the alarming homicide rates in Brazil and especially those registered for young Black men.[15] According to the 2012 report *Mapa da violência 2012: A cor dos homicídios no Brasil* (Map of violence 2012: The color of homicide in Brazil), approximately fifty thousand people are killed each year in Brazil (Waiselfisz, 10). Data from 2002 indicate that there has been a fall in the number of homicides for the White population and an increase in those for the Black population (9). Of the total number of homi-cides, approximately twenty-seven thousand were of young people, and 75 percent of those were Black (10). Owing to the alarming rates of selective mortality, the federal government created the Plano Nacional de Prevenção a Violência contra a Juventude Negra (National Plan to Prevent Violence against Black Youth) in 2012.[16]

As the name of the ESPOCC campaign, Youth Marked to Live, suggests, human rights and the death of young people were the central issues taken up.[17] Rather than be destined for death, the campaign aimed to make local popula-tions of metropolitan Rio de Janeiro aware of the systemic violence commit-ted against predominantly poor, Black youths and mobilize citizens to demand change. The campaign also sought to pressure local and state government agen-cies to abide by five legally established protocols, including discouraging unjustified use of violence (such as shooting firearms from police helicopters) and offering sensitivity training for security agents. In the discussion of the JMV campaign that follows, I consider what it means to make race visible using the tools of a marketing campaign and how this campaign contributed to a broader understanding of affirmative action in Brazil.

The JMV campaign included a wide range of creative and collaborative communication activities reaching different audiences. More traditional marketing materials (such as printed posters and flyers) accompanied online digital materials, including social media (Facebook, Twitter), short commercial spots (on YouTube), and an online petition submitted to the governor of Rio de Janeiro, Sérgio Cabral, to pressure the government to adopt measures to prevent violence. The majority of still images used in the JMV campaign were produced by the Images of the People project. The campaign also relied on community partners to develop a network to distribute materials and increase awareness of the marked levels of violence committed against young Black males in (mostly) poor communities of Rio de Janeiro.

The campaign officially launched on November 10, 2013, in Parque Madureira, a community in the North Zone of Rio de Janeiro. The opening events included a series of debates, dance, storytelling, and musical performances that reached a "downstream" audience (members of the community not involved directly with the observatory but whose raised awareness of their rights was key in the campaign's success). Drawing on a network of community representatives, the campaign then extended to thirteen municipalities with the highest homicide rates.

The date of the launch is notable, as November is generally understood as a month to recognize Black culture in Brazil, with November 20 being designated as the Dia da Consciência Negra (Day of Black Consciousness) in Rio de Janeiro, a day that became a national holiday in 2011.[18] Indeed, one poster created for the campaign states that "every day is a day for Black consciousness."[19] Another poster, produced during the ongoing JMV campaign, warns readers that they could become the next Amarildo, a man whose disappearance and death after being detained by officers of a UPP had sparked protest of police abuse.[20] In this way, the campaign aimed to build on the cultural moment, protest violence committed against the poor, and contribute to developing consciousness of race as a factor contributing to social injustice in Brazil.

Although the campaign was launched in the North Zone of the metropolitan area of Rio, the JMV campaign did not isolate itself from the rest of the city. The campaign sought to reach a broad public who would further support the campaign. To that end, organizers of the JMV campaign targeted the Largo da Carioca, a central plaza in downtown Rio de Janeiro, for two guerrilla marketing activities. The first event, the *ação dos corpos* (body action), involved painting four thousand bodies on the ground in the Largo da Carioca to call attention to the number of people killed each year. Two weeks later, on December 16, 2013, a flash mob occupied the Largo da Carioca. This action involved inviting individuals to participate in the event directly and by way of three widely circulated short online videos featuring actors Lúcio Mauro Filho and Leandro Santana and singer Tico Santa Cruz from the rock band Detonautas.[21] Individuals gathered in the Largo da Carioca and fell to the ground suddenly at a designated time and, like the painted outlines of dead bodies, similarly called attention to the number of young people killed each year.[22]

The JMV Commercial

The official spot for the campaign made race a clear factor in social inequality. Luis Henrique Nascimento, who helped shape the concept of affirmative publicity and served as one of the leaders of the ESPOCC, asserts that young Black men in Brazil die at alarming rates because of racism yet they also begin to be assassinated symbolically at the moment of their birth, given their access to inferior medical care and education and their association in the public imaginary with violence and criminality. He further explains that it is the symbolic that justifies the alarming rates of homicide (Nascimento, interview by the author, Rio de Janeiro, June 29, 2012). That is, the negative position young Black males hold in the imaginary contributes to justifying or excusing the violence committed against them. The JMV campaign not only drew attention to violence committed against young Black youths but also drew attention to racism, questioned a social imaginary that lends support to discrimination, and made race a visible factor in social inequality. By "visible," I mean not only representing racial or ethnic differences but also making transparent the connection between race, ethnicity, and differentiated life experiences in Brazil.

Indeed, the campaign called attention to race overtly and countered a long, complicated history of erasure of Black bodies in Brazil. In his study of race in Brazil, Edward Eric Telles (2004) reveals how race and Black bodies have been elided in political and cultural life through policies and practices ranging from the white supremacy of the nineteenth century to the politics of "whitening" in the early twentieth century and the celebration of miscegenation and racial mixture since the mid-twentieth century. One result of not addressing race has been a failure to develop policies and programs that protect all citizens. By contrast, in the official commercial spot for the JMV campaign, a telescopic sight, as if from a firearm, scans young bodies in the distance and clearly identifies race as a factor that differentiates life experiences.[23] First, a fair-skinned young woman appears in the sight. Then the scope brings into view a young fair-skinned teen talking to a friend. As different people move into the view of the sight, statistical data regarding homicide rates in Brazil appear in intertitles and in voiceover. Those data inform viewers that the chance of death by homicide doubles for young people and is fourteen times higher for young males. Lastly, the scope locks in on a young Black man who is looking off into the distance. The male voiceover notes that the risk of being a victim of homicide is twenty-seven times higher if the individual is young, male, and Black. Then, there is a cut, the scope image disappears, and viewers see a young Black teenager playing football with friends on a neighborhood pitch. The spot ends with the young man breaking the fourth wall and joyfully asserting that his destiny is to live. The ending questions how the Black body has become a target of violence and counters a narrative of criminality associated with the Black male body, placing responsibility for this perspective on the viewer. What is more, the spot challenges other stereotypical beliefs that associate young Black men with poverty, a lack of civility, or dishonesty.

Intervening in cultural beliefs and effecting policy change require more than providing facts. The development of new social identities and cultural values is not a logical process led by data alone. As with most advertising campaigns, the JMV publicity campaign balanced appealing to the intellect as well as emotions in order to promote (in this instance) policy changes to protect civil and human rights. The language of publicity tends to be an emotionally charged form of discourse. Indeed, the process of branding is one that fundamentally involves deploying language that mobilizes desires and cultivates affective relationships between an individual and a presented story about products, places, ideas, and so forth (Escalas 2004; Lerman, Morais, and Luna 2018). In this case, it is a story about people.

Traditional marketing language aims to sell an object by producing certain emotions (such as desire or pleasure), stimulating affective connections to a given product, and cultivating a sense of identity related to the purchase, ownership, and use of that object. By contrast, affirmative publicity aims to cultivate desires and emotions with the aim of seducing people to a new way of being and interacting with others in an urban sphere. That is, affirmative publicity involves using the language and tools of marketing to promote a new paradigm of citizenship. A characteristic particular to affirmative publicity is the subversion of the language and practices of conventional publicity and especially revelation of the mechanisms that generate certain feelings toward an object (or a group of people) (Nascimento 2012; J. Silva, Nascimento, and Salles 2012). The commercial spot just described uses the sight of a gun to re-create the experience of terror and suspense commonly found in the action-thriller movie. (Notably, shock, fear, and confusion are also experiences mobilized by the flash mob and *ação dos corpos* guerrilla marketing events.) By closing with a positive appeal to life, the spot subverts unquestioned fear that prompts attacks on a presumed enemy and the violent imposition of order and security. Rather, fear is converted into emotional connection with the young Black man in an effort to propose new, more just social relations.

In the official commercial spot and the campaign as a whole, race was clearly identified as a factor that contributes to social injustice. However, identifying Blackness as a factor or demographic category itself complicates a long-held celebration of racial and ethnic ambiguity and mixture as central to Brazilian cultural identity. Whereas the United States and South Africa have historically established clearly defined categories and race has been linked to one's ancestry, in Brazil people refer to skin color and other physical features. In fact, the Brazilian census includes the color categories white, brown, and black (*branco, pardo,* and *preto*) and not ethnic origins.[24] What is more, studies show that how an individual identifies oneself can change with time, level of education, gender, and region (Telles 2004, 78–106). Thus, difficulty establishing demographic categories tied to race or color has contributed to difficulty (or resistance) in identifying race or color as a factor contributing to discrimination or inequality.

However, this campaign made race as well as age and gender clear factors in determining levels of violence committed against different individuals. In this way, the campaign called attention to differentiated "vertical relations." In his study of race in Brazil, Telles calls for thinking about discrimination and inequality in terms of vertical and horizontal relations. He notes that in Brazil, influential scholars (including Gilberto Freyre) have tended to focus on levels of sociability and social relations (or "horizontal relations"), which reveal high levels of intermarriage and integration relative to other nations (such as the United States or South Africa).[25] As a consequence, racial hierarchies or conflicts in Brazil have been seen as limited, unproblematic, or temporary (Telles 2004, 223–225). Meanwhile, vertical relations consider economic dimensions as well as an individual's relationship to the state by way of legal protections (219–223). Thus, making race visible in the JMV campaign meant making race a factor in vertical relations whereby race has become a marker not just of class exclusion but of broad social and political status, including security protections that afford the basic human right to live. Indeed, both events held in the Largo da Carioca (the *ação dos corpos* and the flash mob) took place in a central location in the city and denounced the government (local, regional, and federal) for its inaction on issues of racial justice. The campaign challenged the belief that laws or policies that address racial discrimination are not necessary.

Yet making race visible in the JMV campaign also involved rethinking and redeploying long-held cultural values. Identifying race as a factor in inequality runs counter to the myth that Brazil is a racial democracy and that class more than race is the most important factor in discrimination in Brazil. In terms of social marketing, the JMV campaign participated in a "value exchange." A value exchange is a principle asserting that an individual will choose a behavior (or attitude) in exchange for a benefit the individual believes to be of value or for the reduction of a barrier the individual considers important (Lee and Kotler 2011, 18–19). This principle can be brought into the discussion of the JMV affirmative publicity campaign. While the JMV campaign did not involve modifying a behavior (except for the call to sign a petition to pressure government officials), it did tap into ideological benefits and barriers encountered by its target audiences.

These benefits and barriers are simultaneously produced by the concept of a racial democracy (or the belief in the existence of a harmoniously racially and ethnically mixed society). On the one hand, the notion that Brazil is a peaceful, multiracial society is a cornerstone of Brazilian cultural identity. And notwithstanding decades of challenges by social movements and the academy to the notion of Brazil as a racial democracy, it remains a cultural ideal.[26] On the other hand, sustaining the idea that Brazil is a racial democracy further entrenches racial inequality and prevents social progress. The JMV commercial spot presents information that directly contests the notion that Brazil is a racial democracy but then closes with the young Black man embracing his friends and affirming that his destiny is to live. That is, the belief that Brazil is an existing racial democracy (an ideological barrier) is exchanged for the belief that Brazil can become a racial democracy (an ideological benefit). Target audiences are drawn in to embrace the ideal of a racial democracy for the genuine benefit of all citizens.

The goal of the JMV campaign was to value the lives of young Black men and raise awareness about violence committed against them. Just as the concept of affirmative publicity was shaped by the idea of affirmative action, the JMV campaign in turn expanded an understanding of what affirmative action means in Brazil. Affirmative action has been a controversial topic. In a nation that has historically prided itself on its (ostensibly) harmonious race relations, one of the most significant objections to affirmative action policies is that they depend on greater fixity in racial identities than have historically existed (Htun 2004; H. Silva 2000). The challenge becomes how to define race to develop social policies and their implementation. The commercial spot may be critiqued for proposing greater fixity or simplification of racial categories, but self-identified Blacks experience more extreme degrees of violence.[27] A correlation between skin color and inequality is thus drawn, and the emphasis is on valuing life. Whereas affirmative action policies in Brazil have been largely implemented in terms of quotas for higher education and work, the JMV campaign called attention to the fact that inequality involves more than unequal access to education or upward social mobility through employment. The campaign also challenged the idea that race-conscious policies belong somewhere else (e.g., in the United States). Statistics on homicide rates locate the social, political, and cultural problem in the Brazilian context. Ultimately, the campaign challenged the idea that affirmative action is implemented through a quota system. Rather, the alarming rates of homicide committed disproportionately against young Black men demand a different range of race-conscious policies.

Affirming Diversity

The goals of affirmative publicity are greater than intervening in how the language of publicity is mobilized. Indeed, a guiding principle of affirmative publicity is the promotion of new sociability. And as a communicative practice, affirmative publicity aims to propose new paradigms for an integrated city. In addition to the JMV campaign, students and leaders of the ESPOCC produced a series of short videos. If the JMV campaign demanded recognition of young Black men's right to life, the series of short videos further advocates for the right to liberty and equality and a respect for diversity.

The videos not only manifest the goals of alternative media practices but also echo principles proposed by the concept of the "right to the city." French philosopher Henri Lefebvre proposed the idea of the right to the city in the midst of rapid urbanization and commodification of urban space in France in the 1960s in his text *La droit à la ville* (The right to the city, 1968) and further elaborated on the idea in *Espace et politique* (Space and politics, 1973) (Lefebvre 1996). Scholars have taken up Lefebvre's concept of the right to the city in their studies of Brazil as the concept has resonated in a context characterized by informal urban development owing to a speculative land market, clientelistic politics, and an exclusionary legal regime (Brown 2013; Cymbalista 2008; Alfonsin 2004; Rolnik 2007; Edésio Fernandes 2007; Saule Júnior 1999). Notably, a legal structure informed by the concept of the right to the city has been established in Brazil, including the 1988 Brazilian Constitution and the City Statute (Law 10.257/2001), which explicitly recognizes the right to the city as a collective right. Yet in more recent years, scholars have called for moving beyond advocacy and legal commitment to realize the goals of the right to the city more fully (Brown and Kristiansen 2009; Edésio Fernandes 2007). Indeed, a 2010 report from the fifth session of the U.N. World Urban Forum, which was held in Rio de Janeiro, called for acknowledging cultural diversity as a practical step toward making the right to the city a reality (United Nations 2010, 4). A letter presented by Rio de Janeiro at the U.N.-sponsored conference (and published in the 2010 report) recognizes the right to the city as "a new political, cultural, economic, and socio-environmental paradigm for the reconstruction of our cities" (106).

At a time of renewed commodification of urban space, alternative popular media practices such as the affirmative publicity videos helped move the idea of the right to the city forward.[28] These works share with the JMV campaign a similar goal of intervening in belief systems that sustain inequality while they also advocate for respecting diverse lived experiences in the city. While "O atravessador" (The go-between) offers an intersectional view of internalized gender and racial discrimination, the short video "Déjà vu" provides a historical understanding of the city that is diverse and integrated. Two shorter videos are of particular interest, "Roda vida" (Wheels alive) and "Sons da Maré" (Sounds of Maré). Both call for new social relations and promote new understandings of urban space. Whereas "Roda viva" emphasizes the right to the city in terms of physical mobility, "Sons da Maré" challenges the representation (and understanding) of urban peripheries by celebrating the acoustic diversity of the favela Maré.

Appreciating the Everyday

Like the photographs discussed earlier, the short video "Sons da Maré" offers an aesthetic appreciation of the everyday. In this instance, the video emphasizes the experience of hearing different musical styles found playing in the favela. The video begins by following a young woman walking into Maré. She stops when she hears a samba tune and begins to dance. Additional cuts show a young man listening to hip-hop, two women dancing to a northeastern tune (*forró*), and a couple dancing to funk. The juxtaposition of different musical styles suggests the coexistence of disparate social groups. The video develops an aesthetics of the quotidian in the sense that sounds typically heard while walking through Maré are an important backdrop to everyday experiences. In terms of cinematography and editing, the video employs traditional realist strategies of representation. That is, it captures individuals in their surroundings going about their day, enjoying the different sounds of music, with handheld camera, diegetic sound, and ambient lighting.

As a communicative tool guided by the principles of affirmative publicity, the video presents an alternative interpretation of the favela and its diverse cultures. The closing intertitles of "Sons da Maré" state, "Onde alguns veem o caos, vemos multiplicidade" (Where some see chaos, we see multiplicity). In this way the video challenges—much like the photographs—the narrative of order versus chaos that has shaped the perception of favelas as existing outside the "official" city and subsequently neglected by authorities. Conversely, the different styles of music that can be heard while walking in Maré are linked to a cultural richness rather than disorder. What is more, these are styles of music associated with internal migrants from the Northeast (*forró*), the youth culture of Rio's favelas (funk), and Afro-Brazilian musical traditions (samba) widely embraced as a popular expression of Brazilian culture. In this way, "Sons da Maré" operates as an affirmative action in that it advocates for a fundamental equality characterized by a respect for difference.

In his study of how the concept of the right to the city has been developed in Brazil, Edésio Fernandes (2007, 208) characterizes Lefebvre's idea as more of a general political-philosophical platform that has included a number of rights, such as the right to expression and the right to identity in difference and equality. Lefebvre has also been interpreted as proposing a notion of social citizenship that went beyond political and legal conditions to encompass cultural and social dimensions (Edésio Fernandes 2007; Brown 2013). Thus, the juxtaposition of different musical sounds found in "Sons da Maré" places the favela at the intersection of different regions, ethnic and racial groups, and ages in a way that underscores how one urban territory (Maré) forms part of a web of different but shared cultural practices. Thus, these videos participate in one of the key goals of contemporary "other communication" in that they seek to legitimize cultural manifestations emerging from stigmatized locations like Maré (J. Silva and Ansel 2012, 24).

Rethinking Social Mobility

Among the rights that fall under the concept of the right to the city are those of access and the use of urban space that allows for full participation of all citizens in urban life. "Roda viva" illustrates that socio-spatial inclusion means creating an environment that allows for all people to move through and between urban territories without hindrance. The video includes a male voiceover reading a poem-manifesto about ideals of freedom of movement. Viewers see a man in a wheelchair trying to get around in an urban space, presumably a favela. He exerts himself to get over speed bumps, vehicles block him and prevent him from crossing the street, friends (or neighbors) carry him up flights of stairs (because there are no ramps), he negotiates uneven pavement, and so forth.

The voiceover that accompanies these scenes opens with the declaration that he has been waiting a long time: "Estou aqui tem duas horas. Estou aqui todos os dias. Estamos todos aqui. Em nosso caminho, encontramos mais do que queríamos" (I've been here for two hours. I'm here every day. We are all here. In our path, we find more than what we wanted). Thus, the voiceover reflects on a state that affects an individual before emphasizing the communal nature of his situation. The statement takes on the nature of a metaphor: visually we see that he struggles to simply get around, but the struggle for mobility is in practice a struggle to live a full life. The narrator further calls for breaking down barriers, respecting differences, and acknowledging the existence of different lived experiences in the city. The video ends with a quote from Article 5 of the Constitution, which affirms that all are equal before the law and are guaranteed the right to life and liberty, among other rights (Brazil, Senado Federal 1988, 13).[29]

In his original presentation of the concept of the right to the city, Lefebvre argues that the use value of cities as centers of social, political, and cultural life is undermined by commercialization, which creates exchange value in the process of commodifying urban spaces. In turn, this economic process excludes many from the rewards of urban life. Lefebvre argues for a right to the city that includes, among other rights, the right to appropriation (1996, 174). Appropriation includes the right to access, occupy, and use urban space in the pursuit of life and liberty. Text included on the Onlaje website that accompanies "Roda viva" encourages viewers to consider how democracy means thinking about the right to come and go. "Roda viva" thus affirms that a contemporary status of citizenship in Rio de Janeiro must not be predicated on where an individual lives (i.e., in an "official city" or a "subnormal agglomeration") and contests exclusive modes of access between urban territories (such as the gondola project) that do not truly provide socio-spatial integration. Lastly, the video advocates for a new urban sociability whereby socio-spatial inclusion is premised not on economic factors but on civil and human rights.

Both alternative media projects discussed here were informed by commercial practices that sought to cultivate new sensibilities regarding Rio de Janeiro's favelas and promote new ideas about a more democratic, inclusive Brazilian society. The photos of the Images of the People program and the JMV campaign did not simply counter stereotypical representation or increasing commodification of favelas. Rather, they drew on the discursive practices of branding to intervene in how favelas were visually represented and advocated for a new paradigm of citizenship in boom-time Brazil.

5

Favela, Film, Franchise

■■■■■■■■■■■■■■■■■■■■■

The favela holds a contradictory place in Brazilian culture, memory, and history. In Rio's urban landscape, small agglomerations of shacks were present in the nineteenth century but became a "problem" in the twentieth century when concerns with urban hygiene and racist theories of eugenics influenced the nation's elites (Fischer 2014, 12–20). Rio's favelas became identified as home to former slaves and then occupied by soldiers returning from Canudos, a messianic movement in the interior of Bahia that the military eradicated in 1897.[1] In a sense, Rio's favelas in the early twentieth century were born from war. Now, they are frequently the site of urban warfare where militarized police forces combat heavily armed drug syndicates. These communities frequently lack running water, sewage, and paved roads and exist alongside wealthier neighborhoods replete with modern urban infrastructure, doormen, and parking garages.

It is this stark contrast that has made the favela a frequent nodal point for reflecting on Brazilian cultural identity, development, and the country's political evolution. Beatriz Jaguaribe (2007, 100) has written about the portrayal of the favelas in film and literature and notes that they are a locus of the national imagined community but also the failed promise of modernity. Favelas result from inequality. Brazil is known for its marked income inequality that is correlated with spatial, ethnic, and racial segregation. In the "new Brazil," this internal division was one to overcome. In her work on nation branding, Melissa Aronczyk (2013, 37) asserts that the success of a nation brand depends largely on its ability to overcome tensions, especially internal divisions, to gain a competitive advantage through perceptions. Yet what do we make of the repeated portrayal of the favela, especially hyperrealist and spectacular representations in contemporary film? To what degree do contemporary portrayals of the favela reflect concerns with inequality and failed promises of progress?

This chapter considers the representation of the favela as a point of departure for thinking about Brazil's internal divisions and contemporary politics. As noted in chapter 4, the journalist Zuenir Ventura (1994) described Rio de Janeiro as a *cidade partida* (divided city) with protected, prosperous areas and neglected, "no-go" zones. The idea of a "divided city" has become a framework for analyzing contemporary society and Brazil's urban landscapes. Albeit accurate in many ways, the metaphor of a divided city is only partially productive for examining the ideology and representation of favelas in contemporary film. In lieu of this, I propose the franchise as a critical metaphor of analysis. I depart from the idea of the favela as a branded place in contemporary media and consider how the favela as brand operates in a larger socioeconomic exchange. To that end, I draw on the concept of the franchise as a framework to reflect on the action-crime thriller *Tropa de elite* (*Elite Squad*, 2007), its sequel and record-setting box office hit *Tropa de elite 2—O inimigo agora é outro* (*Tropa 2*; *Elite Squad 2: The Enemy Within*, 2010), and the documentary *5x pacificação* (*5x Pacification*, 2012).

Customary understanding of the franchise in film studies emphasizes the marketing of a brand or brand story, including the reappearance of a character or development of a narrative universe. Yet the concept of the franchise allows for a critique of the political and economic incorporation of groups and individuals into a larger organization, as well as the rights of membership in a larger entity. In other words, the idea of the franchise allows for a critique of contemporary citizenship in economic and political terms. Subsequently, my discussion of these three films addresses the territorial, commercial, and political inclusion of the favela into the idea of a new Brazil. Among other questions, I ask of these films, How are contradictions neutralized or erased? How are tensions ostensibly resolved? Notably, these films also reveal the precursors to a negative turn in the development of Brazilian cultural and political identity that foreshadows increased social divisions and the hate-filled rhetoric of the Jair Bolsonaro administration.

Both fiction films directed by José Padilha are notable for their violent, spectacular treatment of efforts to "pacify" the favelas on the eve of an international mega-event and convert them from general menaces to middle-class society to more stable political and economic communities. The blame for Brazilian society's ills proceeds from drug lords in Rio's favelas to corrupt police to an entire political system. *Tropa de elite* further brands the favela as a space for consumption and sustains social hierarchies through authoritarian action.

Tropa 2 identifies the broader political system as the source of the nation's ills. It also portrays the favela as a political and economic emerging space as it maps middle-class discontent. The documentary film *5x pacificação*, a multidirector production by residents from Rio de Janeiro's favelas, stands in critical dialogue with the *Tropa* films regarding inequality and urban violence. Structured as a conversation with multiple stakeholders involved in the pacification process, the documentary focuses on economic insertion of the favelas into the city, its impact on residents, and the development of new relationships between police and favela residents.

All three films reflect on the entrance of the state to enfranchise these communities. The goal is to think about these films against the backdrop of the historical moment, but also to think critically about the repeated representation of favelas in politico-economic terms. After a brief discussion of how the favela has been portrayed in film, I offer reflections on how the franchise can operate as a critical approach for thinking about the frequent return to the favela as a site for filmmakers.

A Brief History of the Favela in Film

The favela has been a site from which key cultural practices have emerged. It is also a location and culture represented in works of literature and film that have historically drawn the curiosity of the nation's middle class. For instance, the novel *Quarto de despejo: Diário de uma favelada* (*Child of the Dark: The Diary of Carolina Maria de Jesus*), published in 1960, was a commercial success as well-heeled Brazilians flocked to bookstores to discover the reflections of a poor semiliterate Black woman who dreamed of a better life. The favela has also appeared regularly in Brazilian films. In the mid-twentieth century, Brazil's urban slums were the setting for several landmark Cinema Novo films, including the collective production *Cinco vezes favela* (*Favela Five Times*, 1962), *Rio, 40 graus* (*Rio, 40 Degrees*, 1955) and *Rio, Zona Norte* (*Rio, Northern Zone*, 1957) by Nelson Pereira dos Santos, and *A grande cidade* (*The Big City*, 1966) by Carlos Diegues. If at first films from this period reflected on urban space with the optimism that revealing inequality would help solve social problems, they are later characterized as offering analyses of the failures of developmentalism and leftist intellectuals (Johnson and Stam 1995, 30–35).

More contemporary films have returned to the favela. The Brazilian film industry had been dismantled in the early 1990s. From approximately 1994 to 2002, the industry revived. During this rebirth (*retomada*)[2] of film production, the favela was once again a setting for filmmakers. Films such as *Orfeu* (Carlos Diegues, 1999), a remake of the French film *Orfeu negro* (*Black Orpheus*, Marcel Camus, 1959), returned to the poor urban neighborhoods of Rio de Janeiro and offered contradictory views of poverty and inequality. *Cidade de Deus* (*City of God*, Fernando Meirelles and Kátia Lund, 2002), which adapts the 1997 semi-autobiographical novel by Paulo Lins and his life in suburban Rio de Janeiro, set the tone for commercial productions representing the favelas with its fast-paced editing, thrilling scenes of violent confrontation between urban factions, seemingly authentic exposé of favela life, and ever-present soundtrack (of samba, funk, and rap). The film was followed by a television series (2002–2005) and film (2007), both titled *Cidade dos homens*. The film's influence extended beyond sequels. Numerous debates took place at film festivals regarding urban violence, and the film reportedly motivated Luiz Inácio Lula da Silva to change public security policies (Meirelles 2003).

The present does not necessarily repeat the past. Ivana Bentes (2003, 122) asserts that more contemporary films lack political perspectives and aesthetic proposals relative to those of the Cinema Novo period. Cinema Novo directors like Glauber Rocha in films and writings, including the manifesto "Uma Estética da Fome" (Aesthetics of hunger), called for disrupting sociological and political assumptions about poverty through an aesthetics that would convey the brutality of hunger and misery. In contrast, Bentes offers that contemporary portrayals naturalize violence, poverty, and misery as typical of favelas through commercial film practices (such as the use of the Steadicam and fast-paced editing). This leads her to assert that we see a transition from the "aesthetics" to the "cosmetics" of hunger whereby "local, historic and traditional subjects [are] wrapped in an 'international' aesthetics" (124–125). What Bentes essentially describes is the branding of the favela whereby profitable narratives are associated with these urban spaces. As discussed further later, the *Tropa* films follow the trajectory of representation of the favela in contemporary Brazilian film and further contribute to an ongoing process of commodification of the favela.

Yet what is it that drives the repeated portrayal of the favela and poverty (more generally) on film? For Bentes, the favelas are a site of contradictory feelings of "fascination as well as horror and repulsion" (2003, 129). The setting of the favela, fast-paced editing, violent exchanges between police and criminal gangs, and other tropes (such as the innocent victim caught in the crosshairs) could lead to asserting that the "favela film" constitutes a sort of genre. However, a different process is taking place with these films. Rather than approach these films in terms of how they display a consistent series of tropes and aesthetics (as with a genre) or established metaphors, the concept of the franchise serves as a framework for thinking about issues of representation and sociopolitical and economic inclusion. In this way, repeated portrayal of the favela and associated poverty can be understood as an attempt to work through the contradictions of neoliberal capitalism that aims to include while excluding and sustains inequality while promising progress.

The Franchise as Critical Metaphor

Franchises abound in modern business, but their broader social, political, and economic significance may go overlooked. Indeed, franchising is a significant capitalist practice in contemporary economies. A franchise is most commonly understood as a business structure intended to expand a business through a licensing relationship. In this sense, a franchisor grants permission to a third party (a franchisee) to act as an agent to conduct business under the umbrella of the larger structure. Restaurants (or chains) are perhaps some of the most readily identified franchises (e.g., McDonald's and Burger King). A consumer can go to different locations of a franchise and at different moments, but expectations for the same experience are generally met.

A franchise involves several components, the most fundamental of which is a brand (generally of a product or service) that is cultivated by an overarching operating system and support. Indeed, franchises are built on brands, and in thinking about a franchise, it is important to consider how a brand is interpreted, consumed, and contextualized. Thus, a franchise is more than just an operating structure; it is about profitable relationships. The process depends on a brand's value (i.e., the qualities associated with a product or service) and the delivery of the branded product or service according to established standards and guidelines. Those relationships are not always equitable. A franchise may offer the impression of equitably including distinct units in a larger structure. Yet they are also notable for directing the majority of the profits toward the franchisor, suppressing the wages of workers, and engaging in labor exploitation (Ehrmann 2013; Edger 2015; Sherman 2011). In this sense, the model of a franchise demands thinking about how a larger structure aiming to include also negotiates and sustains the inequalities of capitalism.

As it relates to film studies, the concept of the franchise has been understood in recent years predominantly in terms of the Marvel Universe, with its series of films populated by a mix of characters that appear, reappear, and cross over into numerous productions. Repetition such as that found with the Marvel films is not new. Amanda Ann Klein and R. Barton Palmer (2016, 1–9) offer that cinema has historically been rooted in the concept of multiplicities, according to which films have repeated and exploited images, narratives, and characters found in previous texts. In addition to evaluating what is repeated and why, Klein and Palmer encourage scholars to consider the relationship between audiences, industry, and culture in relation to multiplicities (14).[3]

However, some ideas concerning the concept of the franchise have been lost or overlooked in film studies. A franchise can be understood as a commercial concept as well as in terms of governance. Indeed, the term calls forth notions of legal rights, citizenship, and social inclusion as well as economic exchanges. This, in turn, involves not only creating or marketing a series of products but also questions of social hierarchies and structures of exchange. Recalling the discussion in the introduction to this book, a brand emerges from the discourses that create a narrative and expectations around not only an object or person but also a place. In her work on branding, Liz Moor (2007) explores the historical connections between brands and imperial projects, which leads her to assert that branding has become a mode of governance over time. In effect, it is a franchise that mobilizes a brand and furthers its symbolic value.

I propose reclaiming some concepts of the franchise to approach the representation of the favela in contemporary film. In this way I extend discussion of the franchise in film studies beyond a distinct series of films by one production company and development of a narrative "universe" (such as the Marvel films) or the reappearance of a character in a series (such as those featuring an action hero like James Bond), to those like *Tropa de elite* that return to the favela as their setting. The concept of the franchise helps think through the negotiations of difference, the apparent inclusion of disparate groups in a larger structure, and different modes of governance that sustain profitable hierarchies. By drawing on the idea of the franchise, I consider not only how film aesthetics help convert the favela into a branded space but also what drives the return to this site in film. Klein and Palmer (2016, 13–14) suggest placing repetitions in dialogue with a larger body of narratives. Following this, we can ask how these films that return to the favela as a site participate in a larger politico-economic system. In other words, what is the political and commercial logic behind the repeated, spectacular portrayal of the favela? And what tensions emerge regarding the portrayal of the favela in the *Tropa* films and the larger narrative of a new Brazil?

The idea of the franchise also helps us to think about the larger discursive practice of branding understood as resolving contradictions. As an economic system, capitalism generally fails at balancing social equality with economic progress and socioeconomic inequalities are constantly (re)negotiated. Adapting the franchise as a model for analyzing these films allows us to identify and critique efforts to ostensibly attain economic progress and inclusion in Brazil at this time.

Trading in Violence: *Tropa de elite*

Tropa de elite recalls several aspects of *Cidade de Deus*, including its spectacular violence, use of the codes of action thrillers, and adaptation of an insider's account of police corruption and favela life. Padilha's film is based on the book *Elite da tropa* (2006), authored by police officers André Batista and Rodrigo Pimentel in collaboration with Luiz Eduardo Soares. Both Batista and Pimentel were members of Brazil's elite special police force (Batalhão de Operações

Policiais Especiais, BOPE), known for its use of military-grade weaponry and tactics.[4] An insider's perspective from the book is conveyed on film with the voiceover of Wagner Moura in the role of Capitão (Captain) Nascimento, who seeks to train a replacement in order for him to retire, as his mental health and family life have suffered considerably during his work as a BOPE officer. In the process of finding his successor, the film exposes corrupt officers who benefit drug traffickers and help sustain a violent urban landscape. The film also exposes the ways in which members of the upper-middle class contribute to ongoing urban violence either by naïvely participating in nonprofit organizations or by directly supporting criminal enterprises by consuming drugs (like cocaine and marijuana). The film's narrative begins in media res as viewers are launched into a tense, violent confrontation related to a larger effort to secure a favela before a papal visit to Rio de Janeiro. A circular structure, which is repeated in the 2010 sequel *Tropa 2*, suggests that the favela is not only a recurring problem but also a departure point for thinking more broadly about corruption and violence in Brazilian society.

Following the premiere at the Rio de Janeiro Film Festival in 2007, *Tropa de elite* sparked debates concerning the representation of violence. Initial critical reception in the Brazilian press focused on whether the film upheld fascist ideology (Caldas 2008). In subsequent critiques, scholars have explored how the representation of urban violence in *Tropa de elite* and other contemporary works of Brazilian film and media reflects the nation's authoritarian past (Marques and Rocha 2010; Sousa 2009), sensationalizes and cements associations between poverty and violence (Hamburger 2007), and can be categorized within an emerging contemporary genre (Lusvarghi 2014).

In his critical reading of the representation of violence in contemporary Latin American cinema, Ignacio Sánchez Prado (2006) notes that violence has become central to the development of new forms of citizenship and cultural imaginaries, especially those projected on an international scale. What is more, his work suggests that violence in Latin American film operates strategically to uphold specific social and political perspectives (39, 46–48). It is the use of violence as a strategic socioeconomic code that is of central importance to understanding how *Tropa de elite* contributes to the branding of Brazil and the transformation of citizenship in contemporary Brazil. *Tropa de elite* not only contributes to branding the favela as a marketable space but also participates in a market of hatred and upholds an ideological perspective that sustains social divisions and hierarchies under the guise of efforts to include marginalized peoples and places.

Producing the Favela and the New Brazil

Tropa de elite is set in a context in which Rio's favelas are undergoing a process of increasing commodification and gradual entrance into the established, formal economy. The favela was integral to the cultivation of a new Brazil, and attempts were made to incorporate the favela into the franchise as nation. (The contradictions of this process are brought up in *5x pacificação*, discussed later.) In addition to the gondola project in the Complexo do Alemão (discussed in chapter 4) and other urban development projects undertaken in preparation for the 2014 World Cup and 2016 Olympics, banks, cell phone companies, and other businesses entered the favelas to capture customers with newfound disposable income.

One of the paradoxical ways that the favela entered into mainstream economic exchange was by way of its illicit allure. Anthropologists John Comaroff and Jean Comaroff (2009) have explored the evolving relationship between culture and the market. Their work underscores that the current historical moment reveals the rampant commodification of human identity. Their observations are salient to the discussion of the representation of the favela in contemporary Brazilian culture, where violence sells. In her ethnography of how "entangled forms of violence, spectacle, and commodification" shape social relations in Rocinha—one of Latin America's largest favelas—Erika Robb Larkins (2015, 5–6) notes that favelas in Brazil have become known in the wider cultural imaginary as places of criminality and narco-trafficking. She further explains that favela violence not only results in numerous deaths but also has become a "commercially viable by-product of an ongoing capitalist enterprise" that has resulted in the favela becoming a site for tourism as well as a setting for video games and other profit-driven expressions (5, 80–108). If the favela has a brand story, it is largely based on spectacular violence.

Of particular interest is how *Tropa de elite* presents the favela as a consumable location and, more specifically, how the film contributes further to an understanding of the favela as a pivotal location in (inter)national politics. Generally, the favela is coded in negative terms. According to Pierre-Mathieu Le Bel's (2018) analysis of the film, (physical) violence almost exclusively takes place in the space of the favela and representations of acts of violence are only available to spectators when they occur in the favela. Indeed, the film's narrative begins with preparations for the pending visit by the pope, who has insisted on staying at a location near one of Rio's favelas. The possibility that the Catholic Church's highest leader would be threatened or awoken by a stray bullet prompts local politicians to call on the BOPE, saviors of urban space in this instance, to secure the location. Peace and violence are thus brought into tension with each other, and the concern for local politicians is how their city appears under the international attention brought by the pope's visit. Notably, the pope did visit Brazil on several occasions,[5] but the narrative device in this instance is slightly allegorical in 2007, at a time when Brazil was in the process of applying to be a host for the 2014 World Cup matches and the 2016 Olympic Games. As discussed previously, international mega-events and the cultivation of Brazil's international image were key components to the Lula and then Rousseff administrations' development plans. In this instance, the favela is recognized less as a component of the nation's identity, as cultural policy would suggest at the time, and prompts, by contrast, concerns about how poverty and violence affect the nation's international reputation.

If the favela is identified as a general threat to urban security and international visitors, *Tropa de elite* also manages to produce urban space in a way that cultivates a sense of authenticity. *Tropa de elite* reiterates the formula of other commercially successful insider accounts of the favela with its tell-all exposé of Brazil's most prestigious (and most militarized) police force. The accusatory and confessional commentary of Captain Nascimento's voiceover appears to provide access to truths and an accurate diagnosis of urban violence and police corruption in Rio de Janeiro. Notably, Padilha originally intended to produce a documentary, following his documentary *Ônibus 174* (Bus 174, 2002), but adjusted plans to avoid the dangers of exposing police corruption (Arantes 2006). It is this documentary mode mapped onto a fictional account that Flora Süssekind (2005, 62) has defined as a kind of "neodocumentalism," frequent in contemporary literary representations of urban Brazil.

The apparent window into the urban soul of Rio de Janeiro is framed by spectacular and hyperrealist aesthetics. In scenes where the police engage drug traffickers in the favelas, hand-held camerawork and tight framing, especially of Captain Nascimento, provide a sense of immediacy. Special effects during "fight" scenes—such as the digitally added sounds of ricochets and explosions of bullets—stimulate audiences' baseline understanding of favelas, which already includes armed confrontation. The tension between heroic, good characters (Nascimento) and bad actors (drug dealers, corrupt cops) provides a simplistic but accessible perspective that further allows audiences to enjoy sensationalist and realist modes of consumption.[6] These instances show how *Tropa de elite* participates in what theorist Jean Baudrillard (2018) has described as a media-made "hyper-reality" whereby representations augment and exaggerate existing characteristics of what truly exists. For Baudrillard, modern life can be generally characterized by engagement with the hyperreal.

Stepping back for a moment from the film, viewers are predisposed in multiple ways to accept spectacle as real. Complementing the observations of Baudrillard, philosopher Guy Debord (1983) has asserted that spectacle is how we come to know the world, understand it, and interact in it. For Debord, social relations have become mediated by images in lieu of direct interactions. Spectacular violence has become a common way of representing the favela and shapes how these urban spaces are known (Robb Larkins 2015; Hamburger 2007). The genre of *Tropa de elite* is also an important factor. The crime thriller situates spectators to seek and interpret information on an emotional quest for apparent truths.[7]

A spectacular and hyperreal representation cultivates a sense of authenticity that is key to discursive practices of branding. Providing "real" and emotionally riveting access to these urban spaces helps make the favela a consumable space. In her work on branding, Sarah Banet-Weiser (2012) examines the transformation of everyday, lived culture—or what we assume to be "authentic"—into brands and the cultures that develop around them. For Banet-Weiser, brands have become a way to express identities, and the language and practices of branding have become an increasingly important mode of citizenship within contemporary capitalism (3–8). Distinct from the photographic representation of the everyday discussed in chapter 4, *Tropa de elite* offers a sense of authenticity by way of the spectacular, taken as real. In turn, the favela becomes a brand and departure point for negotiating contradictions of contemporary political and cultural identity.

Marketing Hate

The concept of a franchise also demands thinking about the engagements and interactions that spectators have with representations. In what ways do individuals support and further a brand and a brand story? How do those engagements cultivate new expressions of cultural and political identities? Days before the premiere of the film at the Rio Film Festival in 2007, a copy of *Tropa de elite* was leaked to the public. Pirated copies were reportedly sold on the streets of Rio de Janeiro as people debated whether the leak was a legitimate crime or a well-crafted viral marketing scheme. Writing about the film's early reception, journalist Aristeu Araújo (2007) attributed the film's phenomenal success to the way its Manichean view of good and bad actors connected with an existing, widespread, class-based hatred and to the fact that the film explored a market niche based on hate.

Although the favela has appeared in action-packed video games such as the popular *Modern Warfare 2, Tropa de elite* was part of a more traditional process of franchising whereby images, characters, and narratives—largely pirated—were included in other media productions (or ad hoc franchises). Milena Szafir (2010, 3) examines the reverberation of *Tropa de elite* in traditional and online media and asserts that these secondary manifestations engaged in a "culture of vigilance" that sought to reform society. She identifies numerous examples of "remixes" whereby pirated versions of video games and YouTube videos included characters from *Tropa de elite*, especially Captain Nascimento, such as remixed versions of Sony PlayStation 2's *Grand Theft Auto, Counterstrike*, and *Tropa de elite Multiplayer Beta*, available to download (59–60) (see figure 5.1). These reappearances of the film and especially Captain Nascimento in video games and on blogs and other websites further contribute to the branding of the favela as a violent urban territory that demands the authoritarian heroism of Captain Nascimento to bring peace and justice.

FIG. 5.1 Moura as Capitão Nascimento in *Tropa de elite.*

Desire to take control of the urban landscape and resolve the ongoing tensions becomes manifest in the broad identification with Captain Nascimento, the everyman, middle-class, heteronormative, White, male hero. Indeed, actor Wagner Moura's star status was so closely connected with the role of Captain Nascimento that audiences rejected his role as a gay lifeguard in *Praia do Futuro* (*Futuro Beach*, Karim Aïnouz, 2014). The role of Captain Nascimento as a modern-day Brazilian hero had significant reverberations in Brazilian society. Audiences, who expected Moura to reiterate his role as an authoritarian, macho, politically incorrect, take-charge leader in *Praia do Futuro*, were left "confused" (Fontanele and Navarro 2014). Audiences could find resonance years later in Jair Bolsonaro, a doppelgänger of sorts for Captain Nascimento. Bolsonaro, a former army captain, also saw his political ascent characterized as fighting against corruption and broad sectors of society.

Spectacular portrayals of the favela and armed conflict cultivated commercial profit and engagement by spectators. What is key is to also consider how spectacular violence in *Tropa de elite* operates as a mode of governance over space and people. Franchises rely on structured networks that provide oversight and unification of different units. The very title of the film, with its reference to an elite group, celebrates social hierarchies. The film sustains social tensions, notably in its representation of race and social relations. Generally, characters' phenotypes and the degree to which they enact or hold some degree of official authority follow social divisions found in Brazilian society along class lines. Captain Nascimento is a heteronormative, White male who appears to exert physical, professional, and intellectual power over children, women, Blacks, and the poor. In the film's strategic code of violence, Black bodies are the targets of violence by predominantly White agents. Notably, the formation of a new hero occurs at the end of the film when the new recruit to the BOPE, Matias, engages in the extrajudicial killing of another Black man, Baiano.

With few exceptions, violence against young Black men and boys is generally not protested but justified in some way. During an invasion of the favela, Captain Nascimento orders the beating and near suffocation of a Black boy, a probable "lookout" for the drug lord, to try to get information. They let him go and he is later killed by the drug gang leaders. Later, the mother confronts Captain Nascimento about the death of her son. In voiceover, we hear Captain Nascimento confess to knowing that letting the boy go would probably lead to his death. But his revelation to viewers serves more as a private confession that seeks compassion for his actions in the pursuit of obtaining an allegedly greater good (urban safety). It also functions to normalize extrajudicial violence as a response to urban insecurity. In his work on the Mexican film *Amores perros* (Alejandro González Iñárritu, 2000), Sánchez Prado (2006, 46–48) observes how violence in the film validates specific social and political perspectives and becomes therapeutic for the middle class. A similar process takes place in *Tropa de elite*. The torture scene of the boy follows a scene in which viewers see Captain Nascimento momentarily paralyzed by anxiety as they enter the favela. Waging violence against an assumed enemy serves as a therapeutic outlet for Nascimento's fear and frustration.

Just as *Tropa de elite* sustains racial and class hierarchies, it also upholds a middle-class point of view and traditional White masculinity. Despite the deaths of Black men, White middle-class victimhood prevails in the film. Captain Nascimento embodies the generalized anxieties and perspective of the urban middle-class spectator whose intimate and public social structures are under threat by urban insecurity. In his introduction to viewers, Nascimento expresses that he is growing tired of going into favelas, and in a subsequent scene, he speaks with his wife, who is pregnant with their first child. Both the job stress and his family status prompt Nascimento to retire from his position. Urban insecurity is thus not a broadly shared problem but one that is framed as an attack on the White, heteronormative family.

If violence can be conceptualized as therapeutic and justified, it is also celebrated. Training scenes for the BOPE and new recruits are particularly important in this instance. Indeed, extended scenes of military-style training constitute a significant portion of the film's narrative. Besides the tests of physical strength and mental stamina, the training scenes are an induction process whereby successful participants are portrayed as honorable and respectable. These training scenes, which are a trope in action films, not only celebrate authoritarianism and militarized police action but also cultivate a desire for law-imposing heroes (Craine and Curti 2009, 6). These scenes contribute significantly to defining contemporary citizenship in Brazil not as enacted by voting or through deliberation but as combating an enemy. It is this perspective of citizenship as an antagonist of moral and political corruption that is continued in *Tropa 2*.

Confronting Corruption: *Tropa de elite 2—O inimigo agora é outro*

Whereas *Tropa de elite* presents the favelas of Rio as a general threat to middle-class society, *Tropa 2* broadens its focus from narcoviolence and police corruption to indict an entire political system that has benefited from the chaos presumably rooted in favelas. If *Tropa de elite* is notable for adapting a firsthand account of police corruption and becoming source material for secondary manifestations (in blogs, video games, and so forth), *Tropa 2* secures a spot in contemporary Brazilian film history for surpassing box office records and becoming the Brazilian film with the greatest number of spectators.[8] The film is also notable for being produced and distributed independently by Zazen, the production company led by José Padilha. As a director, it appears that Padilha has made drug trafficking and the exposure of official corruption a sort of niche. In addition to the *Tropa* films, he has directed the Netflix series *O mecanismo* (*The Mechanism*, 2018–2019), which focuses on the Petrobras scandal revealed in 2014.[9] He has also been the executive producer and directed several episodes of Netflix's *Narcos* (2015–2017),[10] starring Wagner Moura in the first two seasons as legendary Colombian drug lord Pablo Escobar.

The unique production, distribution, and exhibition history of *Tropa 2* is certainly important, but the film is particularly interesting in its apparent effort to resolve sociopolitical contradictions. Here, I wish to explore how the film reflects long-standing political beliefs regarding democratic practices in Brazil and its broader critique of political corruption. Thus, I address the conflicting political and economic logics surrounding the process to enfranchise the favelas. Although it is not possible to claim with any certainty the degree to which the film influenced political attitudes, *Tropa 2* is politically prescient and provides a map of political discontent before the street demonstrations of 2013 and eventual election of right-wing Jair Bolsonaro in 2018.

Tropa 2 was released at a time characterized by the state's escalation of investments in favelas with the ostensible goal of enfranchising these urban territories.[11] Not surprisingly, *Tropa 2* presents the favela as an "opportunity zone" for political and economic development, reflecting public policies of the period. In 2007, Brazil initiated the Programa de Aceleração do Crescimento (Growth Acceleration Program), which provided funds for major infrastructure works throughout the nation. In the first phase of the program, the city of Rio de Janeiro was allotted funds to develop four favela complexes,[12] which were strategically located near future sites for the World Cup and Olympic Games. As noted in chapter 4, the state of Rio de Janeiro launched a "pacification" program for the favelas, the Unidades de Polícia Pacificadora (Police Pacification Units, UPPs), in 2008 whereby elite military police forces initially occupied a favela and ousted drug factions. According to the program, once a territory was under control, military police forces remained stationed in the favelas and, in this way, asserted the arrival of the state in the favelas in order to include these territories in the broader urban and cultural landscape. Indeed, those favelas that were pacified became sites for new publicly and privately funded social programs and services. Both the Programa de Aceleração do Crescimento and the UPPs were central to Rio de Janeiro's city-branding strategies and were elements of the bids to host the World Cup and Olympics.

Mariana Cavalcanti (2007, 2015) has defined the process of increasing state investment in the favelas as "favela consolidation," which she also describes as the story of developing a consensus about the "favela issue." According to Cavalcanti (2015, 110), favela consolidation has been driven by a logic that violence, caused by drug factions, necessitates infrastructure improvements, which increases the social recognition and public visibility of favelas but also furthers stereotypes, unequal power relations, and the cultural "otherness" of the favelas. One consequence is that everyday life in the favelas develops at the intersection of competing agendas set by narcotraffickers, police—often violent and corrupt—and the state. It is this contradictory logic that the metaphor of the franchise helps address, especially in terms of apparent structures of inclusion that sustain economic and political hierarchies.

If in *Tropa de elite* control of the favela concerns public security and corrupt police, then *Tropa 2* further argues that securing the favelas concerns broader economic and political benefits. Various scenes show the favela as an economically profitable space—frequently for illicit advantage. Police debate whether to invade the favela to regain stolen arms (sold by corrupt police officers). Viewers see Rocha, a BOPE police officer, extort money from drug traffickers for their *mesada* (monthly bribe) to continue their dealings. Moments later, the voiceover of Nascimento reflects on Rocha and states that every favela is a powerful market of many items bought and sold.[13] Linked to Rocha, Nascimento's statement presents an obvious critique of his corruption, but interpreted more generally, the comment reflects on what could be possible if state interventions are implemented effectively and without illicit interruption. The "favela issue" that affects broad sectors of society could be potentially resolved. Similarly, various scenes also show the favela as a politically profitable space for corrupt politicians, who enter the favelas and practice classic populist strategies (holding parties, making promises) to secure votes.

In *Tropa de elite*, urban violence, a chronic source of anxiety for people of all classes in Brazil, plays a central role in threatening the structure of the middle-class family and challenges heteronormative White masculinity. *Tropa 2* is set nearly a decade later when Nascimento's nuclear family has become destructured following a divorce from his wife. His role as father and his heteronormative masculinity are further challenged by his ex-wife's new husband, a human rights activist named Diogo Fraga (Irandhir Santos). Nascimento's role as father and ability to raise his son to respect and admire him as a patriarchal figure are challenged by Fraga, who has likely influenced Rafa's opinion of his biological father, leading him to question his authority and moral standing. If the son represents the nation, then the future is caught between differing opinions and approaches to solving social problems.

Tropa 2 upholds an elitist or upper-middle-class point of view. As a mainstream, commercial film, this is largely unsurprising. What is of interest is how the film upholds long-standing political and social conflict under the guise of aiming for an improved society. The film establishes a moralist perspective on Brazil's current political landscape, which further contributes to ideological polarization. Fraga, a history professor, opens the film in a scene in which he provides a lecture on the current state of incarceration in Brazil. He notes that at the current rate, 90 percent of the Brazilian population will be in jail by the year 2081. In making this claim, Fraga fosters fears about violence and criminality and diagnoses the nation as being on the verge of an unprecedented social crisis. That is, he warns that the structure of Brazilian society is deeply flawed. His urgent warning is followed by scenes of a hostage standoff in a Brazilian prison, where Nascimento gives instructions to BOPE offers, including his successor Matias, to confront rioting prisoners in a high-security penitentiary. The opening sequences of *Tropa 2* reference a real incident in 1992 when military police invaded Carandiru Penitentiary in São Paulo, resulting in the death of over a hundred prisoners and condemnation from international human rights agencies. Fraga accuses Nascimento and Matias of human rights violations and, consequently, both men become persona non grata and must regain their status. In this way the narrative follows a trope in the action thriller whereby a hero must seek redemption following unjust treatment. This, in turn, prompts audiences to connect further with the hero and celebrate when he or she regains a position of authority.

The moralist discourse adopted by Fraga and Nascimento in later scenes takes on significance in light of the political moment when the film was released. Fernando Lattman-Weltman (2015) asserts that before the mass protests of June 2013, an ideological polarization had emerged that was similar to that found in the mid-twentieth century. This can be traced to the União Democrática Nacional (Democratic National Union), a political party supported by a conservative group that has been highly influential in the nation's political culture. Lattman-Weltman (34–37) explains that in the present day, *udenismo*[14] becomes manifest in the belief that Brazil's national problems are due to a lack of moral commitment. What is more, *udenista* ideas support a political perspective espousing three core beliefs: poor people do not know how to vote properly, they choose badly, and inappropriate people—often of lower social extraction (like Lula)—are elected to office and mismanage the nation (35–36). Ideas about citizenship began to shift with the election of Lula, whose policies promoted the inclusion and representation of previously marginalized groups. This presented a challenge to elites who held to the belief that the poor and undereducated do not possess the moral ability to vote or lead.

In effect, *Tropa 2* recalls the moralist discourse of the past and provides an elitist critique of politics, including scenes where poor favela residents are essentially bribed to vote for unethical politicians who continue a cycle of oppression, corruption, and urban violence. The story of corruption in *Tropa 2* calls for new leadership. Shortly after Nascimento and Matias are condemned for the incident at the prison, Matias confronts Nascimento regarding his new role in politics and what he is going to be able to change. Matias calls on Nascimento to be a leader, and his question reflects a broader sentiment that the nation has been suffering from a crisis in representation.

The struggle for Nascimento to regain favorable status with his family as well as professionally is part of the process of creating new leadership. His status as a hero is fully reaffirmed at the conclusion of the film when he participates in a Comissão Parlamentar de Inquérito (Parliamentary Investigative Commission, CPI) that is opened to investigate criminal activity in the state of Rio de Janeiro by elected officials. As he is a key witness to testify at the CPI, corrupt police and officials plot to assassinate him beforehand. However, he uncovers the plot and survives the attack, which links back to the opening sequences. At the CPI, Nascimento calls for the end of the military police in Rio de Janeiro and identifies an elected official, Deputy Fortunato, as a leader of one of the largest criminal organizations in the state. He further claims that the state government of Rio de Janeiro is involved in criminal activity, supporting and benefiting from the existence of the favelas. As the camera tracks back during the CPI to close the sequence, Nascimento expresses in voiceover that his goal was to reveal the truth. Yet we see more than the revelation of facts in the ending of *Tropa 2*. Drawing again on the concept of the franchise and how it prompts thinking about networked relationships, these final scenes exploit violence in the favelas as home to political corruption in an effort to call for a new political system.

The final scene of *Tropa 2* reveals a political narrative that seems particularly prescient in light of the impeachment of Dilma Rousseff in 2016 and imprisonment of Lula in 2018.[15] The final aerial shot of *Tropa 2* floats over the capital, Brasília, in a way that is often associated with how films have portrayed favelas perched on the hillsides of Rio de Janeiro. The use of the aerial shot in this instance marks a shift in geopolitical focus and the target of citizen outrage. That is, the final shot offers a cartography of crime and further maps political discontent. Whereas viewers of *Tropa de elite* were encouraged to take sides against urban violence—with the film variously pointing fingers at favelas, drug traffickers, and favela residents generally or corrupt police officers who exacerbate urban insecurity—*Tropa 2* clearly identifies the federal government as being ultimately responsible. Accompanying the aerial shot, the voiceover of the heroic Nascimento offers an integral accusation of current politics as being corrupt, allowing the favelas to be sites of criminality, supporting violence, urban insecurity, and fraud. The film departs from the favela as an "issue" and offers the idea that a military-trained, morally superior leader is needed to solve the problem of corruption that is rooted in the favela. The ending presents the idea that an entire social network needs to be dismantled and purged of corruption. The favela is a branded space that is brought into a political network. There is little effort to seek equitable inclusion here. Rather, sociopolitical profits are directed toward the middle class.

Just after Nascimento threatens that more innocent people will die before this situation changes, there is a cut to his son Rafa in the hospital. In a way that resembles the ending of Lúcia Murat's *Quase dois irmãos* (2004), viewers once again see a young, White member of the upper-middle class as a victim of violence.[16] Viewers are directed to feel more for this character than for the tortured or deceased Black male bodies seen in less contextualized, less narrated visuals in other sequences of the film. Violence again serves as a socioeconomic code to uphold class hierarchies and the network of corruption makes White, middle-class youths innocent victims.

If the film closes as a narrative of good versus evil actors with Nascimento rising to a position of moral authority, the film opens with the disclaimer that despite possible coincidences with reality, the film is a work of fiction.[17] In effect, the film establishes a number of connections with ongoing ideological divisions and appears to capture sentiments of the political landscape that would unfold a few years after the film's release. The June Days of 2013, when citizens took to the streets motivated by different interests and protesting various causes, marked the beginning of the end of the branding period. Political discontent and desire for a truly new Brazil had been planted years earlier. An apparent crisis in representation set in motion the search for a moralistic, antipolitical hero—who appeared years later in the form of Jair Bolsonaro. In the *Tropa* films, the favela serves as a departure point for thinking about political corruption and the argument that the entire network of society is flawed. The potential for a peaceful, civil society was thwarted by corruption that rallied broad sectors of society, who had believed in the promises of progress and the nation's potential as an important emerging nation on the global stage.

Counterpoints to Politico-economic Inclusion in *5x pacificação*

Both *Tropa de elite* and *Tropa 2* present the favela as a site for competing control of political and economic benefits. The favela issue is reiterated as a central problem of Brazilian society, and the arrival of the state, portrayed in both films, can be linked to long-standing political divisions but also the promotion of Rio de Janeiro as an Olympic city and site for international tourists. Spectacular violence connects with preexisting beliefs about the favela and makes the urban space a consumable location.

Reflecting on the spectacular and hyperreal representation of favela violence, Robb Larkins (2015, 84) observes an imbalance in that these portrayals often distort and simplify the lives of people who are rarely given the opportunity to represent themselves. The documentary film *5x pacificação* provides a unique counterpoint to understanding the position of the favela in Brazilian society and the impact of the state's investment in (ostensibly) integrating these urban spaces. The multidirector documentary by young men from the favelas reveals the contradictions involved in the state's investment in these communities. The metaphor of the franchise again allows for discussing the key counterpoints raised in the documentary, especially with regard to intervening in the financial and political dynamic of the favela.

5x pacificação was directed by a team of filmmakers (Cadu Barcelos, Rodrigo Felha, Wagner Novais, and Luciano Vidigal) who are from the favelas they portray. Notably, the documentary was produced by Carlos Diegues, who also produced the film *5x favela—agora por nós mesmos* (*5x Favela, Now by Ourselves*, 2010), an episodic film written and directed by favela residents, including the directors who collaborated on the documentary *5x pacificação*. Both films refer to the Cinema Novo classic multidirector work *Cinco vezes favela* (*Favela Five Times*, 1962), which includes a segment Diegues directed. Although the favela and their experiences were the focus of the 1962 film, favela residents themselves were not the creators of their own representation. *5x pacificação* differs in that not only is it a documentary, but it is also structured as a dialogue among the directors, who in turn interview a broad range of residents of the favelas and other neighborhoods of Rio de Janeiro. In this way the documentary reflects on the pacification process and its impact on the culture, politics, and economic life of the favelas from multiple perspectives.

While they provide new employment opportunities, franchises are often criticized for also reducing the economic diversity of a community. Small, independently owned and operated businesses have difficulty competing with franchised businesses whose parent organizations provide extensive marketing. Similar concerns are raised in *5x pacificação* with regard to the loss of opportunities for some residents of the favelas with the entrance of the UPPs and efforts to develop their economies to capitalize on new consumers. In terms of "gains" experienced following the entrance of the UPPs, favela residents refer to how new businesses enter their communities offering new employment opportunities, where selling drugs had been one of few options previously. In terms of disadvantages, interviewed residents note the loss of cultural-economic diversity when the *bailes funk* (funk balls) were banned because of their frequent sponsorship by local drug lords. These (mostly) open-air dances had been an opportunity for vendors (of food and beverages) who now must find other ways to earn income. Whereas the *Tropa* films lend support to the idea of military-style control of the favelas, in *5x pacificação* interviewed residents of the favelas reveal that control (or pacification) has disrupted their economic opportunities.

The *Tropa* films build on the brand of the favela and cultivate a profitable relationship with this space to critique a political system. Conversely, *5x pacificação* reflects more fully on the potential for the creation of a new culture. The filmmakers gather around a table and talk about an "older" culture and a "new" culture forming that are closely related to past and present relationships with the police. Their discussion is balanced with comments from individuals interviewed in the streets who share their impressions that they have entered a new era. Residents refer to a historical distance between the police and the people, which characterizes a general lack of trust with agents of the state. One woman makes the connection between imposing order and achieving citizenship. For her, legality is an important first step toward inclusion as a citizen. That is, the arrival of the state (in the mode of the UPPs) reflects the possibility of sociopolitical integration.

Yet changing culture and the transformation of citizenship demand people change the way they think about themselves and their relationship to the broader urban sphere. Lefebvre (1991, 1996) has articulated that personal consciousness and urban development coincide. In his call for a theory that transcends representations of space, Lefebvre notes that sociopolitical contradictions are realized spatially. In an effort to resolve contradictions involved in how space is understood, he encourages thinking about how space is not only perceived and conceptualized but also experienced. Theoretical perspectives of Lefebvre find resonance in the social, political, and cultural activism developed in the favelas, of which *5x pacificação* is one example. Indeed, scholar and activist Jorge Luiz Barbosa (2013, 17) calls for recognition of the plurality of lived experiences, practices, and imaginaries to upend hierarchical patterns of representation, understanding, and control of the favelas.

Both *Tropa* films offer a view of citizenship as the claiming of rights, asserting a moral superiority of a central leader over a network of corruption. In contrast, *5x pacificação* advocates for the integration of disparate points of view. A more profound transformation of citizenship will take place by constructing and connecting different spaces through ongoing debate and exchange of ideas.

Rather than offer a top-down dismantling of what is ostensibly "wrong" with Brazilian society, the documentary suggests that the transformation of citizenship in contemporary Brazil can take place more effectively through deliberation. The filmmakers effectively include different points of view regarding the installation of UPPs and their impact on the political and economic structures of the favelas. They juxtapose interviews from people in different parts of the city and in this way contribute to greater social integration. The filmmakers thus assert that the favela is more than a site of struggle or a departure point for thinking about social ills. Rather, they reiterate the idea that urban spaces are a constellation of ideas and experiences within broader contradictory and conflicting dynamics.

Years after the *Tropa* films and several years after the last mega-event that took place in Brazil, the significance of the tone of both films is perhaps more readily captured. The idea of branding Brazil begins to take on less the meaning of promoting ideas about a new Brazil—in a regenerative or commercial sense—and the term's original meaning begins to appear: the scars on the surface of a political body. In one of the interviews included in *5x pacificação*, a man expresses his concerns that the UPPs appear to set the stage for a new era but that social transformation through police action would repeat the mistakes made during the era of the dictatorship.

Violence has returned to the favelas. In February 2018, the federal government ordered the army to take control of policing Rio de Janeiro. Critics warned that the move was authoritarian and could backfire, leading to more violent confrontation (Lessing 2018). The warning was accurate. The death of Marielle Franco in March 2018 at the hands of two police officers marked a watershed moment in the struggle to integrate the favelas and their residents in Brazilian society. Franco had symbolized the contemporary fight for citizenship in Brazil. Originally from Maré, a favela in the North Zone of Rio de Janeiro and home to several of the directors of *5x pacificação*, Franco earned college degrees, served as an elected official, and was an outspoken critic of the UPP program, police brutality, and extrajudicial violence. Her assassination was met with outrage by Brazilians and international condemnation. The moment appeared to mark the erosion of democracy and an end to the promise of progress. Yet demands to develop a new culture that integrates people from diverse backgrounds will certainly continue.

6

Another Good Neighbor?

■ ■

U.S.-Brazil Relations Revisited
On-Screen

Historically, U.S.-Brazil relations have not been entirely productive or equitable. Despite the fact that both are geographically large and populous nations with diverse international commercial ties, the United States and Brazil diverge consistently on policy decisions (Hakim 2015). Culturally, the United States and Brazil have had greater mutual allure. (Brazil has been a site of interest for Europeans as well.) As discussed in chapter 1, cultural policies sought to reshape understanding of Brazil on an international stage and assert new global citizenship in part through its culture. Cultivation of a "new Brazil" was undertaken through the development of international mega-events as well as promotion of Brazilian culture in the arts, especially film.

However, Brazil's new efforts to assert itself as a "serious country" were up against a history of unflattering representation and cultural exchanges during the twentieth century.[1] That is, Brazil had an international brand to counter that foreign films had already shaped significantly. As noted in the introduction, Brazil has been presented to the world in Hollywood (and European) films from the silent screen to the studio-era musicals of Busby Berkeley as a place where bandits could hide and erotic passions could be excited below the equator. In the 1960s, the rhythms of bossa nova populated the airwaves before the image of Brazil largely faded from the North American and European radar, which became concerned more with Cold War strategies and threats of nuclear war.

During the period in question, Brazil reentered North American consumer consciousness. This most recent phase evidenced a return to tropical motifs and exotic sensuality. Late-night television infomercials sold DVDs of exercise routines to help attain the ideal "Brazilian butt lift," after which viewers could quench their thirst with a panoply of new *açaí*-based juice beverages or coconut water. Courageous individuals could grimace as they underwent a formidable and comprehensive Brazilian waxing—unless it was under threat of being banned in their community. And to achieve a polished complexion, the curious could apply foundation made from Amazonian clay.

The period addressed in this book is characterized by the celebration of Brazil becoming a global power and the possibility of a more multipolar world. Yet this shifting global landscape presented a contradiction—if not a threat—to established North-South relations. This chapter addresses the discursive practice of branding in terms of resolving contradictions. The new Brazil was at odds with existing narratives about the nation, especially in foreign films. I address the negotiation of new and old ideas about Brazil in selected Hollywood films that portray U.S.-Brazil relations, including the animated features *Rio* (2011) and *Rio 2* (2014), directed by Carlos Saldanha, as well as the action-packed dramas *The Incredible Hulk* (Louis Leterrier, 2008) and *Fast Five* (Justin Lin, 2011). There is a long history linking the United States and Brazil through film in an effort to intervene in perceptions about the politics and cultures of each nation. During the Good Neighbor era (1933–1945), discussed further shortly, Hollywood films were set in Latin America or included Latin American talent who shared the screen with U.S. actors. If films in the past were part of a larger effort to protect access to resources and markets during World War II, in the present these films capitalize on new audiences and Brazilian cultural identity as a commodity.

Despite differences between the animated films and the action-adventure films, these works replay several tropes found in prior Hollywood (and European) productions. On the one hand, one finds Good Neighbor–era tropes of sexual freedom and amorous liaisons in *Rio* and *Rio 2*. On the other hand, longstanding tropes of Brazil as a place of lawlessness and a refuge for outlaws are repeated in *The Incredible Hulk* and *Fast Five*. While *Rio* and *Rio 2* present slightly more progressive views of Brazil and offer a view of global citizenship, the general repetition of tropes from past Hollywood productions reveals an unwillingness to accept a changing geopolitical landscape.

As outlined in the introduction, renewed interest in Brazil was triggered by global economic forecasting that categorized Brazil as an emerging economy and BRIC nation, which effectively engaged in branding Brazil as a place of economic opportunity. Place-branding expert Simon Anholt (2006) asserts that countries (as well as cities and regions) behave like brands. Similar to goods or services, countries are associated with particular qualities and characteristics. But unlike products, a nation's brand is linked to powers of perception to shape international trade and policy agreements. Anholt further states, "The image of a country determines the way the world sees it and treats it" (105). More than this, brands tell stories, and the branding of a place involves developing narratives about cultural practices, people, and their interpersonal (and international) relationships.

Cinema has played a key role in place branding. Just as Hollywood has been at the heart of creating "Brand America," international cinema has been actively engaged in creating "Brand Brazil" for decades. Whereas quick associations can be made between products and several European nations (Italian fashion, German automobiles, French perfumes, and so forth), there are no recognizable brands or services associated with Brazil. That said, "Brazil"—writ large—is Brazil's biggest, most important international brand and its image has been circulated extensively in the cinema. Film scholar Tunico Amancio (2000) observes that there are hundreds of films from numerous countries across the globe—Iran, Germany, Spain, the United States, and others—in which Brazil appears as a central character. On the eve of several mega-events (the World Cup 2014 and Olympics 2016), film crews were not slowing down as they worked on feature-length and documentary films representing Brazil and its culture. For example, *Fast Five* and *Rio* were among over eighty foreign productions (including movies, television shows, and commercials) that were filmed in Rio de Janeiro in 2011 alone (Oliveira 2012).[2]

(Let's Not) Blame It on Rio

In her study of how Brazil has been imagined throughout its history, Darlene Sadlier (2008, 4) notes that Brazilian national identity has been influenced by the cultures and the politics of other nations, especially France and the United States. Of particular interest are the years of the Good Neighbor Policy (1933–1945) against the backdrop of World War II, when the United States developed cultural policies toward Latin America that constituted, according to Sadlier, "one of the most intensive and developed uses of 'soft power' in U.S. history" (2). Brazilian audiences are quite familiar with foreign (mis)representations of their country. In her documentary film *Olhar estrangeiro* (*The Foreign Eye*, 2006), Lúcia Murat explores ideas about Brazil that have been circulated by international media, primarily foreign film crews that have set their narratives against the backdrop of Brazil without, generally speaking, knowing much at all about its history, its geography, or its people. Murat's documentary includes candid interviews with directors, producers, scriptwriters, and actors involved in some of these cliché-laden films about Brazil in which they sheepishly admit either a general ignorance of Brazil or that their stories about Brazil had little to do with the nation. You could blame it on Rio or blame it on colonialist exoticism, but it was an imaginary of Brazil that they were more interested in. Generally, when foreign films have needed a place that was sensual, tropical, and outside European or U.S. law, Brazil was the place to go.[3]

Indeed, Hollywood cinema has a complicated history of representing Brazil that started in the silent era, became pivotal in transnational politics in the 1930s and 1940s, and continues to the present day. A number of studies have examined Hollywood's depiction of Latin America, noting recurrent motifs such as the barbarous jungles of Brazil, lawless bandits, and "cutthroat savages" (especially during the silent era). For its part, the city of Rio de Janeiro has been constituted as a locus of exotic natural beauty whose magical charm inspires ruffians and skilled seductresses alike. Surveying films from the first half of the twentieth century, film scholars Lisa Shaw and Maite Conde assert that the city of Rio de Janeiro was conceptualized in Hollywood cinema as "a place where sexual license and transgression were virtually inevitable" (2005, 183).

During the era of the Good Neighbor Policy under the Franklin Delano Roosevelt administration, film became a vital tool for linking the United States to Latin America. Since European markets were effectively closed to trade, film sought to form a cultural-political-economic bridge to Latin American markets and cheap commodities. Given that Hollywood films have been a key export for the United States (which became all too clear during the General Agreement on Tariffs and Trade talks in the early 1990s),[4] Hollywood was also looking for an audience. During the 1930s and 1940s, musical extravaganzas were major box office earners and actress Carmen Miranda, in the role of pan–Latin American woman, starred in numerous films, including features such as *That Night in Rio* (Irving Cummings, 1941), *Week-end in Havana* (Walter Lang, 1941), *The Gang's All Here* (Busby Berkeley, 1943), and *Nancy Goes to Rio* (Robert Leonard, 1950). Despite efforts to involve local authorities, these films are riddled with ethnic and linguistic blunders. Alongside musical feature films, animated film constituted part of the Good Neighbor agenda. Walt Disney's *Saludos Amigos* (1942) features Donald Duck on a Latin American tour of discovery, and in *The Three Caballeros* (1944) Donald Duck teams up with his bird friends José (Zé) Carioca (a parrot) and Panchito Pistoles (a rooster) to visit Brazil and Mexico. Both films are structured to combine cartoon fantasy with apparent ethnographic material in live-action and documentary-style segments.

Fast-forward fifty years and we find that Hollywood has returned its gaze to Brazil.[5] This time, the motivating force is less utopic concerns with pan-Americanism and more economic opportunism. (However, economic opportunism also clearly drove Roosevelt's Pan-American agenda.) Journalist Andrew

Stewart (2011), writing in *Variety*, notes that worldwide box office grosses rose for a second straight year in 2010 but the increase was not due exclusively to 3-D megapictures (e.g., *Avatar*, *Toy Story 3*, *Alice in Wonderland*). Rather, the significant growth in box office receipts is attributed to the BRIC countries (Brazil, Russia, India, and China), the top box office territories of 2010. Stewart further notes that, in the specific case of Brazil, one finds a 30 percent increase in box office receipts and a 20 percent increase in attendance, the nation's best box office numbers since 1981. The rise in both attendance numbers and ticket sales can be attributed to the growth of a middle class with more disposable income during the Lula administration (2003–2010). According to the Agência Nacional de Cinema (Brazilian Film Agency, ANCINE), the final box office numbers of 2011 established new records, making Brazil one of the most important global film markets (ANCINCE 2011, 2). This upward trajectory has generally continued, with a slight decrease in spectatorship in 2018 relative to previous years (ANCINE 2019, 12–13).

Brazil has done its best to lure Hollywood. As discussed in chapter 1, cultural policies and programs were designed to welcome international productions. For its part, Hollywood has prepared to take advantage of these shifts. In June 2012, the international arms of Fox and Warner announced they were joining their operations in Brazil, where they would remain separate entities but share resources toward a common goal of cultivating new opportunities. Warner Bros. Pictures International president Veronika Kwan Vandenberg added in a company press release that the initiative aimed to "meet the demands of the rapidly growing Brazilian market" (Time Warner 2012). This venture repeats other recent partnerships in the Brazilian market between Disney and Sony, Paramount and Universal, and Fox and Sony (FilmeB 2012). Hollywood interest in Brazil (and filming in Rio especially) earned the city the nickname "Riollywood" by industry journalist Daniel Oliveira (2012). The film industry newspaper *Variety* has responded to these trends, publishing articles on how to film in Latin America (Newbery, Cajueiro, and Fuente 2012), as well as sponsoring conferences for industry professionals on producing in the BRIC economies.[6] The films discussed here participated in Hollywood trends at the time to seek audiences in Brazil as well as capitalize on international interest in the nation.

Flying Down to Rio (Again): *Rio* and *Rio 2*

Animated films, which have long been transnational, follow trends similar to live-action works. While action-adventure films (discussed later) were heading to Brazil, all U.S.-backed studio animated features from 2011, with the exception of *Rango*, took place abroad (Blair 2011, 17). *Rio* flew to Brazil. *Cars 2* made pit stops in Tokyo, Paris, London, and Italy. *Kung Fu Panda 2* celebrated

Chinese culture and art. And *Puss in Boots* offered a romanticized version of Spain. These choices of setting undoubtedly sought to capture a share of international box office revenues. The effort seemed to bring results. The animated feature *Rio*, directed by the U.S.-based Brazilian Carlos Saldanha and produced by Blue Sky, was the second-most-seen film in Brazil that year, just behind *The Twilight Saga: Breaking Dawn—Part 1* (Bill Condon, 2011), which was also filmed partly in Brazil (ANCINE 2011, 6). Worldwide, *Rio* was the tenth-highest box office earner in 2011 (Padala 2012). In addition to mainstream exhibition venues in Brazil, *Rio* was also included in the Cine Tela Brasil program for 2012, a project launched by filmmakers Laís Bodanzky and Luiz Bolognesi that sets up mobile cinemas in parks and plazas near low-income communities and provides screenings of Brazilian films free of charge.[7] Also outside mainstream channels, copies of the film *Rio* were for sale by street venders in the city's center and in favela communities, indicating its widespread appeal.

Given that animated features may be dubbed in multiple languages, they travel more easily between countries than live-action films. So do birds. The figure of the bird was central in Disney's animated films *Saludos Amigos* and *The Three Caballeros* perhaps because the animal is (relatively) untethered to geopolitical regions and seems to embrace transnational flows.[8] A bird protagonist returns in *Rio* and puts Brazil back on the silver screen. But whereas Disney's 1940s films were primarily designed for a domestic audience and played an important role in introducing Latin America generally to the United States (and elsewhere), Saldanha's *Rio* aims to strike a balance between local and global expectations. As it offers up an image of Brazil and its culture for new generations, the film manages to present modestly more progressive representations of gender but falls short with regard to its representation of race, ethnicity, and class.

Rio narrates the story of Blu (Jesse Eisenberg), a blue macaw who is captured at an early age and taken to the United States, where he is found by Linda (Leslie Mann), a young girl living in Minnesota. An introductory montage sequence of scrapbook-style photos shows how Linda and Blu have grown up together and bonded. They live a peaceful existence in snowy Minnesota until one day when Túlio (Rodrigo Santoro), an ornithologist from Brazil, arrives at Linda's bookstore and urges her to take Blu back to Brazil to mate with the last female blue macaw and save the species. Linda initially refuses Túlio's entreaties to take Blu to Brazil, but she relents when she acknowledges her environmental responsibilities. Shortly after they land in Rio de Janeiro, Blu is abducted by bird smugglers (Marcel, Tipa, and Armando) and the action-adventure to rescue Blu ensues. Along the way, Blu confronts a local crime syndicate of monkeys and marmosets and meets local birds Pedro (will.i.am), Nico (Jamie Foxx), and Rafael (George Lopez) and their bulldog friend Luiz (Tracy Morgan).

The film's one-word title boldly asserts that it aims to present a place. Taking into account the likely youth of the audiences watching the movie, the film establishes cultural identities in simple, dichotomous terms. In other words, identities are constructed largely by following a basic semiotic equation that one's identity can be defined by difference from an *other*. This is evident in the early minutes of the film. The opening sequence, in which colorful birds frolic and twirl through a tropical forest singing joyfully about Rio, abruptly ends when a young blue macaw is captured and tossed in the back of a plane. (It is suggested but never confirmed that Blu had been smuggled to the United States.) Next, there is a cut to a snow-covered landscape with dreary, gray skies where a small brown bird sits immobile and alone on a fence post. White intertitles state in parentheses "(not Rio)" to dispel any doubts and confirm that this space is no longer in Brazil.

In addition to cultural binaries, the film *Rio* repeats a number of other tropes found in Good Neighbor–era films, beginning with the displacement of one or more characters from the United States to Brazil. Like the film *Week-end in Havana*, *Rio* sends its middle-class, straitlaced female protagonist on a trip to the tropics.[9] Once in Rio, Linda's experience fulfills gendered expectations of the North American tourist to Brazil. Actress Mary Kornman famously and enviously asked in the 1933 film *Flying Down to Rio*, "What have these South Americans got below the equator that we haven't?" If we consider this and other films, the answer might be: Carnaval. Linda, who is escorting Blu to the nature center where he will be introduced to Jewel, the last female bird of his species, arrives days before Carnaval celebrations begin. Following a "fish-out-of-water" narrative and sustaining stereotypical expectations of a White, middle-class, midwestern woman from the United States, she reacts prudishly to scantily clad Brazilian women. As an unattached, single female who dislikes leaving her home, Linda seems to present her own threat to the survival of the human species. Fortunately, all she needs is a little time below the equator to bring out her sensuality. In an effort to go incognito and to rescue Blu and Jewel from bird smugglers, she dons a spectacular Carnaval costume, which, notably, incites the passions of Túlio when he sees her. In one significant misstep, Linda then finds herself in full Carnaval gear atop a float heading through the Sambódromo. The humor draws on her not knowing what to do and being well outside her comfort zone. The other female figure in this film, the blue macaw named Jewel (Anne Hathaway), is a savvy and independent bird and her primary goal is seeking and celebrating her freedom. That said, her character repeats the traits assigned Latin American actresses in Hollywood films—she is the street-smart, spitfire Latina woman, recalling roles previously played by Lupe Vélez and Carmen Miranda (Berg 2002, 70–75).

Whereas the female characters in *Rio* follow some established traits, the male characters see some innovation. Neither Blu nor Túlio is presented as a hypermasculine, Latin lover. On the contrary, both display a social awkwardness that is linked to being logical and scientifically oriented. What is more, they are both funny characters but they are not buffoons, another common stereotypical role historically assigned to Latin males in Hollywood films (Berg 2002, 71–72). Túlio's physical clumsiness may draw laughter, but he is a biologist dedicated to the protection of wildlife and Brazil's endangered species, a role that plays into Brazil's developing image as a nation investing in technology and deeply concerned with sustainable development. In 1992 and 2012, Rio de Janeiro hosted the U.N.-sponsored summit on the environment. Both the Lula and Rousseff administrations aimed to improve education and development specifically in the areas of science and technology partly as a response to developments in the energy sector (e.g., the discovery of large oil reserves in Brazil) and to better position the nation as a global political and economic leader.[10]

Similar to films from the past, *Rio* falls short in offering a progressive representation of race, ethnicity, and class. For the English-language version of *Rio*, a multiracial, multiethnic, and multicultural cast lends their voices to the animated figures. For instance, George Lopez, of Mexican heritage, voiced the toucan character Rafael. African American artist will.i.am voiced the character Pedro and Jamie Foxx performed as the character Nico. However, as found in past films, non-Brazilian talent played key roles in the film. Of the main characters, only one was voiced by a native Brazilian, Rodrigo Santoro, in the role of Túlio.

The diversity of the voiceover cast did not translate into a balanced representation of non-Anglo characters. Whereas the lead "human" characters, Túlio and Linda, are fair-skinned, educated, articulate, and on the side of justice, other "human" characters, especially the bird smugglers (Marcel, Tipa, and Armando), are darker-skinned, reside in favelas, engage in illegal activities, and are depicted as irresponsible or incompetent. Notably, Marcel, the leader of the bird-smuggling ring, is given short dreadlocks, gold earrings, a stylish beard, and sunglasses that associate him with Afro-Brazilian urban, hip-hop culture.

In these representations, *Rio* coincides with cinematic predecessors in which darker-skinned Latin Americans have been portrayed as poor, uneducated, and prone to criminality. Initially, the orphaned boy Fernando, who assists Marcel in capturing Blu and Jewel, repeats this trope before his sense of right and wrong urges him to help rescue the birds. In this, the film makes an important gesture to decriminalize young Afro-Brazilian males. Not only is Fernando ultimately presented as a moral character, but he is also humanized as an adopted child of a heteronormative couple. Standing as a newly formed family unit, Túlio, Linda, and Fernando look off into the air as Blu flies off with Jewel and their offspring to a bird sanctuary. This final scene is important in several ways. The multiracial, multiethnic family unit promotes a sense of racial democracy

FIG. 6.1 Túlio, Linda, and Fernando in *Rio*.

in Brazil, which has been questioned for some time but remains a utopic ideal for some (see figure 6.1). Second, the ending suggests that Linda has relocated to Rio de Janeiro so Blu can live in his natural environment. Rio de Janeiro is characterized as a stable place where you can have a good life. It is not just a place to visit on vacation or a city people emigrate from to find better lives elsewhere. Rio is still, however, a place for romance. Whereas in the past White, Anglo-American characters would have brief amorous liaisons with Latin characters, here the love comes to fruition and interethnic, cross-cultural romance flourishes.

Global Citizenship and the Environment in *Rio 2*

The story of romance continues in *Rio 2*. The sequel by Saldanha and his Blue Sky Productions was released a few months before the opening of the 2014 World Cup hosted in Brazil at a time when the nation's outlook was particularly sour.[11] Public criticism questioned the intense investment required to build stadiums to FIFA standards while schools and hospitals were in dire need of upgrades and materials. And just days before the film's release, news broke of a major corruption scandal with the nation's oil company Petrobras.[12] Saldanha's animated sequel is, thus, a colorful, bright work at this historical juncture. Similar to *Rio* and previous animated films by Disney in the 1940s, Saldanha's sequel did not just lift spirits. It helped promote tourism to Rio de Janeiro and Brazil generally (W. Nogueira and Lopes 2017). Whereas *Rio* sets its narrative partly in the city's favela and portrays urban poverty, *Rio 2* furthers other aspects of Brazil's "brand story" as a nation with remarkably beautiful natural landscapes, resources, and "exotic" appeal.

    Rio 2 returns to the Cidade Maravilhosa (Marvelous City)[13] on New Year's Eve and the beach of Copacabana, where celebrants dressed in all white pay homage to the candomblé goddess Iemanjá by offering flowers to the sea.[14] This opening sequence repeats an understanding of Rio de Janeiro as a festive location for visitors. New Year's Eve on Copacabana Beach is second only to Carnaval—represented in *Rio*—for drawing international tourists to Brazil. Among the revelers, viewers are reintroduced to Blu and Jewel, who are now parents to three adolescent offspring. Whereas *Rio* develops a romantic comedy around the adventures of an American woman and her pet bird Blu in Brazil, *Rio 2* focuses further on global citizenship, defined broadly as an understanding that individuals are members of a world community with responsibilities that extend beyond a particular nation or place. In the case of *Rio 2*, questions of global citizenship concern the country's natural beauty, which is portrayed as needing protection while simultaneously offering entertainment and adventure.

The romance also continues with Túlio and Linda, whose reintroduction to viewers finds them on a boat navigating into the Amazon to release a bird from the sanctuary they manage. There, they identify another blue macaw (like Blu) that is understood as an endangered species. Back in Rio de Janeiro, Jewel sees Túlio's announcement of the discovery on television and is inspired to go to the Amazon to connect with other birds of her own species. Reluctantly, Blu agrees to take the family into the "wilderness" on an adventure that follows the tropes of the road trip genre. Seeming to reiterate a scene with Donald Duck from *Saludos Amigos* where the American bird explores the map of South America to discover new lands and friends, the journey of the blue macaws crisscrosses the map of the country, passing through the important cities of Salvador and Manaus, which were coincidentally also destinations for the World Cup matches. In the rainforest, Blu and Jewel serendipitously reconnect with Jewel's parents and her childhood flock. Thus begins a meet-the-parents narrative where the macho, antihuman, rural values of Jewel's father, Eduardo, contrast with Blu's metrosexual identity, slight hypochondria, and preference for human comforts (fanny pack, Swiss army knife, GPS navigation). Eduardo reveals that illegal logging has destroyed their habitat, they are forced to share their grove with a flock of red macaws, and they have struggled to find food—specifically, Brazil nuts. Thus, the macaws' struggle for survival can be read as a threat to Brazilian identity itself given that their food source comes from a tree associated with the nation.

The survival of the blue macaws is further challenged by tribalism between bird communities. Hoping to please his wife and win back her affections, Blu sets off into the forest one morning in search of Brazil nuts, Jewel's preferred breakfast. While he inexpertly tries to cut a nut from the tree, representatives of the rival red macaw flock find him and challenge him to a "duel"—a game strikingly similar to soccer using Brazil nuts in lieu of a ball—to determine who will control the section of rainforest they all desperately need. Blu accidentally scores an own goal, resulting in the loss of the blue macaws' territory.

Yet the film underscores that rival factions (like those in nations, communities, tribes, or flocks of birds) misidentify the source of real conflict. It is not soccer that will determine their fate but the impending destruction of the rainforest by corrupt industrialists. Thus, the film continues the theme of Brazil's natural resources being threatened by corrupt agents, which in *Rio* revolved around smuggled birds and in *Rio 2* concerns massive deforestation. Viewers connect with the plight of the birds, who provide an intimate perspective on trees falling, illegal loggers bulldozing vast areas, and the logging ringleader who openly touts that his practices are illegal. In addition to its advanced computer graphics, colorful characters, and kaleidoscopic sequences set to international music hits, *Rio 2* offers a serious message about global citizenship, economic development, and the environment. Brazil's natural resources have been celebrated in documents since the colonial period. And the (inter)national temptation to pillage that wealth has been historic. With growing concerns about environmental degradation and climate change (brought about significantly by developed nations' [ab]use of fossil fuels), the Amazon rainforest is frequently portrayed metaphorically as the world's lungs. Responsibility as global citizens has been portrayed less as reducing the use of fossil fuels in the North and more as advocating for global ownership and responsibility for this territory and the autonomy of Brazilian governments.

Several years after the release of *Rio 2*, the image of destruction of the rainforest is not an animated fantasy. Since the beginning of the Bolsonaro administration in January 2019, the rate of deforestation has increased dramatically as regulations have been eased or overlooked and miners and loggers encroach on protected lands and pillage the rainforest for its natural resources (Moriyama and Sandy 2019). In retrospect, *Rio 2* offers a warning about the global commodities trade and a veiled warning about the consequences of unchecked neoliberal development at this time.

Global Franchising and Action Thrillers: *The Incredible Hulk* and *Fast Five*

Film scholar Tunico Amancio (2000, 11–13) notes that the most common representations of Brazil in foreign films are of celebrations of the natural landscape and of Brazil as a place for those outside the law. What is more, nature is often presented as savage. This is certainly evident in *Rio*, where monkeys and marmosets steal tourists' wallets, watches, cell phones, and cameras, suggesting that danger and crime are an inherent part of the landscape. As discussed in chapter 5, a number of films from Brazil with wide international distribution—*Cidade de Deus* (2002) and *Tropa de elite* (2007) to name just two—have contributed to an Eros-Thanatos push-pull representation of Rio de Janeiro as simultaneously beautiful and dangerous and have stimulated curiosity for Rio's favelas. One finds a similar equation in recent films from Hollywood such as *Turistas* (John Stockwell, 2006) and *The Twilight Saga: Breaking Dawn, Part 1* (2011). European filmmakers are apparently not immune from the dangerous beauty that Brazil seems to present, as evidenced in the 2009 film *OSS 117: Rio ne répond plus* (*OSS 117: Lost in Rio*), a French parody of James Bond films by actor-director Michel Hazanavicius. These and other films have represented Rio de Janeiro's unique geographic landscape of rising granite mountains, sandy beaches, and peaceful Guanabara Bay. On July 1, 2012, UNESCO declared Rio de Janeiro's landscape a World Heritage site (Paris 2012), solidifying what filmmakers for over a century have already suggested (problematically)—that this space belongs to all of humanity.

If one revisits the history of Hollywood (and European) action-thriller films, it seems inevitable that the high-octane *Fast* series or *The Incredible Hulk* (part of the Marvel Cinematic Universe) would make their way to Brazil. This is not only because of efforts waged by Brazilian film agencies and cultural policies (discussed in chapter 1) to make Rio de Janeiro an audiovisual capital of Latin America. Indeed, numerous action-crime thrillers have historically landed in Brazil, a place to escape international authorities, perhaps because of its lack of extradition treaties with countries in Europe and the United States. In Alfred Hitchcock's *Notorious* (1946), Ingrid Bergman and Cary Grant chase Nazi exiles in Rio de Janeiro. In the British film *Moonraker* (Lewis Gilbert, 1979), Roger Moore as James Bond famously thwarts an outer-space plot and saves the world from mass genocide. In his quest, Bond crisscrosses the globe from the canals of Venice to NASA's Cape Canaveral and through the Amazon jungle, and he then spends a significant time fighting evil against the backdrop of Rio de Janeiro.

In the discussion that follows, I consider *The Incredible Hulk* and *Fast Five*, action-adventure films set in Brazil and partly in the favelas of Rio de Janeiro. Both recall tropes from past portrayals of Brazil, which contradicts efforts to present a new Brazil. In this regard, nation-branding expert Anholt (2006, 117) asserts that a nation's brand is difficult to change and the best that managers of a nation brand can hope for is to accentuate the positive and downplay the negative in a country's external communications. The representation of Brazil in both films reveals an ongoing negotiation of U.S.-Brazil relations against the backdrop of shifting North-South relations.

While stereotypes and clichés abound in a good number of films that represent favela communities and Brazil more generally, it is not just the inaccuracies that are of interest but also the relationships of power that a film like *Fast Five* communicates. In other words, it is important to explore what it means to represent the favela and take up this space in terms of what it represents to Brazilians, as well as what it represents for those outside the circle of the

emerging economies. Just as Jim O'Neill (O'Neill et al. 2005) famously celebrated Brazil as an emerging BRIC nation and new global power, additional
global economic forecasting called for a shift in global economic policymak-
ing. At this historic juncture, North-South hierarchies were questioned and
the balance of global power appeared to be shifting. In chapter 5, I discussed
how the favela was taken up in contemporary Brazilian films as a space to negotiate contradictions in Brazilian society related to socioeconomic inclusion
and discontent related to corruption. Brazilian productions deployed spectacular violence as a way to critique corruption and presumably enfranchise
the favelas as socioeconomically profitable spaces. Similarly, Hollywood was
(once again) drawn to preexisting narratives of violence and criminality associated with Brazil's lower-income communities for its action-adventure films.
In Hollywood productions like *Fast Five* and *The Incredible Hulk*, the favela is
a setting that serves as a space to negotiate perceived threats to U.S. status as a
global power.

The Incredible Hulk

The Incredible Hulk is an important example of a trend to build on the illicit
allure of Brazil's favelas and deploy spectacular violence as a mode of branding
and governance. Action films like *The Incredible Hulk* tend to perform well
domestically and internationally. While the 2003 version of the Marvel character in *The Hulk*, directed by Ang Lee, was generally rejected by fans and
deemed a failure at the box office, the 2008 version, directed by Louis Leterrier,
earned approximately the same box office revenues worldwide but diverged in
terms of fan reviews posted to Rotten Tomatoes.[15] *The Incredible Hulk* and *Iron
Man* are the first films in the Marvel Cinematic Universe, the highest-grossing
film franchise in history.[16] Yet *The Incredible Hulk* fell short of *Iron Man*, which
quickly surpassed expectations (DiOrio 2008).

The Incredible Hulk opens with sequences that retell the origin story of the
superhero before cutting to a shot of Dr. Bruce Banner (Edward Norton) hiding in a dimly lit warehouse.[17] White intertitles indicate the number of days
he has gone without an episode (i.e., becoming angered and transforming into
the monstrous, green character). A second cut to an aerial shot floats over a
favela and white intertitles establish the location as "Rocinha Favela—Brazil."
However, the film was actually shot in the community of Tavares Bastos and
not Rocinha, one of Latin America's largest and Rio de Janeiro's most visible
and (in)famous favelas. The opening sequence is accompanied by a soundtrack
that combines a score common to action films (i.e., dramatic orchestra music),
police sirens (to characterize the space as a criminal hangout), and other sounds
to ensure spectators understand this space to be an underdeveloped location
(dogs barking, roosters crowing, children yelling in streets).

While few Brazilian characters with speaking parts appear in the film, numerous tropes of Brazil abound. Similar to the portrayal of the favela in *Fast Five* discussed later, *The Incredible Hulk* upholds the idea that the favela exists as a site of refuge for fugitives. In this instance, Bruce Banner hides out in Rocinha to escape U.S. military forces who pursue him. Legal jurisdictions aside, the U.S. military eventually invades the favela to find Banner, who escapes in daring chase scenes through narrow favela passageways and across rooftops as if an experienced parkour athlete.

If the favela is a hideout for criminals, Brazil also offers refuge in other senses. Portrayals of Brazil have suggested that the nation is a tropical paradise where Americans and Europeans could not just find adventure but also connect with nature and recover from the ills of industrial society. (Notably, *Rio 2* develops this get-back-to-nature narrative when Jewel wants to reconnect with other birds of her species.) The idea of Brazil as a place of natural refuge and recovery is underscored by the shot of Bruce Banner waking from an episode as the Hulk. Half-naked, exhausted, and lying on rocks at the foot of a waterfall (located in the National Park of Tijuca), Banner awakes as if in a garden of Eden where he is reborn as a defenseless human. In the next scene, he speaks in broken Portuguese to a man driving a truck, who responds in Spanish and informs him he has (miraculously) landed in Guatemala.

Brazil is also a setting that provides a potential source for a medicinal cure of the gamma illness that afflicts Bruce Banner and causes him to become the Hulk. Under the guidance of Mr. Blue, the code name of a scientist working in the United States who communicates over an encrypted network, Bruce locates a unique, presumably rare white flower that he uses as a base to prepare a potion to help cure him of his condition. In this way, the film positively characterizes Brazil as a location where plant medicines and potential cures may be found among its diverse flora. However, a man with indigenous features hands the package with the coveted white flower to Banner in a way that is suggestive of criminal behavior, as if dealing drugs on a street corner. What is beautiful and beneficial is framed as existing outside the bounds of legality and mainstream society.

The Incredible Hulk also sustains long-standing cultural, ethnic, and economic hierarchies. While immigrants to the United States or Europe are frequently portrayed as having few skills or working illegally in secret or on the margins of industrial operations, Bruce Banner has accepted a day laborer's position at a beverage bottling factory while he learns to control his anger with an aikido master. He is called on regularly by the plant manager to offer his engineering know-how to fix broken machinery that no other worker can repair, and the manager offers him a salaried position because he apparently demonstrates intelligence and talent. Thus, the film reiterates a stereotypical, hierarchical belief in American ingenuity and superior abilities relative to the presumed incompetence of so-called Third World producers.

This sense of supremacy translates into the portrayal of Brazilian exports. At the bottling factory, Banner cuts his finger fixing an electrical device that controls the conveyor belt. A drop of his blood falls into the greenish-yellow beverage—which is referred to as *guaraná*, a popular carbonated beverage in Brazil—and the contaminated bottle is packaged and put on a shipping pallet. A shot captures a shipping label clearly indicating the product will be sent from Brazil to the United States, where a man—Marvel Comics creator Stan Lee in a cameo appearance—later falls sick and dies of apparent gamma illness. In the past, Brazil-U.S. economic exchanges have been portrayed on-screen in terms of food exports from Brazil to the United States. Indeed, the opening sequences of *The Gang's All Here* (1943) famously portray Carmen Miranda as bringing with her coffee beans and fruit in exchange for North American good wishes. However, rather than importing fun and variety, Brazil's favorite soft drink in this instance causes a sci-fi illness and death.

In addition to members of the U.S. military, the American protagonist of *The Incredible Hulk* can freely roam the world. As found in other globe- or world-trotting superhero action films, Bruce Banner leaves Brazil (after an episode transforms him into the Hulk). As noted earlier, he awakes in Guatemala and walks to the state of Chiapas in Mexico. While trying to avoid the detection of authorities, Banner apparently walks across the landscape and returns to his home on the East Coast, partly following a route through Central America and Mexico that thousands of migrants have followed in recent years. Yet as a superhero scientist, he travels unimpeded. Requiring viewers to suspend disbelief, he obtains food, lodging, and clothing without any apparent credentials or money. Banner can apparently inhabit and travel through Latin America taking advantage of resources and opportunities as needed. The film eventually relocates to New York City and Toronto. *The Incredible Hulk* may have started in and departed from Brazil in this iteration of the comic series, but other films of the Marvel Cinematic Universe have returned to Brazil, including the 2018 films *Avengers: Infinity War* (Anthony Russo and Joe Russo) and *Black Panther* (Ryan Coogler) that, respectively, traveled to the Lençóis Maranhenses National Park (in the state of Maranhão) and Iguaçu Falls on the border between Brazil and Argentina.

Fast Five

The *Fast* franchise has similarly traversed the globe. Not coincidentally, the success of the *Fast* films has led it to locations where car cultures thrive. In addition to racing through the streets of Los Angeles and Miami, the cast and crew made their way to Japan (Tokyo), a country proud of its car manufacturing industry.[18] The fifth film in the series lands in Brazil, also a country with a strong auto industry and a culture that embraces auto racing,[19] and where the largest television network (TV Globo) regularly broadcasts Grand Prix auto racing events. In this respect, Brazil is a logical pit stop for the *Fast* franchise. Yet Brazil is also a prime location given that the film's multiethnic, multiracial cast finds a demographic parallel there. According to Mary Beltrán (2005, 50), the rise in "multiculti" Hollywood action films with multiracial and multiethnic casts (such as *The Fast and the Furious*) embodies contemporary shifts in U.S. demographics and ethnic identities. Including a more diverse cast and international locations also helps capture global audiences, who represent a significant percentage of a blockbuster film's total box office receipts. Industry journalist Glenn Whipp (2013) asserts that Hollywood has tried to make films seem less American, which presumably means less White, male, and Anglo.

These efforts have yielded positive results. The action-thriller *Fast Five* also did well in Brazilian box offices, ranked as the eighth-highest-grossing film of 2011 and sandwiched between the animated features *Puss in Boots* (seventh) and *Cars 2* (ninth) (ANCINE 2011, 6).[20] Worldwide, *Fast Five* held the position as the sixth-highest-grossing film in 2011. In terms of unauthorized distribution and exhibition, *Fast Five* was not widely available from street vendors but it was reported by TorrentFreak to be the most downloaded film of 2011 (Van der Sar 2011).

The narrative of *Fast Five* develops predictable plot points for an action-adventure film. The viewer is reintroduced to the car gang leader, Dominic "Dom" Toretto (Vin Diesel). Having been sentenced to hard time, Dom is seen in the opening scene dressed in an orange jumpsuit and being transported by bus to a maximum-security prison. Fortunately, his car-racing colleagues show up and, through their daring maneuvers, manage to tip the bus over, leading to his escape. The following sequence is a montage of on-the-scene news reporters covering the incident. The reporters help weave together the narrative and story. They are looking for Dominic Toretto, Mia Toretto (Jordana Brewster),[21] and former FBI agent Brian O'Conner (Paul Walker). The last news reporter states that there is an international manhunt for these fugitives and builds suspense and mystery when she states, "But despite every eye in the country looking for them, where Toretto and O'Connor are now is anyone's guess."

The pursuit continues in Brazil. There is a cut to black and a full pause of darkness and silence (for five seconds). Then the sounds of a lilting cavaquinho quietly emerge a few seconds before graceful aerial shots appear of the Christ the Redeemer statue, a panoramic view of Sugarloaf Mountain, the beaches, and the favelas in the Zona Sul (Vidigal, Rocinha). The geography speaks for itself, and it is apparent that Rio de Janeiro is where the story will continue. In Brazil, the car gang finds refuge before taking on the city's most powerful drug lord, Hernán Reyes (Joaquim de Almeida), to steal his money and free the favelas from his oppression. But U.S. agent Hobbs (Dwayne Johnson) is after them and goes to Rio to impose justice.

Unlike the animated feature *Rio*, which was directed by Rio native Carlos Saldanha to help prevent gross misrepresentations of Brazil, *Fast Five* was not so fortunate. Journalist Nelito Fernandes (2012, 46) suggests that several absurd misrepresentations may make the film entertaining for Brazilian viewers. In a similar vein, writer Edu Fernandes (2011) draws up a list of the most egregious mistakes in the film. Examples include drug dealers using U.S. dollars; a train crisscrossing a flat, desert-like landscape; a drug lord hiding in the posh neighborhood of Leblon; non-Brazilian actors speaking Portuguese with marked accents; and gross historical inaccuracies regarding the colonial period presented by Portuguese actor Joaquim de Almeida in the role of a wealthy drug lord with the Hispanic name Reyes.

The inaccuracies extend to the actual locations where scenes are shot. Most of the car action and chase scenes were actually shot in Puerto Rico, and warehouse scenes were filmed in Atlanta. Although the favelas of Rio figure prominently in the film, not a single favela scene in the film was actually shot in Rio de Janeiro. Instead, urban neighborhoods in Puerto Rico served as substitutes. Notably, *Fast Five* includes aerial establishing shots of (ostensibly) Rio's favelas, which were produced with technical assistance provided by the Rio Film Commission. Despite his efforts to promote Rio de Janeiro as a location for a variety of film genres, Steve Solot reports that the interests of foreign producers are still tied to Rio's favelas, beaches, and Carnaval (N. Fernandes 2012, 44). *Fast Five* is not unique in this instance. (As discussed in chapter 5, Brazilian cinema has also made the favelas the setting for action-crime dramas.) That said, *Fast Five* accurately includes aerial shots of Rio de Janeiro's main attractions—Corcovado and the Christ the Redeemer statue, Sugarloaf Mountain, the beaches, the Flamengo neighborhood (the Aterro), and some locations downtown, including the beautiful Metropolitan Theater and Cinelândia.

In *Fast Five*, the favela is once again a space where foreign outlaws can hide out, presuming that they will go incognito among the local population. The favela in *Fast Five* is stereotypically depicted as a place of danger. However, local gang members are easily controlled by American, male characters. After the opening bus-crash sequence, Mia and Brian are next observed driving on the streets of Rio de Janeiro. They have managed to obtain a car, and they drive into a favela clinging to a hillside. Shots through wire fences and from high angles register their actions. At one moment, the camera pulls back to reveal a young man with a machine gun and a walkie-talkie, through which he informs others that "they have arrived." Accompanied by slow, foreboding music, high-angle shots continue to emphasize Mia and Brian's vulnerability as they walk up some steps in the favela. When Brian sees that they are surrounded by armed locals, he tells Mia they should get out of there. The tension is suddenly broken when a man yells out in Portuguese (with a thick American English accent), telling them to wait. The young men lower their guns and Vince, a colleague from Los Angeles, suddenly appears from a house. Besides the improbability that a foreigner would be able to integrate into and take over the leadership of a favela, this scene coincides with expectations that the favelas are dangerous spaces filled with gun-toting young men of color.

That said, in this and other scenes, *Fast Five* represents the favela as a relatively clean, organized space that, despite criminal elements, can be controllable by well-armed U.S. forces who assert their assumed global authority. Not only is Vince apparently able to find a home in the favelas of Rio de Janeiro, but so can American police forces. On a mission to capture Dom and his gang of car thieves, U.S. agent Hobbs invades the favela in a manner that is akin to tactics used by the Batalhão de Operações Policiais Especiais, the special police forces charged with entering the favelas and routing out drug traffickers. Agent Hobbs and his entourage enter the favela in armored vehicles, wear military combat-style clothing, and subdue the local population by their show of force.

The favelas are a significant part of Rio de Janeiro's urban history, and the criminal gangs and violence associated with them were certainly a concern for Brazilian officials on the eve of several international mega-events. But they were also a key place brand element and major tourist draw. In a brief case study of Brazil, Anholt observes that "Brand Brazil" has the potential to be a strong youth brand, including various negative associations (such as pollution, overpopulation, poverty, crime, and corruption), which are "within the brand print of Brazil" (2006, 112). He does not fail to recognize that these "negative associations" are clearly problematic for the people who have to live with them. However, overall, Anholt argues that these associations contribute to the development of a strong brand whose richness draws on "a complex and intriguing mix of many different elements" (112).

The favelas and violence associated with them are part of a contradictory attraction. They offer a preconceived notion of danger that combines with natural geographic beauty. However, their apparent manageability is significant for what it represents to international travelers. After the Christ statue, Sugarloaf Mountain, and the beaches of the Zona Sul, the favelas are one of the most visited sites by tourists to Rio de Janeiro. Indeed, at the U.N. Rio+20 conference in June 2012, a number of international delegations specifically requested to visit Rio's favelas.[22] However, if international tourists take inspiration from films such as *Fast Five* or *The Incredible Hulk* and visit Rio's favelas looking for an adventure travel experience, they may be disappointed (or pleased?) to see that they will find tight-knit urban neighborhoods inhabited by hardworking, peace-loving people. That said, some locations continue to be plagued by

FIG. 6.2 Agent Hobbs asserting authority in *Fast Five*.

authoritarian, extrajudicial violence committed by criminal factions and official forces.

Replaying imperialist tropes, the American male characters in *Fast Five* are depicted as heroes who help liberate the people of the favela from the drug lord Reyes in what is ultimately a veiled reference to real-life, ongoing pacification programs[23] (see figure 6.2). In one scene, Dom breaks into the home of local police officer Elena Neves (played by the blond Spanish actress and model Elsa Pataky). He corners her and, during their exchange, asks her why she has continued to reside in the favela. Explaining why she stays and her motivations for revenge, she states, "My husband was a good police officer, an honest man. We both grew up here. Two years ago, he was murdered in the street right outside our door. Reyes owns this favela now. He gives things to people. But everything has a price. People here need a new start. They need to be free." Her statement offers a critique of local populist political practices, which were a central point of attack for films like *Tropa de elite* and its 2010 sequel. She also calls for change and reinvention of these urban spaces. Yet just as she supports the police in the mode of mourning her deceased husband, she also mourns the loss of good authority. This creates an opening and convenient justification for the American character to rescue innocent people and restore places to their potential.

Part of *Fast Five*'s transnational appeal is that it extends "Brand America" at the same time that it develops "Brand Brazil" by addressing particular anxieties on both sides of the equator. Spectators get well-trodden visions of U.S. brute force taking over an unruly space, recalling action flicks from the 1980s such as *Rambo 2* (G. Cosmatos, 1985) that helped assert and defend U.S. authority after its post-Vietnam failures and engagement in a power struggle with the Soviet Union. However, the days of the United States being an unquestioned global leader have ended. What we find in the film *Fast Five* is a *saudosista*[24] mode of masculinity that is a response to what Fareed Zakaria (2012) has described as a "post-American world." Zakaria is referring not to the precipitous decline of the United States, as some have misinterpreted, but rather to "the rise of the rest" in a more multipolar world (1–5). The male action-adventure heroes in *Fast Five* are not completely ready for this transition. Numerous scenes show U.S. American male characters using old and new technologies. Men seek rewards by fixing cars, using flame torches, and chasing trains to rob them as if it were the Wild West. But most importantly, their brute American military-style force is defined as an international good that subdues a local evil.

According to Efe Sevin (2011, 157–159), place branding involves perceptions of a location that are held by external and internal audiences, and what is more, it is a communicative activity that arises from disagreements about a place's image. In the case of Brazil's nation brand and the image of Rio de Janeiro, there are a number of contradictory elements—violence and beauty, romance and hatred, corruption and justice. This chapter has addressed how the animated films *Rio* and *Rio 2* and the action-adventure films *The Incredible Hulk* and *Fast Five* contributed to the process of branding Brazil. These films sought to work through some of the contradictions related to the emergence of a new Brazil and negotiate U.S.-Brazil relations. Whereas *Rio* and *Rio 2* manage to present ideas about global citizenship that calls on citizens of all nations to take note of environmental degradation, overall these films sustain established hierarchies whereby U.S. characters and narratives reign over Latin Americans. In this way, these contemporary films continue a history of linking the United States to Latin America through film. It appears that both nations have still not figured out how to be "good neighbors" on-screen.

Conclusion

■ ■ ■ ■ ■ ■ ■ ■ ■ ■ ■ ■ ■ ■ ■ ■ ■ ■ ■ ■

States of Upheaval:
The Marks That Linger

The period from 2003 to 2014 was a unique moment in Brazil's history. The nation's economy was strong, fueled by Chinese demand for commodity exports. As a newly declared BRIC nation, foreign direct investment flowed into the country. Yet several years after the historical period in question, the assertion that Brazil is an emerging global power seems less plausible, if not unfashionable, notwithstanding the fact that China, India, and Russia continue to assert themselves as leading economies and political actors in the current era.

For Brazil, the excitement surrounding the nation's status as an emerging nation appears to have dissipated. Following the period of international megaevents, hope and excitement for Brazil faded from international press. Attention shifted away from Brazil until the election in 2018 of right-wing president Jair Bolsonaro and environmental destruction of the Amazon caught the world's attention. Thousands of fires, most likely started by (il)legal miners and ranchers, have devastated forests across the Amazon. Smoke originating from far away filled the skies over São Paulo in August 2019, setting off international alarms. In response to expressions of international concern, Bolsonaro publicly offended allies like France's president Emmanuel Macron. Ironically, not long before, Brazil had appeared to be a new global actor (or "bridge") in reshaping international negotiations (Burges 2013). Nearly a year prior, the National Museum of Brazil had suffered a catastrophic fire. Reflecting on the losses suffered at the National Museum, biology professor Dalton de Souza Amorim observed that the destruction of anthropological collections represented an incalculable loss, as the museum held the only recordings of people whose nations had disappeared (Gorman 2018). It seemed that the Brazil that was coming into being in 2003 bore little relation to the nation fifteen years later. The images of both the National Museum and the Amazon in flames operate as a point of departure for thinking about the transformation of citizenship, as well as the more general social and cultural accomplishments and backtracking of the branding and Bolsonaro periods. It seemed as though over a decade of sociopolitical progress and the "new Brazil" were also up in flames.

The branding period began to come to a close with a global economic slowdown. In 2012, the Brazilian economy ranked sixth, placing it behind Germany and France but ahead of most European nations, including the U.K. Similar to the economies of other Latin American countries, Brazil's economy has historically depended on international factors and has been largely a commodity exporter. The branding period discussed in this book coincided with an international demand for commodities. As Campello and Zucco note, it was the demand for commodities and the availability of foreign capital that allowed for sociopolitical advances of the Partido dos Trabalhadores (Workers' Party) government from 2003 to 2014. Following a fall in commodity prices and low investor confidence due to the nation's internal political crisis, Brazil then entered the worst recession on record and millions were left unemployed. It seemed that it was not Brazilian cultural identity or productions that were vital exchangeable commodities; it was soybeans, coffee, beef, iron ore, and sugar.

Popular protests also signaled the end of the branding period. Although protests initially were a reaction in June 2013 to an increase in the regular bus fare in the city of São Paulo, popular mobilization began in other major Brazilian cities and included a range of complaints. Long-standing political differences had reemerged. Notwithstanding portrayals in mainstream media or the sectors of the Brazilian intelligentsia that framed the protests as evidence of institutional malfunction, Fernando Lattman-Weltman (2015, 36–37) asserts that the June Days of 2013 were not new to Brazil and demonstrate democratic vitality.

The same cannot easily be said of subsequent events. Both the 2014 World Cup and the 2016 Olympics were envisioned to showcase the long-awaited arrival of a new Brazil on the world stage. The loss to Germany in the final of the World Cup further devastated the spirits of people already disgruntled by the revelation of massive corruption schemes involving Petrobras and the high costs of hosting the matches to FIFA's standards. Weeks before the opening ceremony of the Olympics in Rio de Janeiro, the city coffers were empty, there was little popular support for the games, and the Olympics generally symbol-ized the failure of political promises and the nation's apparent, perennial inabil-ity to live up to its potential.

It seemed as though the politicians who had crafted the strategic affirma-tion of a new Brazil were either in jail, heading to jail, or waiting for verdicts. Dilma Rousseff was impeached in 2016, and Luiz Inácio Lula da Silva was con-victed of money laundering and passive corruption in mid-2017. Michel Temer, who served as president following Rousseff's impeachment, was also accused of passive corruption and sentenced to jail. Finally, the assassination of Marielle Franco in March 2018 stopped the nation. Franco had embodied the new Brazil as a Black lesbian from the periphery who earned university degrees and became active in further developing her community through politi-cal work. Her death signaled a return to authoritarian, extrajudicial violence as well as the shocking retraction of social and urban development that had invested in favelas to foster economic growth.

The period addressed in this book began at a high moment in Brazil's demo-cratic trajectory. As discussed in chapter 2, faith in the future and political progress appears in films from the dictatorship cycle that mark a separation from the authoritarian past. Yet whereas Lula's political ascent can be charac-terized by alliances among disparate groups (that Rousseff was not able to main-tain), Jair Bolsonaro seems invested in attacking diverse groups and fomenting division. The presidential election of 2018 represented a turn to authoritarian-ism, and rather than making steady progress toward the expansion of rights and inclusion, Brazil under Bolsonaro seems to have taken steps backward from democracy. Bolsonaro, who was elected with the support of a powerful con-servative lobby composed of evangelicals, gun advocates, and the agri-business industry, took office in January 2019. Shortly after his inauguration, he signed a series of executive orders dismantling progressive cultural programs, social policies of inclusion, and environmental protections.

Several corruption scandals certainly contributed to dividing the nation, but Bolsonaro has contributed to the marked increase in political polarization with a rampant "us versus them" hate-filled populist rhetoric. A review of Bolsona-ro's first year in office reads like a surrealist script. The ultraconservative presi-dent has rejected the creative economy. He has made culture an enemy and embraced exploitation of the nation's natural resources. As mentioned earlier, recent invasions by illegal miners and loggers in the Amazon region with tacit approval from Bolsonaro to exploit the nation's natural resources signal the clo-sure of a soft-power moment whereby Brazil's cultural heritage was presented as a significant commodity. The arts are just one enemy targeted by Bolsonaro. In a country that recently celebrated and strategically sought to expand under-standing of citizenship and inclusion, Bolsonaro has criticized feminists, expressed homophobia toward Brazil's LGBTQ citizens, and been generally dismissive of the rights demanded by the indigenous, Afro-Brazilians, and other groups. The Bolsonaro administration has set a tone that fosters conservative, divisive ideas regarding gender and sexuality. As the newly appointed minister of the Estado da Mulher, da Família e dos Direitos Humanos (State of Women, Family, and Human Rights), Damares Alves, an evangelical pastor, declared that the nation would enter a "new era" where boys wear blue and girls wear pink. A hateful mode of conservatism has fostered attacks on gays and lesbians, including the censorship of a graphic novel that included a gay kiss at the Bienal do Livro no Rio de Janeiro (Rio International Book Fair). What is more, Bolsonaro has appointed individuals to lead government agencies despite the fact that they have expressed no faith or interest in the missions of those entities. For instance, Sérgio Nascimento de Camargo was appointed head of the Fundação Cultural Palmares, an agency dedicated to human rights and Afro-Brazilian culture. However, Camargo has openly called for the end of the Black movement in Brazil. More recently, Bolsonaro defied health experts amid a global health pandemic in 2020 and interacted with supporters at mass gatherings. He seemed to be less a classic populist politician engaging with his supporters and more a megalomaniac with little regard for public health and humanity.

While we may no longer frequently talk about Brazil as an emerging nation or part of a new political and economic bloc (i.e., the BRICs), Brazil most certainly participates in a changing global reality characterized by shifts in power, increasing polarization, democratic insecurity, and popular protest of authoritarianism and inequality and, as noted earlier, is at the forefront of climate change. Brazil may not currently rank among the top economies of the world as it did at the height of the branding period, but it remains and will continue to be an important geopolitical actor. It governs one of the largest landmasses—of rich yet fragile territory—and it has the fifth-largest population. It is a significant nuclear power and a leading agricultural producer, including of biofuels. It is also home to the Amazon, which, despite rampant deforestation and degradation in recent years, absorbs significant amounts of carbon dioxide and produces 20 percent of the world's rainwater, which will be a vital natural resource in years to come.

If it is challenging to describe Brazil's current context, is impossible to accurately predict the nation's future economic, social, and political landscapes. The period from 2003 to 2014 in Brazil was shaped by utopian impulses. Global politics and economic shifts offered apparent openings to a new middle class and new political, democratic practices. Profitable, utopian ideals mobilized desires to construct a more egalitarian nation and seek systematic reform. Branding was a mode to present a new nation and shape ideas about citizenship in Brazil. However, branding is a discursive practice informed by capitalism and, as such, may fail at achieving socioeconomic equality. Rather than see

Acknowledgments

This book began years ago as I was trying to think about how to address changes taking place in Brazil. Circumstances allowed me to have the honor of meeting Hongmei Li, who was similarly interested in changes taking place in China at the time. Her encouraging words were the spark to this multiyear endeavor.

No monograph is a solitary undertaking. I received generous support from Ana M. López, who read early drafts of proposals and chapters and offered vital input about this book in its earliest stages. Catherine Benamou graciously read drafts of chapters that were in desperate need of constructive criticism. I am deeply grateful for the support these two women have shown. They are outstanding leaders and patient, thoughtful mentors in the field. I am equally indebted to Salomé Aguilera Skvirsky for offering input on early versions of proposals and asking probing and motivating questions. João Luiz Vieira expressed interest and enthusiasm when I really needed feedback. (We will find Tara, João. Tomorrow is another day!) I thank Kátia da Costa Bezerra for her assistance as I prepared the final manuscript. I have admired her work and I enjoyed meeting her in Maré. Stephanie Dennison and Tamara Falicov patiently listened to me talk about this project at Society for Cinema and Media Studies conferences when I needed to articulate some early thoughts on the book's structure and chapters. Thank you for listening! Looking out over downtown Atlanta, I have truly enjoyed and benefited from the insightful and stimulating conversations with Caroline Machado de Azevedo.

In Brazil, I deeply appreciate the warm welcome I received at the Observatório de Favelas (Slum Observatory), as well as in the communities in the North Zone of Rio de Janeiro. Joanna Mazza introduced me to the Imagens do Povo (Images of the People) project and spoke with me at length about their work. Francisco Valdean provided contacts to speak with photographers. Marcos (Ratão) Diniz graciously shared his photographs and offered valuable insights into his work. I am grateful for the solidarity and willingness to help. As part of the Escola Popular de Comunicação Crítica (Popular School of Critical Communication), I was greeted enthusiastically by Thiago Araújo Ansel, who shared his expertise on alternative media in Rio de Janeiro. Similarly, Luis Henrique Nascimento welcomed me into his home to discuss the evolution of ideas about affirmative publicity, which helped me shape my own understandings of branding. I also thank Eduardo Alves for taking the time to discuss citizenship, cultural production in the *comunidades*, and the work of the Slum Observatory in the fight for social justice. In addition to research assistance, I am thankful for the kind friendship and support I have received from Ana Pessoa and her family. *Muito obrigada.* Lastly, Eunice Gutman and Susana Fuentes welcomed me into their homes and helped make sure things were okay when nothing seemed to be okay at all.

Portions of chapter 1 originally appeared in the article "Branding Brazil through Cultural Policy: Rio de Janeiro as Creative, Audiovisual City," *International Journal of Communication* 10 (2016): 3022–3041.

Passages in chapter 2 appeared in the essay "Memory, Youth, and Regimes of Violence in Recent Hispanic and Lusophone Cinemas," in *Beyond Tordesillas: New Approaches to Comparative Luso-Hispanic Studies*, edited by Robert Patrick Newcomb and Richard A. Gordon, 204–219 (Columbus: Ohio State University Press, 2017).

Revised and updated sections of chapter 6 were originally published in "Another Good Neighbor? Hollywood's (Re)embracing of Brazil in *Rio* (2011) and *Fast Five* (2011)," *Revista Canadiense de Estudios Hispánicos* 37, no. 1 (Autumn 2012): 67–85.

I received grants at various stages of this project from the Department of World Languages and Cultures at Georgia State University in the form of summer research support that assisted with travel to Brazil to conduct field research and visit archives. I deeply appreciate the patience and generosity of my colleagues and institution. As a Humanities Center Research Fellow at Georgia State University in the spring of 2020, I benefited from the kind and thoughtful input offered by Audrey Goodman, Joe Perry, Denise Davidson, and Dan Weiskopf. Finally, I would like to thank my family, who listened to me compassionately as I talked for untold hours about Brazil and this book. My parents have provided consistent encouragement that has kept me going. My husband, David, has been incredibly supportive in the final stages of finishing the manuscript.

Lastly, I thank Nicole Solano at Rutgers University Press for supporting this project. It has been wonderful working with her and her team as we moved forward in the midst of a global pandemic.

Filmography

Ação entre amigos. Directed by Beto Brant. 1998; São Paulo: Video Três, 2014. DVD.

A grande cidade. Directed by Carlos Diegues. 1966; Rio de Janeiro: Globo Video, 1980. VHS.

A memória que me contam. Directed by Lúcia Murat. 2012; São Paulo: Imovision, 2013. DVD.

Anos rebeldes. Directed by Dennis Carvalho, Sílvio Tendler, and Ivan Zettel. 20 episodes. 1992; Rio de Janeiro: Rede Globo; Som Livre, Globo Video, 2003. DVD.

Araguaya—a conspiração do silêncio. Directed by Ronaldo Duque. 2004; São Paulo: Paris Filmes, 2007. DVD.

As brasileiras. Directed by Cris D'Amato, Tizuka Yamasaki, and Daniel Filho. 11 episodes. 2012; Rio de Janeiro: Rede Globo; Manaus, Brazil: AMZ Mídia, Som Livre, Globo Marcas, 2012. DVD.

As cariocas. Directed by Daniel Filho, Cris D'Amato, and Amora Mautner. 10 episodes. 2010; Rio de Janeiro: Rede Globo; Manaus, Brazil: AMZ Mídia, Som Livre, Globo Marcas, 2011. DVD.

Avengers: Infinity War. Directed by Anthony Russo and Joe Russo. 2018; Burbank, CA: Buena Vista Home Entertainment, 2018. DVD.

Avenida Brasil. Directed by André Câmara, Gustavo Fernández, Paulo Silvestrini, Thiago Teitelroit, José Luiz Villamarim, Amora Mautner, and Ricardo Waddington. 179 episodes. 2012; Rio de Janeiro: Rede Globo; Manaus, Brazil: Som Livre, TV Globo, 2016. DVD.

Batismo de sangue. Directed by Helvécio Ratton. 2006; Manaus, Brazil: AMZ Mídia Industrial, 2007. DVD.

Black Panther. Directed by Ryan Coogler. 2018; Burbank, CA: Marvel Studios; Buena Vista Home Entertainment, 2018. Blu-Ray.

Cabra-Cega. Directed by Toni Venturi. 2004; Barueri, Brazil: Europa Filmes, 2006. DVD.

Carlota Joaquina, princesa do Brazil. Directed by Carla Camurati. 1995; Barueri, Brazil: Europa Filmes, 2000. DVD.

Cheias de charme. Directed by Maria de Médicis, Allan Fiterman, Natália Grimberg, and Carlos Araújo. 143 episodes. 2012; Rio de Janeiro: Rede Globo, https://globoplay.globo.com/cheias-de-charme/t/ZHd9f7R1d2/.

Cidadão Boilesen. Directed by Chaim Litewski. 2009; Manaus, Brazil: Imovision, 2009. DVD.

Cidade de Deus. Directed by Fernando Meirelles and Kátia Lund. 2002; Santa Monica, CA: Miramax, Lionsgate, 2014. DVD.

Cidade dos homens. Directed by Fernando Meirelles, Kátia Lund, and Paulo Lins. 19 episodes. 2002–2005; Rio de Janeiro: Rede Globo; New York: Palm Pictures, 2006. DVD.

Cidade dos homens. Directed by Paulo Morelli. 2007; Santa Monica, CA: Lionsgate, 2013. Blu-Ray.

Cinco vezes favela. Directed by Joaquim Pedro de Andrade, Miguel Borges, Marcos de Farias, Carlos Diegues, and Leon Hirszman. 1962; Santana de Parnaiba, Brazil: Frontlog, 1988. VHS.

5x favela—agora por nós mesmos. Directed by Manaíra Carneiro, Wagner Novais, Rodrigo Felha, Cacau Amaral, Luciano Vidigal, Cadu Barcellos, and Luciana Bezerra. 2010; Manaus, Brazil: Sony Pictures Home Entertainment, 2011. DVD.

5x pacificação. Directed by Cadu Barcelos, Rodrigo Felha, Wagner Novais, and Luciano Vidigal. 2012; Rio de Janeiro: H2O Filmes, 2013. DVD.

Dhoom 2. Directed by Sanjay Gadhvi. 2006; Long Island City, NY: Yash Raj Films USA, 2007. DVD.

Diário de uma busca. Directed by Flávia Castro. 2010; Manaus, Brazil: AMZ Midia, 2012. DVD.

Dois Córregos—verdades submersas no tempo. Directed by Carlos Reichenbach. 1999; São Paulo: Versátil Home Video, 2000. DVD.

Dois filhos de Francisco. Directed by Breno Silveira. 2005; Manaus, Brazil: Sony Pictures Home Entertainment, 2013. DVD.

Dzi Croquetes. Directed by Tatiana Issa and Raphael Alvarez. 2009; Manaus, Brazil: Imovision, 2010. DVD.

Fantástico. "Marilene Jesus vence o concurso da empregada mais cheia de chame do Brasil." Aired July 22, 2012, on Rede Glob., https://globoplay.globo.com/v/2053147/.

Fast Five. Directed by Justin Lin. 2011; Universal City, CA: Universal Studios Home Entertainment, 2011. DVD.

Flying Down to Rio. Directed by Thornton Freeland. 1933; Burbank, CA: Turner Entertainment; Warner Home Video, 2011. DVD.

The Gang's All Here. Directed by Busby Berkeley. 1943; Glendale, CA: Twilight Time, Red Jam; Beverly Hills, CA: 20th Century Fox Home Entertainment, 2016. Blu-Ray.

Guerra de Canudos. Directed by Sérgio Rezende. 1997; Culver City, CA: Sony Pictures Home Entertainment, 2013. DVD.

Hoje. Directed by Tata Amaral. 2011; Rio de Janeiro: H2o Distribuidora de Filmes, 2013. DVD.

The Incredible Hulk. Directed by Louis Leterrier. 2008; Universal City, CA: Universal Studios Home Entertainment, 2008. DVD.

Iron Man. Directed by Jon Favreau. 2008; Burbank, CA: distributed by Buena Vista Home Entertainment, 2019. Blu-Ray.

Lamarca. Directed by Sérgio Rezende. 1994; Manaus, Brazil: Paramount, 2005. DVD.

Los rubios. Directed by Albertina Carri. 2003; New York: Women Make Movies, 2017. DVD.

Moonraker. Directed by Lewis Gilbert. 1979; Beverly Hills, CA: Twentieth Century Fox Home Entertainment, 2012.

Nancy Goes to Rio. Directed by Robert Leonard. 1950; Hollywood, CA: Warner Bros. Entertainment, 2017. DVD.

Notorious. Directed by Alfred Hitchcock. 1946; New York: Criterion Collection, 2019. DVD.

O ano em que meus pais saíram de férias. Directed by Cao Hamburger. 2006; New York: City Lights Home Entertainment, 2008. DVD.

Olhar estrangeiro. Directed by Lúcia Murat. 2006; Barueri, Brazil: Europa Filmes, 2008. DVD.

O mecanismo. Directed by José Padilha, Marcos Prado, Felipe Prado, and Daniel Rezende. 2 seasons (2018–). Netflix.

Ônibus 174. Directed by José Padilha. 2002; New York: Hart Sharp Video, 2004. DVD.

O quatrilho. Directed by Fábio Barreto. 1995; São Paulo: Paramount, 2005. DVD.

O que é isso, companheiro? Directed by Bruno Barreto. 1997; Montreal, Quebec: Alliance Atlantis, 2010. DVD.

Orfeu. Directed by Carlos Diegues. 1999; New York: New Yorker Video, 2002. DVD.

Orfeu negro. Directed by Marcel Camus. 1959; Irvington, NY: Criterion Collection, 2010. DVD.

Os Desafinados. Directed by Walter Lima Jr. 2008; Rio de Janeiro: Tambellini Filmes, 2008. DVD.

O Sol—caminhando contra o vento. Directed by Martha Alencar and Tetê Moraes. 2006; Rio de Janeiro: Videofilmes, 2006. DVD.

OSS 117: Rio ne répond plus. Directed by Michel Hazanavicius. 2009; Chicago: Music Box Films, 2010. DVD.

Praia do Futuro. Directed by Karim Aïnouz. 2014. Culver City, CA: Strand Releasing Home Video, 2015. DVD.

Quase dois irmãos. Directed by Lúcia Murat. 2004; Manaus, Brazil: Casablanca Filmes, 2009. DVD.

Que bom te ver viva. Directed by Lúcia Murat. 1989; New York: Women Make Movies, 2014. DVD.

Rambo 2. Directed by G. Cosmatos. 1985; Santa Monica, CA: Lionsgate, 2008. DVD.

Rio. Directed by Carlos Saldanha. 2011; Los Angeles: 20th Century Fox Home Entertainment, 2011. DVD.

Rio 2. Directed by Carlos Saldanha. 2014; Los Angeles: 20th Century Fox Home Entertainment, 2014. DVD.

Rio, 40 graus. Directed by Nelson Pereira dos Santos. 1955; Rio de Janeiro: Rio Filme Home Video, 1997. VHS.

Rio, Zona Norte. Directed by Nelson Pereira dos Santos. 1957; Manaus, Brazil: Bretz Filmes, Regina Filmes Video, 2017. DVD.

Saludos Amigos. Directed by Wilfred Jackson Jack Kinney, Hamilton Luske, Bill Roberts, and Normal Ferguson. 1942; Burbank, CA: Walt Disney Studios Home Entertainment, 2008. DVD.

Salve Jorge. Directed by Marcos Schechtman, Frederico Mayrink, João Paulo Jabur, Alexandre Klemperer, Adriano Melo, and Luciano Sabino. 179 episodes. 2012–2013; Rio de Janeiro: Rede Globo, https://globoplay.globo.com/salve-jorge/t/PqbGyWsY8F/.

Se eu fosse você. Directed by Daniel Filho. 2006; Manaus, Brazil: 20th Century Fox Home Entertainment, 2006. DVD.

Tatuagem. Directed by Hilton Lacerda. 2013; Manaus, Brazil: Imovision, 2014. DVD.

That Night in Rio. Directed by Irving Cummings. 1941; Beverly Hills, CA:
20th Century Fox Home Entertainment, 2016. DVD.

The Three Caballeros. Directed by Norman Ferguson Clyde Geronimi, Jack Kinney,
Bill Roberts, and Harold Young. 1944; Burbank, CA: Walt Disney Studios Home
Entertainment, 2008. DVD.

Tropa de elite. Directed by José Padilha. 2007; Universal City, CA: Universal Pictures
Home Entertainment, 2008. DVD.

Tropa de elite 2—O inimigo agora é outro. Directed by José Padilha. 2010; New York:
Flatiron Film Company, 2011. DVD.

Turistas. Directed by John Stockwell. 2006; Beverly Hills, CA: 20th Century Fox;
Vaughan, ON: Criterion-on-Demand, 2013. eVideo.

Uma longa viagem. Directed by Lúcia Murat. 2011; Rio de Janeiro: Copacabana Filmes
e Produções, 2012. DVD.

Uma noite em 67. Directed by Renato Terra and Ricardo Calil. 2010; Petrópolis,
Brazil: Bretz Filmes, 2015. DVD.

Week-end in Havana. Directed by Walter Lang. 1941; Beverly Hills, CA:
20th Century Fox Home Entertainment, 2006. DVD.

Zuzu Angel. Directed by Sérgio Rezende. 2006; São Paulo: Warner Bros. Entertainment, 2006. DVD.

Notes

Introduction

1 Painted before the victory of Germany over Brazil months later, the image of the young boy references that of a photograph taken in 1982 of a boy sad after the loss of the national team to Italy.

2 The free trade agreement is known as Mercosul in Portuguese and Mercosur in Spanish.

3 See also Boito, Berringer, and Morton 2014; Boito 2018.

4 The strategic, economic role of culture is presented in the government publication *Programa cultural para o desenvolvimento do Brasil* (Brazil, Ministério da Cultura, 2006) and further developed in the *Plano da Secretaria da Economia Criativa: Políticas, diretrizes e ações, 2011–2014* (Brazil, Ministério da Cultura, 2011).

5 For instance, Melissa Aronczyk (2013, 34–39, 82–106) discusses nation-branding campaigns in Spain led by official tourism boards and consulting firms that worked for the Polish government.

6 Among numerous publications, see, for example, the collection of essays *Spaces of Capital* (Harvey 2001).

7 Throughout this text I use the term *favela* to refer to urban communities that frequently began as informal settlements but have organized and become established urban neighborhoods. The term has become more commonly used in English-speaking contexts despite being disfavored by some in Brazil. On occasion, I also use the term *comunidade* (community), which is preferred by some groups as being a more politically correct (and respectful) term.

8 Regarding the portrayals of how Brazil was "imagined" during the early colonial period, see Sadlier 2008, 9–62.

9 Pêro Vaz de Caminha was a scribe aboard the ship helmed by Pedro Álvares Cabral that discovered Brazil in 1500.

10 Regarding this, see the documentary by Lúcia Murat, *Olhar estrangeiro* (*The Foreign Eye*, 2006), as well as the study by Tunico Amancio, *O Brasil dos Gringos* (2000).

11 In short, the *mensalão* scandal involved the monthly payment from Workers' Party (Partido dos Trabalhadores) officials to elected deputies in exchange for votes in favor of legislation proposed by the ruling party.

12 See, for example, García Canclini 2001; Saes 2016.
13 Saad-Filho identifies these groups as right-wing oligarchs who lost influential positions, several prominent capitalists, large segments of the working class, and the unionized urban and rural working class.
14 For an excellent overview of changes to film culture, including discussion of actions taken during the Bolsonaro administration, see Dennison 2019.

Chapter 1 Branding Brazil through Cultural Policy

1 The titles of these programs translate to the English as approximately Living Culture (Cultura Viva), More Culture (Mais Cultura) and Culture Coupon (Vale Cultura).
2 In addition to numerous independent theses, dissertations, and articles, several book-length studies of the Cultura Viva program and the Pontos de Cultura have been published by the Instituto de Pesquisa Econômica Aplicada (Applied Economics Research Institute, IPEA), including Frederico A. Barbosa da Silva and Herton Ellery Araújo, eds., *Cultura Viva: Avaliação do programa—arte, educação e cidadania* (Brasília, Brazil: IPEA, 2010); IPEA, *Coordenação de Cultura, Cultura Viva: As práticas dos pontos e pontões* (Brasília, Brazil: IPEA, 2011); and Frederico Barbosa and Lia Calabre, eds., *Pontos de Cultura: Olhares sobre o Programa Cultura Viva* (Brasília, Brazil: IPEA, 2011).
3 For example, according to research conducted in the state of São Paulo, approximately 67 percent of the projects affiliated with the Pontos de Cultura network are dedicated to audiovisual production.
4 The *retomada* (rebirth) is a period in Brazilian film history when production was renewed following the dismantling of funding and film agencies in the early 1990s. For a more in-depth discussion of the *retomada* in Brazilian cinema, see Oricchio 2003; Nagib and Rosa 2002; C. Rêgo and Rocha 2010.
5 Other organizations include the Escola Popular de Comunicação Crítica, which I discuss extensively in chapter 4; Central Única das Favelas, which is dedicated primarily to Black youths; Centro de Criação de Imagem Popular; ArtCult; Tá na Rua; Opção Brasil; Casa de Cultura Tainã; Rede Mocambos; and the Instituto Educarte.
6 The *chanchada* is a form of popular musical film comedy in Brazil that frequently developed themes of carnival. For more on the *chanchada*, see W. Meirelles 2005; Catani and Souza 1983; Dennison and Shaw 2004.
7 I thank the anonymous reviewer for clarifying these dates.
8 These agencies include ANCINE, the Instituto do Patrimônio Histórico e Artístico Nacional, the Instituto Brasileiro de Museus, the Fundação Biblioteca Nacional, the Fundação Casa de Rui Barbosa, the Fundação Cultural Palmares and the Fundação Nacional de Artes.

Chapter 2 Negotiating the Past in the Dictatorship Film Cycle

1 Regarding new notions of citizenship in Brazil, see, for example, Perlman 2010; Holston 2008.
2 This commission is considered a key victory for the families of the dead and disappeared. The publication can be found at https://www.gov.br/mdh/pt-br /centrais-de-conteudo/memoria-e-verdade/direito-a-memoria-e-a-verdade-2013

-comissao-especial-sobre-mortos-e-desaparecidos-politicos/view. Last accessed November 13, 2020.

3 In 2013, Herzog's death certificate was changed to officially state that he died of torture while in custody. A documentary film, *Vlado—30 anos depois* (João Batista de Andrade, 2005), includes interviews with people who knew and loved Herzog.

4 The site also goes by the name Centro de Referências para as Lutas Políticas no Brasil (1964–1985). The National Archive oversees the site, which is charged with providing information to the public on Brazil's political history.

5 Such is the case of the films *O que é isso, companheiro?*, *Zuzu Angel*, and *Batismo de sangue*.

6 The photo refers simultaneously to prisoners released after the kidnapping of the ambassador of Germany (Ehrenfried Anton Theodor Ludwig Von Holleben) in June 1970 and that of the ambassador of the United States (Charles Elbrick) in September 1969.

7 In Portuguese, Stuart's letter to his mother reads, "Todo homem, por si só, influência a natureza do futuro. Através de nossas vidas nós criamos ações que resultam na multiplicação de reações. Esse poder, que todos nós possuímos, esse poder de mudar o curso da história é o poder de Deus."

8 See Hildegard Angel's statement in "Zuzu Angel" n.d.

9 Audiences familiar with Chico Buarque's music will know that this song is a veiled critique of the dictatorship whose upbeat samba rhythm and seemingly optimistic message escaped military officials before being censored until 1978.

10 *Feijoada* refers to a popular black bean stew as well as the gathering of friends or family to eat the stew.

11 For instance, in Spain one finds a number of films featuring young protagonists that reflect on the Franco period, including *El espíritu de la colmena* (1973), *Cría cuervos* (1979), *La lengua de las mariposas* (1999), *Los girasoles ciegos* (2008), and, more recently, the Catalan film *Pá negre* (2010). Mexican director Guillermo del Toro has directed two films that feature young protagonists in a reflection on the Spanish Civil War and Franco period, *El espinazo del diablo* (2001) and *El laberinto del fauno* (2006). From Argentina, we find several films that detail the experiences of children whose lives were unknowingly affected by the atrocities of the military regime, including *Los rubios* (2003), *Botín de guerra* (2000), *Los pasos perdidos* (2001), and *Cautiva* (2004). Critiques of government policies and inequality are notably treated in Luis Buñuel's *Los olvidados* (1950, Mexico) and Hector Babenco's *Pixote* (1980, Brazil).

12 These films are *Batismo de sangue*, *Cabra-Cega*, *O ano em que*, *Os Desafinados*, *Zuzu Angel*, and the documentary film *O Sol—caminhando contra o vento*.

13 Amaral worked with a theatrical style of acting previously in the four-part miniseries *Trago comigo* (2009), which aired on TV Cultura. In this miniseries, actors in a theater re-create experiences from the dictatorship.

Chapter 3   Courting the New Middle Class on Primetime TV

1 While the term "suburban" holds generally positive connotations in the United States and refers to communities of mostly middle- and upper-class residents, in Brazil it refers to locations where individuals of lower economic means live and where developed infrastructure may be lacking.

2 During his first term, Luiz Inácio Lula da Silva created government bodies to address gender (Secretaria de Políticas para as Mulheres) and racial (Secretaria de Políticas de Promoção da Igualdade Racial) equality issues.

3 *As brasileiras* does not technically adapt episodes, but it is inspired by Porto's work, according to opening credits.

4 The contemporary ending contrasts with the rather sad ending found in the 1967 text, where Nadia cries herself to sleep after her older lover leaves.

5 For critical analyses of the carnivalesque in Brazil, see Matta 1977, 1983.

6 The television adaptation changed the title to "the tormented one" (*a atormentada*) from "the separated one" (*a desquitada*). The term *desquite* refers to a marital separation (especially before divorce became legal in 1977). The term *desquitada* holds pejorative connotations for women, who often experienced discrimination and social exclusion once separated.

7 For more on the challenges in developing a new civil code, see Grinberg 2001.

8 The highly successful *Avenida Brasil* (2012) aired at the coveted nine o'clock slot, while *Cheias de charme* (2012) preceded it at the seven o'clock one. Although it held a smaller share of the audience relative to *Avenida Brasil*, *Cheias de charme* was quite successful and a film spin-off was in development, but it has not been released.

9 Electronic styles of *forró* and *brega* music associated with the North and Northeast of Brazil.

10 For example, birth rates have decreased and bone marrow donations have gone up. After the broadcast of *Duas Caras* (2007–2008), which featured Brazilian television's first Afro-Brazilian hero, the Brazilian census of 2010 showed a marked increase in the number of citizens who self-identified as Black.

11 Between 2005 and 2015, access to the internet exploded in Brazil, going from about 13 percent of households to 58 percent (B. Santos 2016).

12 The actresses selected the winner on July 22, 2012, and the episode was aired on July 27, 2012.

13 The videos of the four finalists can be viewed in Fantástico 2012.

14 The segment on *Fantástico* from July 22, 2012, showing the final selection can be found in Fantástico 2012.

Chapter 4 Selling Citizenship in Alternative Media

1 The secretary of culture of the state of Rio de Janeiro sought to stimulate and strengthen cultural production in Rio de Janeiro beginning in 2008; it created a grant program for visual arts in 2011.

2 The photographs discussed in this chapter come from this published collection.

3 For instance, the event "Superfícies" (Surfaces) took place in October 2018 and included exhibits "Entre a Maré e Alemão: relatos visuais do cotidiano" and "Encruzilhadas." For more information, see "Galpão Bela Maré" n.d.

4 Edmilson de Lima, *Wesley da Silva brinca na frente das casas marcadas para demolição*, 2011, in Ripper, Gastaldoni, and Mazza 2012, 16.

5 Léo Lima, *Criança soltando pipa sobre a laje*, 2011, in Ripper, Gastaldoni, and Mazza 2012, 80–81.

6 Marcos (Ratão) Diniz, *Nevinha em sua casa na Rua de Alegria*, 2011, in Ripper, Gastaldoni, and Mazza 2012, 128–129.

7 Pierre Lambert proposed his idea of two Brazils in the text *Os dois Brasis* (1957; São Paulo: Companhia das Letras, 1967).

8 The Complexo do Alemão is a group of favelas in a region in the North Zone of Rio de Janeiro.

9 Lacking funding from the local and regional government, operation of the gondola discontinued in 2016.

10 A. F. Rodrigues, *Vista para o Morro das Palmeiras, Teleférico*, 2011, in Ripper, Gastaldoni, and Mazza 2012, 22–23.

11 In early 2018, Brazil's lower house of Congress and Senate approved a military takeover of security in Rio de Janeiro.

12 A. F. Rodrigues, *Pai corre com seu filho durante a Ocupação Militar no Conjunto de Favelas do Alemão*, 2010, in Ripper, Gastaldoni, and Mazza 2012, 113.

13 For example, see Santoro 1989; Festa and Silva 1986; Peruzzo and Otre 2015.

14 Among other categories of marketing, affirmative publicity also shares some characteristics with "cause promotion" (or "cause marketing"), but affirmative publicity differs significantly in that it is more specifically concerned with issues of social inequality related to race and class.

15 The campaign was overseen by the ESPOCC but benefited from logistical support provided by the nongovernmental organization Meu Rio, ICCO Cooperation, and the Federal University of Rio de Janeiro and sponsorship by the state oil company Petrobras and the Brazilian federal government.

16 The program was launched in 2012 and went by the name Juventude Viva (Youth Alive). For more information, see Brazil 2018.

17 Notably, the JMV campaign was followed a year later by the campaign Jovem Negro Vivo (Black Youth Alive), sponsored by Amnesty International in Brazil.

18 Before becoming a national holiday, the date was understood as marking the death in 1695 of Zumbi dos Palmares, leader of a community of escaped slaves (*quilombo*) that resisted the Portuguese for nearly one hundred years.

19 In Portuguese, "Todo dia é dia da consciência negra."

20 On July 14, 2013, Amarildo de Souza disappeared after being detained by UPP police for questioning. Police officers were later charged with torturing and murdering him.

21 For the videos calling for participation, see ESPOCC 2013a, 2013b, 2013d.

22 For a video of the event, see ESPOCC 2013c.

23 See ESPOCC 2014 for the video.

24 Individuals self-classify their color (or race) on the Brazilian census as one of five categories: *branca, preta, parda, amarela,* or *indígena.* The category "indigenous" does consider ethnic origin but in a limited way.

25 Gilberto Freyre authored the text *Casa grande e senzala* (1933), which became an influential text for several North American scholars studying slavery, race, and race relations.

26 For example, Florestan Fernandes reportedly challenged the myth of Brazil's racial democracy in the 1950s, later publishing the text *A integração do negro na sociedade de classes* (São Paulo: Dominus Editora, 1965).

27 According to the report *Mapa da violência 2012* the race or color of homicide victims was established by official death certificates that classified individuals based on preexisting documentation (from census data) as well as external agents (Waiselfisz 2012, 8).

28 These videos appeared on the digital platform Onlaje (http://www.espocc.org.br /onlaje/index.html) hosted by the Slum Observatory (site no longer available). They ranged from 1:30 to 11:00 in length. Production of the videos was made possible by the Slum Observatory with support from ICCO Cooperation and the Fundo-Carioca and financial support from Petrobras and the Brazilian federal government.

29 Article 5 of the Brazilian Constitution states, "Todos são iguais perante a lei, sem distinção de qualquer natureza, garantindo-se aos brasileiros e aos estrangeiros residentes no País a inviolabilidade do direito à vida, à liberdade, à igualdade, à segurança e à propriedade."

Chapter 5   Favela, Film, Franchise

1 The war in Bahia was famously treated in the novel *Os sertões* by Euclides da Cunha (1902).

2 See chapters 1 and 2 for a discussion of the *retomada*.

3 See also the discussion of film cycles in chapter 2.

4 Notably, both officers appear in the documentary *Notícias de uma guerra particular* (*News from a Personal War*, Kátia Lund and João Moreira Salles, 1999), where they discuss the military-style training and weaponry used to combat drug traffickers in Rio de Janeiro.

5 Among other papal visits, Pope John Paul II visited Rio de Janeiro in 1997 and Pope Benedict XVI visited São Paulo in May 2007, just a few months before the film was released in Brazil on October 12, 2007. More recently, Pope Francis visited Rio de Janeiro in 2013.

6 A similar observation is made by Felicia Chan and Valentina Vitali (2010) with regard to *Cidade de Deus*.

7 See discussion of the thriller in chapter 2.

8 *Tropa 2* surpassed *Dona Flor e seus dois maridos* (Bruno Barreto), which had held the top position since 1976. *Tropa 2* has since been surpassed by the religious bio-drama *Nada a perder* (2018) and the biblical *Os dez mandamentos—o filme* (2016) by director Alexandre Avancini.

9 The Netflix series first aired in March 2018 and draws on the investigations into the Operaçao Lava Jato (Operation Car Wash) as its background material. The series was renewed for a second season, airing in May 2019.

10 Netflix announced in 2018 that season 4 of *Narcos* would reset as a new series, *Narcos: Mexico*.

11 This is not to say that the state had not intervened in the favelas in the past. Throughout the twentieth century, the government implemented various programs to eradicate the favelas, remove residents, and combine urbanization projects with social programs. For more on the subject, see Zaluar and Alvito 1998.

12 These were Cantagalo and Pavão/Pavãozinho; Rocinha; Alemão; and Manginhos.

13 In Portuguese, Nascimento states, "Toda favela é um mercado poderoso de muita coisa comprada e vendida."

14 *Udenismo* is a term for the political perspective associated with the political party and matches the initials of the political party, "UDN."

15 Lula was tentatively released in November 2019, and he continues to exhaust appeals of his conviction.

16 See the discussion of Murat's film in chapter 2.

17 The statement in Portuguese reads, "Apesar de possíveis coincidências com a realidade, este filme é uma obra de ficção."

Chapter 6   Another Good Neighbor?

1 The critique is attributed to Charles de Gaulle, who visited Brazil in the late 1960s and allegedly stated on his departure from Rio de Janeiro, "This is not a serious country."

2 Other notable examples include U.S. director Spike Lee's documentary project *Go Brazil Go*, for which he traveled to Rio de Janeiro; the adaptation of the 2001 French novel *Rouge Brésil*, which began production at this time; and British director Julien Temple's *Children of the Revolution*, which started filming.

3 Notwithstanding the important exception of Orson Welles, who, undertaking the task to make a documentary on the subject of Carnaval in Brazil, strived to offer a more authentic representation of Brazil in the unfinished film *It's All True*. For more information, see Benamou 2007.

4 During these talks, the U.S. film industry, defended by Jack Valenti, sought to retain unrestricted market access for audiovisual products. For their part, European film industries sought to uphold restricted market access for films, television programs, and other audiovisual works.

5 The focus here is on films from the United States. Other notable films from the period include the U.K.-Brazil coproduction *Trash* (Stephen Daldry and Christian Duurvoort, 2014), the French James Bond parody *OSS 117: Rio ne répond plus* (*OSS 117: Lost in Rio*, Michel Hazanavicius, 2009), and the Bollywood film *Dhoom 2* (Sanjay Gadhvi, 2006).

6 A *Variety* BRIC summit was held in Los Angeles on June 15, 2012.

7 For more information on the Cine Tela Brasil project, see http://www.cinetelabrasil.com.br/cine-tela-brasil.

8 Walt Disney's *Saludos Amigos*, which premiered in Rio de Janeiro in 1942, showcases Donald Duck flying to different locations in South America, making friends and exploring Latin America. This animated film was followed by *The Three Caballeros* (1944), featuring Donald Duck, who opens presents from his friends from Latin America, including the Brazilian parrot José "Zé" Carioca and the Mexican rooster Panchito Pistoles.

9 The protagonist of *Week-end in Havana*, American Nan Spencer (Alice Faye), goes on a cruise to Cuba.

10 For instance, one component of Brazil's retooling of its image abroad has been its support of educational exchanges such as the program Ciência Sem Fronteiras (Science without Borders), launched on July 26, 2011.

11 *Rio 2* appeared in Brazilian theaters in March 2014, whereas the release date was April for the United States and other locations. The 2014 World Cup opened June 12 and ended July 13, 2014.

12 The Petrobras scandal, referred to as Operaçao Lava Jato (Operation Car Wash), is an ongoing criminal investigation into money laundering and bribes by officials for construction contracts.

13 Cidade Maravilhosa is a nickname for the city of Rio de Janeiro attributed to the writer Coelho Neto as well as the song by André Filho that was later popularized by Carmen Miranda.

14 Iemanjá is a deity in Candomblé of West African (Yoruban) origin. In Brazil, Iemenjá is associated with water, and on New Year's Eve, people gather on Copacabana Beach and make offerings to the sea with the hopes that the goddess will grant their wishes in the new year.

15 Users of Rotten Tomatoes gave Ang Lee's 2003 version a 29 percent positive rating compared with a 70 percent favorable rating for *The Incredible Hulk* (2008).

16 *The Incredible Hulk*, which was released just a few weeks after *Iron Man*, features *Iron Man* protagonist Tony Stark (Robert Downey Jr.). Stark appears at the end of the film meeting up with General Ross, who had pursued Bruce Banner. *The Incredible Hulk* closes with Stark telling Ross they are "putting a team together," which refers to the Avengers and serves as the departure point for the Avengers series of the Marvel franchise.

17 I wish to thank David Duckworth for drawing out the significance of this opening sequence and its relation to the trajectory of Marvel Comics.

18 The *Fast and the Furious* franchise began in 2001. Thus far there have been eight films in the series, which has recently included the spin-off *Fast & Furious Presents: Hobbs & Shaw* (2019). *Fast & Furious 9* is anticipated to be released in 2021.

19 Auto racing is generally respected, so much so that the country mourned the death of driver Ayrton Senna, whose name has subsequently been lent to numerous streets and avenues.

20 It is curious to note that among the seventeen highest-grossing foreign films from 2011, only two were comedies, while six were animated films and nine were fantasy-adventure films—all editions of film franchises directed toward younger audiences (ANCINE 2011, 2).

21 It should be noted that Jordana Brewster is an American actress who was born in Panama to a Brazilian mother. She speaks a few phrases of Brazilian Portuguese in the film.

22 Anecdotal reports from people living in the Complexo do Alemão based on site visits I made in 2012 and 2014 indicate that riding on the *teleférico* (cable car), installed in the area after police pacification units took over the region, had become a new tourist activity. See also chapter 4 for a discussion of photographs of the cable car.

23 For more on the police pacification units, see chapters 4 and 5 here.

24 The term *saudosista* comes from the noun *saudade*, a Portuguese word meaning something akin to sad "longing" or "yearning."

References

Agénor, Pierre-Richard, and Otaviano Canuto. 2013. "Gender Equality and Economic Growth in Brazil." Policy research working paper, World Bank, Washington, DC.

Alfonsin, Jacques Távora. 2004. *A função social da cidade e da propriedade privada urbana como propriedade de funções*. Belo Horizonte, Brazil: Editora Fórum.

Álvarez, Sonia. 1990. *Engendering Democracy in Brazil: Women's Movements in Transition Politics*. Princeton, NJ: Princeton University Press.

Amancio, Tunico. 2000. *O Brasil dos gringos: Imagens no cinema*. Niterói, Brazil: Intertexto.

ANCINE (Agência Nacional do Cinema). 2006. *Relatório de atividades: 5 anos*. Brasília, Brazil: Ministério da Cultura.

———. 2011. *Informe anual de acompanhamento de mercado 2011: Filmes e bilheterias*. Brasília, Brazil: ANCINE.

———. 2018. *Diversidade de gênero e raça nos longa-metragens brasileiros lançados em salas de exibição 2016*. Rio de Janeiro: Observatório Brasileiro do Cinema e do Audiovisual, ANCINE.

———. 2019. *Anuário Estatístico do Cinema Brasileiro*. Brasília, Brazil: ANCINE.

Andrade, Luciana Vieira Rubim, and Marlise Miriam de Matos Almeida. 2017. "A criminalização da violência contra as mulheres no Brasil: De legítima defesa da honra à violação dos direitos humanos." *Revista Sociais e Humanas* 30 (2).

Andreasen, Alan R. 1994. "Social Marketing: Its Definition and Domain." *Journal of Public Policy and Marketing* 13 (1): 108–114.

———. 2006. *Social Marketing in the 21st Century*. Thousand Oaks, CA: SAGE.

Anholt, Simon. 2006. *Brand New Justice: How Branding Places and Products Can Help the Developing World*. Oxford: Elsevier Butterworth-Heinemann.

———. 2007. *Competitive Identity: The New Brand Management for Nations, Cities and Regions*. Basingstoke, UK: Palgrave Macmillan.

Appadurai, Arjun. 1986. "Introduction: Commodities and the Politics of Value." In *The Social Life of Things: Commodities in Cultural Perspective*, edited by Arjun Appadurai, 3–63. Cambridge: Cambridge University Press.

Arantes, Silvana. 2006. "'Tropa de Élite' de José Padilha explica por que polícia 'é o que é.'" *Folha de São Paulo*, December 29, 2006. https://www1.folha.uol.com.br /folha/ilustrada/ult90u67237.shtml.

Araújo, Aristeu. 2007. "Tropa de Élite." *Revista Moviola—Revista de cinema e artes*. October 1, 2007. http://www.revistamoviola.com/2007/10/01/tropa-de-elite/ (site no longer available).

Aronczyk, Melissa. 2013. *Branding the Nation: The Global Business of National Identity*. Oxford: Oxford University Press.

Aronczyk, Melissa, and Devon Powers. 2010. "Introduction: Blowing Up the Brand." In *Blowing Up the Brand: Critical Perspectives on Promotional Culture*, edited by Melissa Aronczyk and Devon Powers, 1–26. New York: Peter Lang.

Arvidsson, Adam. 2006. *Brands: Meaning and Value in Media Culture*. London: Routledge.

Atencio, Rebecca J. 2011. "A Prime Time to Remember: Memory Merchandising in Globo's *Anos Rebeldes*." In *Accounting for Violence: Marketing Memory in Latin America*, edited by Ksenija Bilbija and Leigh A. Payne, 41–68. Durham, NC: Duke University Press.

Avelar, Idelber. 1999. *The Untimely Present: Postdictatorial Latin American Fiction and the Task of Mourning*. Durham, NC: Duke University Press.

Bacha, Edmar L. 1973. "Sobre a dinâmica do crescimento da economia industrial subdesenvolvida." *Pesquisa e Planejamento Econômico* 3 (4): 937–952.

Bacha, Edmar L., and Lance Taylor. 1976. "The Unequalizing Spiral: A First Growth Model for Belindia." *Quarterly Journal of Economics* 90:197–218.

Banet-Weiser, Sarah. 1999. *The Most Beautiful Girl in the World: Beauty Pageants and National Identity*. Berkeley: University of California Press.

———. 2012. *Authentic^{TM}: The Politics of Ambivalence in a Brand Culture*. New York: New York University Press.

Barbar, Tathiana. 2012. "Cineastas fazem manifesto em defesa da Comissão da Verdade." *Folha de São Paulo*, June 3, 2012. http://www1.folha.uol.com.br/poder /1057759-cineastas-fazem-manifesto-em-defesa-da-comissao-da-verdade.shtml.

Barbosa, Jorge Luiz. 2013. "Favela: Solo cultural da cidade." In *Solos culturais*, edited by Jorge Luiz Barbosa and Caio Gonçalves Dias, 17–27. Rio de Janeiro: Observatório de Favelas.

Barros, Mariana. 2015. "Faxina completa." *Veja*, May 11, 2015. https://veja.abril.com.br /brasil/faxina-completa/.

Bastos, Gláucia Soares. 1992. "Pall-Mall Rio." In *A crônica: O gênero, sua fixação e suas transformações no Brasil*, edited by Antônio Candido, 225–233. Campinas, Brazil: Unicamp.

Bastos, Mônica Rugai. 2001. *Tristezas não pagam dívidas: Cinema e política nos anos da Atlântida*. São Paulo: Olho d'Agua.

Baudrillard, Jean. 2018. *Simulacra and Simulation*. Translated by Sheila Faria Glaser. Ann Arbor: University of Michigan Press. First published 1981.

Beauchesne, Kim, and Alessandra Santos. 2011. "Introduction: The Theory and Practice of the Utopian Impulse in Latin America." In *The Utopian Impulse in Latin America*, edited by Kim Beauchesne and Alessandra Santos, 1–26. New York: Palgrave Macmillan.

Bell, Vikki. 2011. "The Politics of 'Memory' in the Long Present of the Southern Cone." In *The Memory of State Terrorism in the Southern Cone: Argentina, Chile, and Uruguay*, edited by Francesca Lessa and Vincent Druliolle, 209–221. New York: Palgrave Macmillan.

Beltrán, Mary. 2005. "The New Hollywood Racelessness: Only the Fast, Furious, (and Multiracial) Will Survive." *Cinema Journal* 44 (2): 50–67.

Benamou, Catherine L. 2007. *It's All True: Orson Welle's Pan-American Odyssey* (Berkeley: University of California Press.

Bentes, Ivana. 2003. "The Sertão and the Favela in Contemporary Brazilian Film." In *The New Brazilian Cinema*, edited by Lúcia Nagib, 121–137. London: I. B. Tauris in association with the Centre for Brazilian Studies, University of Oxford.

Berg, Charles Ramírez. 2002. *Latino Images in Film: Stereotypes, Subversion, and Resistance*. Austin: University of Texas Press.

Bezerra, Kátia da Costa. 2018. *Postcards from Rio: Favelas and the Contested Geographies of Citizenship*. New York: Fordham University Press.

Bilbija, Ksenija, and Leigh A. Payne. 2011. "Time Is Money: The Memory Market in Latin America." In *Accounting for Violence: Marketing Memory in Latin America*, edited by Ksenija Bilbija and Leigh A. Payne, 1–40. Durham, NC: Duke University Press.

Blair, Ian. 2011. "Tales Unfold Far, Far Away." *Variety*, November 16, 2011, 17.

Boes, Tobias. 2012. *Formative Fictions: Nationalism, Cosmopolitanism, and the Bildungsroman*. Ithaca, NY: Cornell University Press.

Boito, Armando, Jr. 2007. "Class Relations in Brazil's New Neoliberal Phase." Translated by Rosana Resende. *Latin American Perspectives* 34 (5): 115–131.

———. 2018. *Reforma e crise política no Brasil: Os conflitos de classe nos governos do PT*. Campinas, Brazil: Editora da Unicamp.

Boito, Armando, Tatiana Berringer, and Gregory Duff Morton. 2014. "Social Classes, Neodevelopmentalism, and Brazilian Foreign Policy under Presidents Lula and Dilma." *Latin American Perspectives* 41, no. 5 (September): 94–109.

Bost, David. 2009. "*No pasó nada* and *Machuca*: *Bildungsroman* as Historical Understanding." *Latin Americanist* 53 (2): 49–60.

Brannan, Matthew J., Elizabeth Parsons, and Vincenza Priola, eds. 2011. *Branded Lives: The Production and Consumption of Meaning at Work*. Northampton, MA: Edward Elgar.

Brayner, Sonia. 1992. "Machado de Assis: Um cronista de quatro décadas." In *A crônica: o gênero, sua fixação e suas transformações no Brasil*, edited by Antônio Candido, 407–417. Campinas, Brazil: Unicamp.

Brazil, Ministério da Cultura. 2006. *Programa cultural para o desenvolvimento do Brasil*. Brasília, Brazil: Ministério da Cultura.

———. 2011. *Plano da Secretaria da Economia Criativa: Políticas, diretrizes e ações, 2011–2014*. Brasília, Brazil: Minstério da Cultura.

Brazil, Secretária Especial dos Direitos Humanos. Comissão Especial sobre Mortos e Desaparecidos Políticos. 2007. *Direito à verdade e à memória: Comissão Especial sobre Mortos e Desaparecidos Políticos*. Brasília: Secretaria Especial dos Direitos Humanos.

Brazil, Secretária Nacional de Juventude. 2018. *Plano Juventude Viva: Um levantamento histórico*. Brasília, Brazil: Secretaría Nacional de Juventude.

Brazil, Senado Federal. 1988. Constituição da República Federativa do Brasil. Brasília, Brazil: Senado Federal.

Brittos, Valerio Cruz, and Cesar Ricardo Siqueira Bolaño. 2005. *Rede Globo: 40 anos de poder e hegemonia*. São Paulo: Paulus.

Brown, Alison. 2013. "The Right to the City: Road to Rio 2010." *International Journal of Urban and Regional Research* 37 (3): 957–971.

Brown, Alison, and Annali Kristiansen. 2009. *Urban Policies and the Right to the City: Rights, Responsibilities and Citizenship*. Paris: UNESCO.

Burges, Sean W. 2009. "Brazil: Toward a (Neo)liberal Democracy." In *Governance after Neoliberalism in Latin America*, edited by Jean Grugel and Pía Riggirozzi, 195–216. New York: Palgrave Macmillan.

———. 2013. "Brazil as a Bridge between Old and New Powers?" *International Affairs* 89 (3): 577–594.

Calabre, Lia, ed. 2013. *Políticas culturais: Informações, territórios e economia criativa*. São Paulo: Itaú Cultural; Rio de Janeiro: Fundação Casa de Rui Barbosa.

Caldas, Pedro. 2008. "O (ab)uso da palavra fascismo: A recepção de Tropa de Elite." *Viso: Cadernos de estética aplicada* 2 (4): 46–56.

Campello, Daniela and Cesar Zucco Jr. 2015. "Understanding the Increasing Popularity of Brazilian Presidents." In *Emergent Brazil: Key Perspectives on a New Global Power,* edited by Jeffrey Needell, 51–67. Gainesville: University of Florida Press.

Campos, Carmen Hein de. 2015. "Feminicídio no Brasil: Uma análise crítico-feminista." *Sistema Penal & Violência* 7 (1): 103–115.

Cardoso, Adalberto, and Edmond Préteceille. 2017. "Classes médias no Brasil: Do que se trata? Qual seu tamanho? Como vem mudando?" *Dados: Revista de Ciências Sociais* 60 (4): 977–1023.

Catani, Afrânio Mendes, and José Inácio de Melo Souza. 1983. *A chanchada no cinema brasileiro*. São Paulo: Brasiliense.

Cavalcanti, Mariana. 2007. "Of Shacks, Houses and Fortresses: An Ethnography of Favela Consolidation in Rio de Janeiro." PhD diss., University of Chicago.

———. 2015. "Pacification Urbanism: A View from Rio's Old Industrial Suburbs." In *Emergent Brazil: Key Perspectives on a New Global Power*, edited by Jeffrey Needell, 108–126. Gainesville: University of Florida Press.

Chalhoub, Sidney, Margarida de Souza Neves, and Leonardo Affonso de Miranda Pereira. 2005. *História em cousas miúdas: Capítulos de história social da crônica no Brasil*. Campinas, Brazil: Unicamp.

Chalmers, Vera. 1992. "A crônica humorística de O Pirralho." In *A crônica: O gênero, sua fixação e suas transformações no Brasil*, edited by Antônio Candido, 193–211. Campinas, Brazil: Unicamp.

Chan, Felicia, and Valentina Vitali. 2010. "Revisiting the 'Realism' of the Cosmetics of Hunger: *Cidade de Deus* and *Ônibus 174*." *New Cinemas: Journal of Contemporary Film* 8 (3): 15–30.

Chin, Elizabeth. 2001. *Purchasing Power: Black Kids and American Consumer Culture*. University of Minnesota Press: Minneapolis.

Clark, Michael. 1987. "Humor and Incongruity." In *The Philosophy of Laughter and Humor,* edited by John Morreall, 139–155. Albany: State University of New York Press.

Cleveland, Kimberly. 2019. *Black Women Slaves Who Nourished a Nation: Artistic Renderings of Black Wet Nurses of Brazil*. Amherst, NY: Cambria.

Comaroff, John L., and Jean Comaroff. 2009. *Ethnicity, Inc*. Chicago: University of Chicago Press.

Conde, Maite. 2012. *Consuming Visions: Cinema, Writing, and Modernity in Rio de Janeiro*. Charlottesville: University of Virginia Press.

Cooper, Dana, and Claire Phelan, eds. 2014. *Motherhood and War: International Perspectives*. New York: Palgrave Macmillan.

Craine, James and Giorgio Hadi Curti. 2009. "A(u)tuando o Rio: a lei, o desejo e a produção da cidade em Tropa de elite, de José Padilha / (En)acting Rio: law, desire and the production of the city in Jose Padilha's Tropa de elite." *Pro-Posições* 20 (3): 87–108.

Cunha, Rodrigo de Moura e. 2006. "Memória dos ressentimentos: A luta armada através do cinema brasileiro dos anos 1980 e 1990." MA thesis, Pontífica Universidade Católica do Rio de Janeiro.

Cymbalista, Renato, ed. 2008. *The Challenges of the Democratic Management of Brazil: The Right to the City*. São Paulo: Instituo Polis; Fundação Ford.

D'Araujo, Maria Celina Soares, ed. 2014. *Redemocratização e mudança social no Brasil*. Rio de Janeiro: FGV editora.

Debord, Guy. 1983. *Society of the Spectacle*. Detroit: Black and Red.

Dennison, Stephanie. 2019. *Remapping Brazilian Film Culture in the Twenty-First Century*. New York: Routledge.

Dennison, Stephanie, and Lisa Shaw. 2004. *Popular Cinema in Brazil, 1930–2001*. Manchester, UK: Manchester University Press.

De Oliveira, Fabrício Augusto, and Paulo Nakatani. 2000. "The Real Plan: Price Stability with Indebtedness." *International Journal of Political Economy* 30 (4): 13–31.

De Santana Pinho, Patricia, and Elizabeth B. Silva. 2010. "Domestic Relations in Brazil: Legacies and Horizons." *Latin American Research Review* 45 (2): 90–113.

De Souza, Julia Filet-Abreu. 1980. "Paid Domestic Service in Brazil." *Latin American Perspectives* 7 (1): 35–63.

DiOrio, Carl. 2008. "'Iron Man' Bolts Past $300 Million at Box Office." *NewsDaily*, June 19, 2008. https://web.archive.org/web/20080627123040/http://www.newsdaily.com/stories/n19296777-ironman/.

Doles, Steven. 2016. "Cycle Consciousness and the White Audience in Black Film Writing: The 1940–1950 'Race Problem' Cycle and the African American Press." In *Cycles, Sequels, Spin-Offs, Remakes, and Reboots: Multiplicities in Film and Television*, edited by Amanda Ann Klein and R. Barton Palmer, 80–95. Austin: University of Texas Press.

Donoghue, Courtney Brannon. 2014. "The Rise of the Brazilian Blockbuster: How Ideas of Exceptionality and Scale Shape a Booming Cinema." *Media, Culture and Society* 36 (4): 536–550.

Druliolle, Vincent. 2011. "Remembering and Its Places in Postdictatorship Argentina." In *The Memory of State Terrorism in the Southern Cone*, edited by Francesca Lessa and Vincent Druliolle, 15–41. New York: Palgrave Macmillan.

Dyer, Richard. 2012. *Heavenly Bodies: Film Stars and Society*. Hoboken, NJ: Taylor and Francis. First published 1986.

Economist. 2011. "Domestic Labour: The Servant Problem." December 17, 2011. https://www.economist.com/christmas-specials/2011/12/17/the-servant-problem.

Edger, Chris. 2015. *Franchising: How Both Sides Can Win*. Faringdon, UK: Libri.

Ehrmann, Thomas. 2013. *Network Governance: Alliances, Cooperative and Franchise Chains, Contributions to Management Science*. Heidelberg, Germany: Springer Verlag.

Escalas, Jennifer Edson. 2004. "Narrative Processing: Building Consumer Connections to Brands." *Journal of Consumer Psychology* 14 (1/2): 168–180.

ESPOCC (Escola Popular de Comunicação Crítica). 2013a. "FlashMob #JMV." YouTube video, 0:27. Posted December 7, 2013. https://www.youtube.com/watch?v=27m8WmWd_UM.

———. 2013b. "FlashMob #JMV." YouTube video, 0:28. Posted December 11, 2013. https://www.youtube.com/watch?v=eFREVi8eRho.

———. 2013c. "#JMV FlashMob." YouTube video, 1:44. Posted December 19, 2013. https://www.youtube.com/watch?v=XYA8j6z29k8&feature=youtu.be.

———. 2013d. "#JMV Leandro Santana." YouTube video, 0:17. Posted December 16, 2013. https://www.youtube.com/watch?v=JOs3DjtjnUk.

———. 2014. "#JMV 30"." YouTube video, 0:41. Posted January 16, 2014. https://www.youtube.com/watch?v=Kt5XUZBIals.

Fantástico. 2012. "Marilene Jesus vence o concurso da empregada mais cheia de chame do Brasil." Globoplay video, 10:08. Posted July 22, 2012. https://globoplay.globo.com/v/2053147/.

Federação das Indústrias do Estado do Rio de Janeiro. 2008. "A cadeia da indústria criativa no Brasil." In *Estudos para o desenvolvimento do Estado do Rio de Janeiro*, 13–23. Rio de Janeiro: Federação das Indústrias do Estado do Rio de Janeiro.

Fernandes, Edésio. 2007. "Constructing the 'Right to the City' in Brazil." *Social and Legal Studies* 16 (2): 201–219.

Fernandes, Edu. 2011. "Veja cinco erros que 'Velozes e Furiosos' comete ao retratar o Brasil." *UOL Cinema*, May 4, 2011.

Fernandes, Nelito. 2012. "O Rio que eles veem." *Época*, February 6, 44–46.

Festa, Regina Dalva, and Carlos Eduardo Lins da Silva, eds. 1986. *Comunicação popular e alternativa no Brasil*. São Paulo: Edições Paulinas.

Fico, Carlos. 1997. *Reinventando o otimismo: Ditadura, propaganda e imaginário social no Brasil*. Rio de Janeiro: Fundação Getúlio Vargas.

Fischer, Brodwyn M. 2014. "A Century in the Present Tense: Crisis and the Intellectual History of Brazil's Informal Cities." In *Cities from Scratch*, edited by Brodwyn M. Fischer, Bryan McCann, and Javier Auyero, 9–67. Durham, NC: Duke University Press.

Flew, Terry. 2012. *The Creative Industries: Culture and Policy*. Los Angeles: SAGE.

———. 2013. *Creative Industries and Urban Development: Creative Cities in the 21st Century*. London: Routledge.

Florida, Richard L. 2002. *The Rise of the Creative Class: And How It's Transforming Work, Leisure, Community and Everyday Life*. New York: Basic Books.

Fonseca, Manuel A. R. da. 1998. "Brazil's Real Plan." *Journal of Latin American Studies* 30 (3): 619–639.

Fonseca, Pedro. 2009. "Rio defende com emoção 1a Olimpíada na América do Sul." *O Globo*, October 2, 2009. http://g1.globo.com/Noticias/Mundo/0,,MUL1327017-5602,00-rio+defende+com+emocao+a+olimpiada+na+america+do+sul.html.

Fontanele, Marina, and Fredson Navarro. 2014. "Reação homofóbica deixa fucionários de cinema constrangidos." *O Globo*, May 21. http://g1.globo.com/se/sergipe/noticia/2014/05/reacao-homofobica-deixa-funcionarios-de-cinema-constrangidos.html.

Forsey, Jane. 2013. "Appraising the Ordinary—Tension in Everyday Aesthetics." *Proceedings of the European Society for Aesthetics* 5:237–245.

French, Jeff, and Ross Gordon. 2015. *Strategic Social Marketing*. London: SAGE.

Fung, Anthony. 2016. "Strategizing for Creative Industries in China: Tensions in Nation Branding." *International Journal of Communication* 10:3004–3021.

"Galpão Bela Maré recebe a Mostra Superfícies." n.d. Observatório de Favelas. Accessed October 8, 2020. http://of.org.br/sem-categoria/galpao-bela-mare-recebe-a-mostra-superficies/.

García Canclini, Néstor. 2001. *Consumers and Citizens: Globalization and Multicultural Conflicts*. Cultural Studies of the Americas. Minneapolis: University of Minnesota Press.

Gil, Gilberto. 2003. "Discurso de posse do Ministro da Cultura Gilberto Gil." *Folha de São Paulo*, January 2, 2003. https://www1.folha.uol.com.br/folha/brasil/ult96u44344.shtml.

Gledhill, Christine. 1991. *Stardom: Industry of Desire*. London: Routledge.

Goldstein, Donna. 2014. *Laughter Out of Place: Race, Class, Violence, and Sexuality in a Rio Shantytown*. California Series in Public Anthropology, vol. 9. Berkeley: University of California Press.

Goodman, Josh. 2013. "Brazil's Domestic Servants Get Work Equality." Bloomberg, April 11, 2013. https://www.bloomberg.com/news/articles/2013-04-11/brazils-domestic-servants-get-work-equality.

Gorman, James. 2018. "The Brazil Museum Fire: What Was Lost." *New York Times*, September 4, 2018. https://www.nytimes.com/2018/09/04/science/brazil-museum-fire.html.

Gorulho, Luciane. 2012. "BNDES Support to the Audiovisuals Sector." In *The Brazilian Audiovisual Industry: An Explosion of Creativity and Opportunities for Partnerships*, edited by Steve Solot, 85–100. Rio de Janeiro: Latin American Training Center.

Greenberg, Miriam. 2008. *Branding New York: How a City in Crisis Was Sold to the World*. New York: Routledge.

Grinberg, Keila. 2001. *Código civil e cidadania*. Rio de Janeiro: Jorge Zahar.

Haapala, Arto. 1998. "Strangeness and Familiarity in the Urban Environment." In *The City as Cultural Metaphor: Studies in Urban Aesthetics*, edited by Arto Haapala, 108–125. Lahti, Finland: International Institute of Applied Aesthetics.

———. 2005. "On the Aesthetics of the Everyday: Familiarity, Strangeness, and the Meaning of Place." In *The Aesthetics of Everyday Life*, edited by Andrew Light and Jonathan M. Smith, 39–55. New York: Columbia University Press.

Hakim, Peter. 2015. "The Strange Case of the Missing Relationship: Brazil and the United States." In *Emergent Brazil: Key Perspectives on a Global Power*, edited by Jeffrey D. Needell, 275–289. Gainesville: University Press of Florida.

Hamburger, Esther. 2005. *O Brasil antenado: A sociedade da novela*. Rio de Janeiro: Jorge Zahar Editor.

———. 2007. "Violência e pobreza no cinema brasileiro recente: Reflexões sobre o espetáculo." *Novos Estudos* 78:113–128.

Harmeling, Colleen, Jordan Moffett, Mark J. Arnold, and Brad Carlson. 2016. "Toward a Theory of Customer Engagement Marketing." *Journal of the Academy of Marketing Science* 45:312–335.

Harvey, David. 2001. *Spaces of Capital*. New York: Routledge.

Hirsch, Marianne. 2008. "The Generation of Postmemory." *Poetics Today* 29 (1): 103–128.

Hokenson, Jan. 2006. *The Idea of Comedy: History, Theory, Critique*. Madison, NJ: Fairleigh Dickinson University Press.

Holston, James. 2008. *Insurgent Citizenship: Disjunctions of Democracy and Modernity in Brazil*. Princeton, NJ: Princeton University Press.

Hopewell, John. 2013a. "City of Rio Builds Rio's Film-TV Future." *Variety*, October 1, 2013. https://variety.com/2013/film/global/city-of-rio-builds-rios-film-tv-future-1200684904/.

———. 2013b. "Rio de Janeiro Launches Films from Rio." *Variety*, October 7, 2013. https://variety.com/2013/film/global/rio-de-janeiro-launches-films-from-rio-1200702897/.

———. 2019. "Cinema do Brasil Fights to Secure Its Future." *Variety*, May 16, 2019. https://variety.com/2019/film/features/cinema-do-brasil-fights-to-secure-its-future-1203216839/.

Howkins, John. 2001. *The Creative Economy: How People Make Money from Ideas.* Harmondsworth, UK: Penguin.

Htun, Mala. 2004. "From 'Racial Democracy' to Affirmative Action: Changing State Policy on Race in Brazil." *Latin American Research Review* 39 (1): 60–89.

Ind, Nicholas. 2001. *Living the Brand: How to Transform Every Member of Your Organization into a Brand Champion.* London: Kogan Page.

———, ed. 2003. *Beyond Branding: How the New Values of Transparency and Integrity Are Changing the World of Brands.* London: Kogan Page.

Ind, Nicholas, Clare Fuller, and Charles Trevail. 2012. *Brand Together: How Co-creation Generates Innovation and Re-energizes Brands.* London: Kogan Page.

Ind, Nicholas, and Oriol Iglesias. 2016. *Brand Desire: How to Create Consumer Involvement and Inspiration.* London: Bloomsbury Information.

Instituto Brasileiro de Geografia e Estatística. 2016. *Pesquisa Nacional por Amostra de Domicílios (PNAD): Síntese de indicadores 2015.* Rio de Janeiro: Instituto Brasileiro de Geografia e Estatística.

International Labour Organization. 2013. *Domestic Workers across the World: Global and Regional Statistics and the Extent of Legal Protection.* Geneva: International Labour Organization.

International Monetary Fund. 2013. *Brazil: Technical Note on Consumer Credit Growth and Household Financial Stress.* Vol. 13 of 149. Washington, DC: International Monetary Fund.

Jaguaribe, Beatriz. 2007. "Cities without Maps: Favelas and the Aesthetics of Realism." In *Urban Imaginaries: Locating the Modern City*, edited by Alev Çinar and Thomas Bender, 100–120. Minneapolis: University of Minnesota Press.

Jara, Daniela. 2016. *Children and the Afterlife of State Violence: Memories of Dictatorship.* New York: Palgrave Macmillan.

Jess-Cooke, Carolyn. 2009. *Film Sequels: Theory and Practice from Hollywood to Bollywood.* Edinburgh: Edinburgh University Press.

Johnson, Randal, and Robert Stam. 1995. "The Shape of Brazilian Film History." In *Brazilian Cinema*, edited by Randal Johnson and Robert Stam, 15–51. New York: Columbia University Press.

Joyce, Samantha Nogueira. 2012. *Brazilian Telenovelas and the Myth of Racial Democracy.* Lanham, MD: Lexington.

Joyce, Samantha Nogueira, and Monica Martinez. 2017. "From Social Merchandising to Social Spectacle: Portrayals of Domestic Violence in TV Globo's Prime-Time Telenovelas." *International Journal of Communication* 11:220–236.

Kalandides, Ares, and Jaime Hernandez-Garcia. 2013. "Slum Tourism, City Branding and Social Urbanism: The Case of Medellin, Colombia." *Journal of Place Management and Development* 6 (1): 43–51.

Kaneva, Nadia. 2012. *Branding Post-Communist Nations: Marketizing National Identities in the "New" Europe.* New York: Routledge.

Kehl, Maria Rita. 2010. "Tortura e sintoma social." In *O que resta da ditadura: A exceção brasileira*, edited by Edson Teles and Vladimir Safatle, 123–132. São Paulo: Boitempo.

Kilbourn, Russell J. A. 2010. *Cinema, Memory, Modernity: The Representation of Memory from the Art Film to Transnational Cinema*. New York: Routledge.

Kingstone, Peter R. 2018. *The Political Economy of Latin America: Reflections on Neoliberalism and Development after the Commodity Boom*. New York: Routledge.

Klein, Amanda Ann. 2011. *American Film Cycles: Reframing Genres, Screening Social Problems, and Defining Subcultures*. Austin: University of Texas Press.

Klein, Amanda Ann, and R. Barton Palmer. 2016. Introduction to *Cycles, Sequels, Spin-Offs, Remakes, and Reboots: Multiplicities in Film and Television*, edited by Amanda Ann Klein and R. Barton Palmer, 1–21. Austin: University of Texas Press.

Klein, Naomi. 2010. *No Logo*. 10th anniversary ed. New York: Picador.

Kushigian, Julia A. 2003. *Reconstructing Childhood: Strategies of Reading for Culture and Gender in the Spanish American Bildungsroman*. Lewisburg, PA: Bucknell University Press.

Lattman-Weltman, Fernando. 2015. "Brazilian Spring or Brazilian Autumn? First Impressions of the June Days of 2013." In *Emergent Brazil: Key Perspectives on a New Global Power*, edited by Jeffrey D. Needell, 31–48. Gainesville: University of Florida Press.

Lazzara, Michael J. 2011. "Justice and Its Remainders: Diamela Eltit's *Puño y letra*." In *The Memory of State Terrorism in the Southern Cone*, edited by Francesca Lessa and Vincent Druliolle, 87–106. New York: Palgrave Macmillan.

Lebeau, Vicky. 2008. *Childhood and Cinema*. London: Reaktion.

Le Bel, Pierre-Mathieu. 2018. "War in Rio: The City Goes to the Movies." *Articulo: Journal of Urban Research* 15. https://doi.org/10.4000/articulo.3403.

Leddy, Thomas. 2005. "The Nature of Everyday Aesthetics." In *The Aesthetics of Everyday Life*, edited by Andrew Light and Jonathan M. Smith, 3–22. New York: Columbia University Press.

———. 2012. *The Extraordinary in the Ordinary: The Aesthetics of Everyday Life*. Peterborough, ON: Broadview.

Lee, Nancy, and Philip Kotler. 2011. *Social Marketing: Influencing Behaviors for Good*. 4th ed. Thousand Oaks, CA: SAGE.

Lefebvre, Henri. 1991. *The Production of Space*. Translated by Donald Nicholson-Smith. Cambridge, MA: Blackwell.

———. 1996. *Writings on Cities*. Translated by Eleonore Kofman and Elizabeth Lebas. Cambridge, MA: Blackwell.

Lerman, Dawn, Robert J. Morais, and David Luna. 2018. *The Language of Branding: Theories, Strategies, and Tactics*. New York: Routledge.

Lessa, Francesca, and Vincent Druliolle, eds. 2011. *The Memory of State Terrorism in the Southern Cone: Argentina, Chile, and Uruguay*. New York: Palgrave Macmillan.

Lessing, Benjamin. 2018. "Brazil's Federal Intervention in Rio's Drug Wards Has an Authoritarian Feel—and Could Backfire." *Washington Post*, March 2, 2018. https://www.washingtonpost.com/news/monkey-cage/wp/2018/03/02/brazils-federal-intervention-in-rios-drug-wars-has-an-authoritarian-feel-and-could-backfire/.

Levitas, Ruth. 1990. *The Concept of Utopia*. Syracuse, NY: Syracuse University Press.

Lievesley, Geraldine, and Steve Ludlam. 2009. "Introduction: A 'Pink Tide'?" In *Reclaiming Latin America: Experiments in Radical Social Democracy*, edited by Geraldine Lievesley and Steve Ludlam, 1–18. London: Zed.

Loock, Kathleen. 2016. "Retro-Remaking: The 1980s Film Cycle in Contemporary Hollywood Cinema." In *Cycles, Sequels, Spin-Offs, Remakes, and Reboots:*

Multiplicities in Film and Television, edited by Amanda Ann Klein and R. Barton Palmer, 277–298. Austin: University of Texas Press.

Lopes, Guilherme, Lia Baron, Mariana Darsie, Marina Ferraz, Natália Lackeski, and Sofia Barreto. 2014. "A Implementação de Rede Carioca de Pontos de Cultura: Um movimento de descentralização e de reconhecimento do território." V Seminário Internacional: Políticas Culturais, Rio de Janeiro, May 7–9.

Lopez, Telê Porto Ancona. 1992. "A crônica de Mário de Andrade: Impressões que historiam." In *A crônica: O gênero, sua fixação e suas transformações no Brasil*, edited by Antônio Candido, 165–188. Campinas, Brazil: Unicamp.

Lury, Celia. 2004. *Brands: The Logos of the Global Economy*. International Library of Sociology. Routledge: London.

Lury, Karen. 2010. *The Child in Film: Tears, Fears and Fairytales*. London: I. B. Tauris.

Lusvarghi. 2014. "Law, Urban Violence and Order: Cop Shows as a Brazilian TV Genre." *CINEJ Cinema Journal* 3 (1): 107–125.

Machado, Marta Rodríguez de Assis, ed. 2015. *A violência doméstica fatal: O problema do feminicídio íntimo no Brasil*. Coleção diálogos sobre a justiça. Brasília, Brazil: Ministério da Justiça, Secretaria da Reforma do Judiciário.

Mackert, Jürgen, and Bryan S. Turner. 2017. "Introduction: A Political Economy of Citizenship." In *The Transformation of Citizenship*, edited by Jürgen Mackert and Bryan S. Turner, 1–12. London: Routledge.

Maguire, Geoffrey. 2017. *The Politics of Postmemory: Violence and Victimhood in Contemporary Argentine Culture*. Cham, Switzerland: Palgrave Macmillan.

Maier, Elizabeth, and Nathalie Lebon, eds. 2010. *Women's Activism in Latin America and the Caribbean: Engendering Social Justice, Democratizing Citizenship*. New Brunswick, NJ: Rutgers University Press.

Mango, Agustin. 2013. "Rio de Janeiro Expands Studio Capability prior to World Cup, Olympics." *Variety*, September 18, 2013. http://www.hollywoodreporter.com/news/rio-de-janeiro-expands-studio-631693.

Marques, Ângela Cristina Salgueiro, and Simone Maria da Rocha. 2010. "Representações fílmicas de uma instituição policial violenta: Resquícios da ditadura militar em Tropa de Elite." *FAMECOS: Mídia, cultura e tecnologia* 17 (2): 49–58.

Marsh, Leslie L. 2012. *Brazilian Women's Filmmaking: From Dictatorship to Democracy*. Urbana: University of Illinois Press.

———. 2017a. "Memory, Youth, and Regimes of Violence in Recent Hispanic and Lusophone Cinemas." In *Beyond Tordesillas: New Approaches to Comparative Luso-Hispanic Studies*, edited by Robert Patrick Newcomb and Richard A. Gordon, 204–219. Columbus: Ohio State University Press.

———. 2017b. "Women, Gender and Romantic Comedy in Brazil: Love on the High Seas in *Meu passado me condena* (2013) and *S.O.S. mulheres ao mar* (2014)." *Feminist Media Histories* 3 (2): 98–120.

———. 2017c. "Women's Filmmaking and Comedy in Brazil: Anna Muylaert's *Durval discos* (2002) and *É proibido fumar* (2009)." In *Latin American Women Filmmakers: Production, Politics, Poetics*, edited by Deborah Martin and Deborah Shaw, 149–171. London: I. B. Tauris.

Marsh, Leslie L., and Hongmei Li. 2016. "The Global Middle Classes: Towards the Study of Emergent Citizenship." In *The Middle Class in Emerging Societies: Consumers, Lifestyles and Markets*, edited by Leslie L. Marsh and Hongmei Li, 1–16. New York: Routledge.

Marshall, T. H. 1950. *Citizenship and Social Class and Other Essays*. Cambridge: Cambridge University Press.

Matta, Roberto da. 1977. *Ensaios de antropologia estrutural: o Carnaval como um rito de passagem*. Petrópolis, Brazil: Editora Vozes.

———. 1983. *Carnavais, malandros e heróis: para uma sociologia do dilema brasileiro*. Rio de Janeiro: Zahar.

McCann, Bryan. 2012. "A View from the Corner Bar: Sérgio Porto's Satirical Crônicas and the Democradura." *HAHR: The Hispanic American Historical Review* 92 (3): 507–535.

Meeuf, Russell, and Raphael Raphael, eds. 2013. *Transnational Stardom: International Celebrity in Film and Popular Culture*. New York: Palgrave Macmillan.

Meirelles, Fernando. 2003. "Interview: Fernando Meirelles Talks *City of God*." By Ed Gonzales. *Slant*, August 27, 2003.

Meirelles, William Reis. 2005. *Paródia & chanchada: Imagens do Brasil na cultura das classes populares*. Londrina, Brazil: Eduel.

Mesquita, Cláudia. 2008. *De Copacabana à Boca do Mato: O Rio de Janeiro de Sérgio Porto e Stanislaw Ponte Preta*. Rio de Janeiro: Edições Casa de Rui Barbosa.

Mizejewski, Linda. 2015. *Pretty/Funny: Women Comedians and Body Politics*. Austin: University of Texas Press.

Mizejewski, Linda, Victoria Sturtevant, and Kathleen Rowe Karlyn, eds. 2017. *Hysterical! Women in American Comedy*. Austin: University of Texas Press.

Moor, Liz. 2007. *The Rise of Brands*. Berg: Oxford.

Moreira de Sá, Vanessa Mendes. 2016. "Brazil: Netflix, VPNS and the 'Paying' Pirates." In *Geoblocking and Global Video Culture*, edited by Ramon Lobato and James Meese, 158–166. Amsterdam: Institute of Network Cultures.

Moriyama, Victor, and Matt Sandy. 2019. "'The Amazon Is Completely Lawless': The Rainforest after Bolsonaro's First Year." *New York Times*, December 9, 2019.

Morreall, John. 1987. "Funny Ha-Ha, Funny Strange, and Other Reactions to Incongruity." In *The Philosophy of Laughter and Humor*, edited by John Morreall, 188–207. Albany: State University of New York Press.

Nagib, Lúcia, and Almir Rosa. 2002. *O cinema da retomada: Depoimentos de 90 cineastas dos anos 90*. São Paulo: Editora 34.

Naremore, James. 1988. *Acting in the Cinema*. Berkeley: University of California Press.

Nascimento, Luis Henrique. 2012. *Publicidade afirmativa*. Rio de Janeiro: Observatório de Favelas.

Navitski, Rielle E. 2017. *Public Spectacles of Violence: Sensational Cinema and Journalism in Early Twentieth-Century Mexico and Brazil*. Durham, NC: Duke University Press.

Nelson, Alice A. 2011. "Marketing Discontent: The Political Economy of Memory in Latin America." In *Accounting for Violence: Marketing Memory in Latin America*, edited by Ksenija Bilbija and Leigh A. Payne, 339–364. Durham, NC: Duke University Press.

Neri, Marcelo Cortes. 2011. *A nova classe média: O lado brilhante da base da pirâmide*. São Paulo: Editora Saraiva.

Nery, Laura. 2005. "Cenas da vida carioca: O Rio no traço de Raul Pederneiras." In *História em cousas miúdas: Capítulos de história social da crônica no Brasil*, edited by Sidney Chalhoub, Margarida de Souza Neves, and Leonardo Affonso de Miranda Pereira, 435–458. Campinas, Brazil: Unicamp.

Newbery, Charles, Marcelo Cajueiro, and Anna Marie de la Fuente. 2012. "On Verge of Rush in Pic Production: How to Shoot a Film in Latin America 2012." *Variety*, May 5, 2012. https://variety.com/2012/film/news/on-verge-of-rush-in-pic -production-1118053176/.

Nogueira, Carol. 2012. "Empregadas domésticas lutam por direitos há quase meio século." Câmara dos Deputados, December 14, 2012. https://www.camara.leg.br /noticias/392343-empregadas-domesticas-lutam-por-direitos-ha-quase-meio-seculo/.

Nogueira, Wilson de Souza, and Rafael de Figueiredo Lopes. 2017. "A Amazônia em Rio 2: Clichês culturais cinematográficos para a promoção turística." *Turismo & Sociedade* 10 (1): 1–18.

O'Connor, Justin, and Xin Gu. 2013. "Developing a Creative Cluster in a Postindustrial City: CIDS and Manchester." In *Creative Cities and Urban Development: Creative Cities in the 21st Century*, edited by Terry Flew, 43–55. New York: Routledge.

Oliveira, Daniel. 2012. "Welcome to Riollywood." Infosur, January 5, 2012. http:// infosurhoy.com/en_GB/articles/saii/features/economy/2012/05/01/feature-02.

O'Neill, Jim, Dominic Wilson, Roopa Purushothaman, and Anna Stupnytska. 2005. "How Solid Are the BRICs?" Global Economics Paper 134, Goldman Sachs, New York.

Oricchio, Luiz Zanin. 2003. *Cinema de novo: Um balanço crítico da retomada*. São Paulo: Estação Liberdade.

Padala, Satya Nagendra. 2012. "Top 10 Box Office Hits of 2011." *International Business Times*, January 12, 2012. http://www.ibtimes.com/articles/280608/20120112/top -10-box-office-hits-2011.htm?page=all.

Paris, Natalie. 2012. "Rio de Janeiro Awarded UNESCO World Heritage Status." *Telegraph* (UK), July 2, 2012. https://www.telegraph.co.uk/travel/destinations /south-america/brazil/rio-de-janeiro/articles/Rio-de-Janeiro-awarded-UNESCO -World-Heritage-status/.

Paschoalick, Jonas Pereira, and Luciana Rodrigues. 2014. "Por Dentro da Rede: Delineando o Impacto da Implantação da Rede de Pontos de Cultura nas Entidades de Ribeirão Preto/SP." V Seminário Internacional: Políticas Culturais, Rio de Janeiro, Brazil, May 7–9.

Perlman, Janice. 2010. *Favela: Four Decades of Living on the Edge in Rio de Janeiro*. New York: Oxford University Press.

Peruzzo, Cicilia Krohling, and Maria Alice Campagnoli Otre, eds. 2015. *Comunicação popular, comunitária e alternativa no Brasil: Sinais de resistência e de construção da cidadania*. São Bernardo do Campo, Brazil: UMESP.

Pike, Andy. 2011. *Brands and Branding Geographies*. Northampton, MA: Edward Elgar.

Poblete, Juan. 2016. "Cinema and Humor in Latin America: An Introduction." In *Humor in Latin American Cinema*, edited by Juan Poblete and Juana Suárez, 1–28. New York: Palgrave Macmillan.

Pochmann, Marcio. 2012. *Nova classe média? O trabalho na base da pirâmide social brasileira*. São Paulo: Boitempo Editorial.

———. 2014. *O mito da grande classe média: Capitalismo e estrutura social*. São Paulo: Boitempo Editorial.

Podalsky, Laura. 2011. *The Politics of Affect and Emotion in Contemporary Latin American Cinema: Argentina, Brazil, Cuba, and Mexico*. New York: Palgrave Macmillan.

Porto, Sérgio. 2010. *As cariocas*. Rio de Janeiro: Editora Nova Fronteira Participações.

Prefeitura do Rio. n.d. *Porto Maravilha*. Rio de Janeiro: Prefeitura do Rio.

Prieto Larraín, María Cristina. 2011. "Branding the Chilean Nation: Socio-cultural Change, National Identity and International Image." PhD diss., Leiden University.

Ramos, Ana Flávia Cernic. 2005. "Política e humor nos últimos anos da monarquia: A série 'Balas de Estalo.'" In *História em cousas miúdas: Capítulos de história social da crônica no Brasil*, edited by Sidney Chalhoub, Margarida de Souza Neves, and Leonardo Affonso de Miranda Pereira, 87–121. Campinas, Brazil: Unicamp.

Ramos, Fernão Pessoa. 2003. "Humility, Guilt and Narcissism Turned Inside Out in Brazil's Film Revival." In *The New Brazilian Cinema*, edited by Lúcia Nagib, 65–84. New York: I. B. Tauris, in association with the Centre for Brazilian Studies, University of Oxford.

Rancière, Jacques. 2007. *The Future of the Image*. New York: Verso.

Rapoza, Kenneth. 2013. "Brazil's 'Poor' Middle Class, and the Poor That No Longer Serve Them." *Forbes*, January 22, 2013.

Rêgo, and Carolina Rocha, eds. 2010. *New Trends in Argentine and Brazilian Cinema*. Bristol: Intellect.

Rêgo, Daniela Domingues Leão. 2007. "Imagem e política: Estudo sobre o Cine Jornal Brasileiro (1940–1942)." MA thesis, Instituto de Artes, Universidade de Campinas.

Reis, Ana Carla Fonseca. 2008. Introduction to *Economia criativa: Como estratégia de desenvolvimento: Uma visão dos países em desenvolvimento*, edited by Ana Carla Fonseca Reis, 14–49. São Paulo: Itaú Cultural.

Ridenti, Marcelo. 2004, "Resistência e mistificação da resistência armada contra a ditadura: Armadilhas para pesquisadores." In *O golpe e a ditadura militar: Quarenta anos depois (1964–2004)*, edited by Daniel Aarão Reis Filho, Marcelo Ridenti, and Rodrigo Patto Sá Motta, 53–65. Bauru, Brazil: Editora da Universidade do Sagrado Coração.

Riofilme. 2014. *Riofilme: Resultados de 2009 a 2013*. Rio de Janeiro: Prefeitura do Rio.

Ripper, João Roberto, Dante Gastaldoni, and Joana Mazza, eds. 2012. *Imagens do povo*. Rio de Janeiro: Nau.

RMCMC (Rio: Mais Cinema, Menos Cenário). 2014. *Carta aberta*. Rio de Janeiro: RMCMC.

Robb Larkins, Erika. 2015. *The Spectacular Favela: Violence in Modern Brazil*. Berkeley: University of California Press.

Rocha, Ana Raquel Coelho, and Angela da Rocha. 2016. "Meanings Attached to Cruises by Emerging Consumers: A Study Using Participant Observation." In *The Middle Class in Emerging Societies: Consumers, Lifestyles and Markets*, edited by Leslie L. Marsh and Hongmei Li, 85–102. New York: Routledge.

Rolnik, Raquel. 2007. *A cidade e a lei: Legislação, política urbana e territórios na cidade de São Paulo*. São Paulo: FAPESP, Studio Nobel.

Rosas-Moreno, Tania Cantrell. 2014. *News and Novela in Brazilian Media: Fact, Fiction, and National Identity*. Lanham, MD: Lexington Books.

———. 2017. "Brazilian Telenovelas and Social Merchandising." *ReVista* 17 (1): 50–53, 66.

Rubim, Antonio Albino Canelas. 2010. *Políticas culturais no governo Lula*. Salvador, Brazil: Editora da UFBA.

Rubin, Martin. 1999. *Thrillers*. Cambridge: Cambridge University Press.

Saad-Filho, Alfredo. 2003. "New Dawn or False Start in Brazil? The Political Economy of Lula's Election." *Historical Materialism* 11 (1): 3–21.

———. 2007. "Neoliberalism, Democracy and Economic Policy in Brazil." In *Political Economy of Brazil: Recent Economic Performance*, edited by Philip Arestis and Alfredo Saad-Filho, 7–23. New York: Palgrave Macmillan.

Sadlier, Darlene Joy. 2008. *Brazil Imagined: 1500 to the Present*. Austin: University of Texas Press.

———. 2009. "Introduction: A Short History of Film Melodrama in Latin America." In *Latin American Melodrama: Passion, Pathos, and Entertainment*, edited by Darlene Joy Sadlier, 1–18. Urbana: University of Illinois Press.

Saes, Décio. 2016. *Cidadania e classes sociais: Teoria e história*. São Bernardo do Campo: UMESP.

Salvi, Valentina. 2011. "The Slogan 'Complete Memory': A Reactive (Re)-signification of the Memory of the Disappeared in Argentina." In *The Memory of State Terrorism in the Southern Cone*, edited by Francesca Lessa and Vincent Druliolle, 43–61. New York: Palgrave Macmillan.

Sammons, Jeffrey L. 1991. "The Bildungsroman for Nonspecialists: An Attempt at a Clarification." In *Reflection and Action: Essays on the Bildungsroman*, edited by James N. Hardin, 26–45. Columbia: University of South Carolina Press.

Sánchez Prado, Ignacio M. 2006. "*Amores perros*: Exotic Violence and Neoliberal Fear." *Journal of Latin American Cultural Studies* 15 (1): 39–57.

Santana, A.P.D. 2012. "New Directions in the Public Sector for Expansion of Audiovisual Activities." In *The Brazilian Audiovisual Industry: An Explosion of Creativity and Opportunities for Partnerships*, edited by Steve Solot, 61–71. Rio de Janeiro: Latin American Training Center.

Santoro, Luiz Fernando. 1989. *A imagem nas mãos: O vídeo popular no Brasil*. São Paulo: Summus Editorial.

Santos, Bárbara Ferreira. 2016. "Apesar de expansão, acesso à internet no Brasil ainda é baixo." *Exame*, December 22, 2016.

Santos, Márcia de Souza. 2010. "A ditadura de ontem nas telas de hoje: Representações do regime militar no cinema brasileiro contemporâneo." MA thesis, Instituto de Ciências Humanas, História, Universidade de Brasília.

Santos, Wilq Vicente dos. 2014. "O Novo Cenário da Produção e Difusão Audiovisual no Contexto das Transformações nas Políticas Públicas." V Seminário Internacional: Políticas Culturais, Rio de Janeiro, Brazil, May 7–9.

Saule Júnior, Nelson. 1999. *Direito à cidade: Trilhas legais para o direito às cidades sustentáveis*. São Paulo: Polis, Max Limonad.

SAv (Secretariat of Audiovisual). 2010. *Relatório de gestão, Nov/2007–Abr/2010: Brasil, um país de todas as telas*. Rio de Janeiro: Secretária do Audiovisal, Minstério da Cultura.

Schiavo, Marcio Ruiz. 2006. "Dez anos de merchandising social." Intercom—Sociedade Brasileira de Estudos Interdisciplinários da Comunicação, XXIX Congresso Brasileiro de Ciências da Comunicação, September 6–9. http://www.portcom.intercom.org.br/pdfs/120978737171710494144163695234717744651.pdf.

Schmidt, Benito Bisso. 2008. "Cicatriz aberta ou página virada? Lembrar e esquecer o golpe de 1964 quarenta anos depois." *Anos 90* 14 (26): 127–156.

Schneider, Nina. 2014. *Brazilian Propaganda: Legitimizing an Authoritarian Regime*. Gainesville: University of Florida Press.

Seliprandy, Fernando. 2013. "O monumental e o íntimo: Dimensões da memória da resistência no documentário brasileiro recente." *Estudos Históricos (Rio de Janeiro)* 26 (51): 55–72.

Sevin, Efe. 2011. "Thinking about Place Branding: Ethics of Concept." *Place Branding and Public Diplomacy* 7 (3): 155–164.

Shaw, Lisa. 2006. "Vargas on Film: From the Newsreel to the *Chanchada*." In *Vargas and Brazil: New Perspectives*, edited by Jens R. Hentschke, 207–225. New York: Palgrave Macmillan.

Shaw, Lisa, and Maite Conde. 2005. "Brazil through Hollywood's Gaze: From the Silent Screen to the Good Neighbor Policy Era." In *Latin American Cinema: Essays on Modernity, Gender and National Identity*, edited by Lisa Shaw and Stephanie Dennison, 180–208. Jefferson, NC: McFarland.

Sherman, Andrew J. 2011. *Franchising and Licensing: Two Powerful Ways to Grow Your Business in Any Economy*. 4th ed. New York: American Management Association.

Silva, Hélio, Jr. 2000. "Do racismo legal ao princípio da ação afirmativa: A lei como obstáculo e como instrumento dos direitos e interesses do povo negro." In *Tirando a máscara: Ensaios sobre o racismo no Brasil*, edited by Antônio Sérgio Alfredo Guimarães and Lynn Huntley, 359–388. São Paulo: Editora Paz e Terra.

Silva, Jailson de Souza e. 2012a. "Carta para Zuenir Ventura." In *O novo carioca*, edited by Jailson de Souza e Silva, Jorge Luiz Barbosa, and Marcus Vinicius Faustini, 19–21. Rio de Janeiro: Mórula Editorial.

———. 2012b. "O simbólico também institui o real." In *Imagens do povo*, edited by João Roberto Ripper, Dante Gastaldoni, and Joana Mazza, 13–14. Rio de Janeiro: Nau.

Silva, Jailson de Souza e, and Thiago Araújo Ansel. 2012. *Mídia e favela: Comunicação e democracia nas favelas e espaços poplares: Levantamento de mídia alternativa*. Rio de Janeiro: Observatório de Favelas.

Silva, Jailson de Souza e, Luis Henrique Nascimento, and Écio Salles. 2012. *Publicidade afirmativa: Plano político pedagógico*. Rio de Janeiro: Observatório de Favelas.

Silveira, Sérgio Amadeu da, Murilo Bansi Machado, and Rodrigo Tarchiani Savazoni. 2013. "Backward March: The Turnaround in Public Cultural Policy in Brazil." *Media, Culture and Society* 35 (5): 549–564.

Smith, Jonathan M. 2005. Introduction to *The Aesthetics of Everyday Life*, edited by Andrew Light and Jonathan M. Smith, ix–xv. New York: Columbia University Press.

Smuts, Aaron. 2008. "The Desire-Frustration Theory of Suspense." *Journal of Aesthetics and Art Criticism* 66 (3): 281–290.

Solot, Steve, ed. 2012. "The Rio Film Commission: Programs, Incentives and Support." In *The Brazilian Audiovisual Industry: An Explosion of Creativity and Opportunities for Partnerships*, edited by Steve Solot, 279–292. Rio de Janeiro: Latin American Training Center.

———. 2015. "Uma imagem vale mais que mil palavras." *Cultura e Mercado*, January 6, 2015.

Sousa, Ramayana Lira de. 2009. "Violent Imagens and the Images of Violence: The Politics of Violence in Urban Space in Contemporary Brazilian Cinema." PhD diss., Universidade Federal de Santa Catarina.

Souza, André de, Catarina Alencastro, and Luiza Damé. 2012. "Verdade sem ressentimento." *O Globo*, May 17, 3–4, O País.

Souza, Jessé. 2017. *A elite do atraso: Da escravidão à Lava Jato*. Rio de Janeiro: Leya.

Souza, Maria Luiza Rodrigues. 2007. "Um estudo das narrativas cinematográficas sobre as ditaduras militares no Brasil (1964–1985) e na Argentina (1976–1983)." PhD diss., Instituto de Ciências Sociais, Universidade de Brasília.

Stampa, Inez Terezinha, and Vicente Rodrigues. 2016. *Ditadura e transição democrática no Brasil: O golpe de estado de 1964 e a (re)construção da democracia.* Rio de Janeiro: Arquivo Nacional.

Stewart, Andrew. 2011. "Global Power Shift: Emerging Economies, Technology Help Rev Record Worldwide Grosses." *Variety*, January 15, 2011.

Surowiec, Pawel. 2017. *Nation Branding, Public Relations and Soft Power: Corporatizing Poland.* New York: Routledge.

Süssekind, Flora. 2005. "Desterritorialização e forma literária: Literatura brasileira contemporânea e experiência urbana." *Literatura e Sociedade* 10 (8): 60–81.

Szafir, Milena. 2010. "Retóricas audiovisuais (o filme Tropa de Elite na cultura em rede)." MA thesis, Universidade de São Paulo.

Szondi, György. 2007. "The Role and Challenges of Country Branding in Transition Countries: The Central and Eastern European Experience." *Place Branding and Public Diplomacy* 3 (1): 8–20.

Távora, Lina Rocha Fernandes. 2011. "Cinema de Intimidade: Proposta de gênero para o novo cinema brasileiro." MA thesis, Universidade de Brasília.

Taylor, Astra, dir. 2005. *Zizek!* Zeitgeist Films. eVideo.

Teles, Edson, and Vladimir Safatle, 2010. "Apresentação." In *O que resta da ditadura: A exceção brasileira*, edited by Edson Teles and Vladimir Safatle, 9–12. São Paulo: Boitempo.

Telles, Edward Eric. 2004. *Race in Another America: The Significance of Skin Color in Brazil.* Princeton, NJ: Princeton University Press.

Time Warner. 2012. "Warner Bros. Pictures International and Fox International Announce Formation of New Joint Operation in Brazil." Press release.

Torres, I. 2012. "Branding Slums: A Community-Driven Strategy for Urban Inclusion in Rio De Janeiro." *Journal of Place Management and Development* 5 (3): 198–211.

Turino, Célio. 2010. *Pontos de Cultura: O Brasil de baixo para cima.* 2nd ed. São Paulo: Anita Garibaldi.

UNCTAD (United Nations Conference on Trade and Development). 2000. *Tenth Session, Plan of Action.* Bangkok, Thailand: UNCTAD.

———. 2002. *Report of the Expert Meeting on Audiovisual Services: Improving Participation of Developing Countries.* Geneva: UNCTAD.

———. 2004. *Creative Industries and Development.* Geneva: UNCTAD.

United Nations. 2010. *The Right to the City: Bridging the Urban Divide.* Rio de Janeiro: World Urban Forum.

Vandaele, Jeroen. 2002. "Humor Mechanisms in Film Comedy: Incongruity and Superiority." *Poetics Today* 23 (2): 221–249.

Van der Sar, Ernesto. 2011. "Top 10 Most Pirated Movies of 2011." TorrentFreak, December 24, 2011. http://torrentfreak.com/top-10-most-pirated-movies-of-2011 -111223/.

Veblen, Thorstein. 1918. *Theory of the Leisure Class.* New York: B. W. Huebsch. First published 1899.

Veja. 2015. "Crise faz número de domésticas crescer no país." June 8, 2015. https://veja .abril.com.br/economia/crise-faz-numero-de-domesticas-crescer-no-pais/.

Ventura, Tereza. 2014. "Notas sobre cultura, diversidade e inclusão social." V Seminário Internacional: Políticas Culturais, Rio de Janeiro, Brazil, May 7–19.

Ventura, Zuenir. 1994. *Cidade partida.* São Paulo: Companhia das Letras.

Verevis, Constantine. 2016. "Vicious Cycle: *Jaws* and Revenge-of-Nature Films of the 1970s." In *Cycles, Sequels, Spin-offs, Remakes, and Reboots: Multiplicities in Film and Television*, edited by Amanda Ann Klein and R. Barton Palmer, 96–111. Austin: University of Texas Press.

Vieira, João Luiz. 2003. "*Chronically Unfeasible*: The Political Film in a Depoliticized World." In *The New Brazilian Cinema*, edited by Lúcia Nagib, 85–94. London: I. B. Tauris in association with the Centre for Brazilian Studies, University of Oxford.

Waiselfisz, Julio Jacobo. 2012. *Mapa da violência 2012: A cor dos homicídios no Brasil*. Rio de Janeiro: Centro Brasileiro de Estudos Latino-Americanos and Facultad Latinoamericana de Ciencias Sociales; Brasília, Brazil: Secretaria de Políticas de Promoção da Igualdade Racial.

Wernick, Andrew. 1991. *Promotional Culture: Advertising, Ideology, and Symbolic Expression*. London: SAGE.

Whipp, Glenn. 2013. "Why Hollywood Movies Seem Less American: 'Fast Five' Goes on the Beach in Rio." *Chicago Sun Times*, Roger Ebert's Journal. Accessed July 12, 2013. http://blogs.suntimes.com/ebert/movies-1/why-hollywood-movies-seem-less .html (site no longer available).

Williams, Daryle. 2001. *Culture Wars in Brazil: The First Vargas Regime, 1930–1945*. Durham, NC: Duke University Press.

Williams, Erica Lorraine. 2013. *Sex Tourism in Bahia: Ambiguous Entanglements*. Urbana: University of Illinois Press.

Wilson, Julie A. 2018. *Neoliberalism*. New York: Routledge.

Wylde, Chris. 2012. *Latin America after Neoliberalism: Developmental Regimes in Post-crisis States*. New York: Palgrave Macmillan.

Xavier, Ismail. 1997. *Allegories of Underdevelopment: Aesthetics and Politics in Modern Brazilian Cinema*. Minneapolis: University of Minnesota Press.

———. 2003. "Brazilian Cinema in the 1990s: The Unexpected Encounter and the Resentful Character." In *The New Brazilian Cinema*, edited by Lúcia Nagib, 39–63. London: I. B. Tauris in association with the Centre for Brazilian Studies, University of Oxford.

Yang, Fan. 2016. *Faked in China: Nation Branding, Counterfeit Culture, and Globalization*. Bloomington: Indiana University Press.

Zakaria, Fareed. 2011. *The Post-American World. Release 2.0*. New York: Norton.

Zaluar, Alba, and Marcos Alvito, eds. 1998. *Um século de favela*. Rio de Janeiro: Editora Fundação Getulio Vargas.

Zaverucha, Jorge. 2010. "Relações civil-militares: O legado autoritário da Constituição brasileira de 1988." In *O que resta da ditadura: A exceção brasileira*, edited by Edson Teles and Vladimir Safatle, 41–76. São Paulo: Botempo.

Zuazo, Pedro. 2012. "'Cheias de charme': Vencedora do concurso do 'Fantástico' canta e dança com as Empreguetes." *Extra Globo*, July 26, 2012.

"Zuzu Angel." n.d. Memórias da Ditadura. Accessed October 6, 2020. http:// memoriasdaditadura.org.br/biografias-da-resistencia/zuzu-angel/.

Zweig, Stefan. 1941. *Brazil: Land of the Future*. Translated by Andrew St. James. New York: Viking.

Index

About the Author

LESLIE L. MARSH specializes in Latin American film and media studies, focusing on Brazil and more broadly on questions of citizenship. She is the author of *Brazilian Women's Filmmaking: From Dictatorship to Democracy* (2012) and coeditor of *The Middle Class in Emerging Societies: Consumers, Lifestyles, and Markets* (2016).